Apocalypse of the Word

The Life and Message of George Fox (1624-1691)

by Douglas Gwyn

Friends United Press
Richmond, Indiana

Library of Congress Cataloging-in-Publication Data

Gwyn, Douglas, 1984–
  Apocalypse of the word.

    Bibliography: p.
    Includes index.
    1. Fox, George, 1624-1691.   2. Quakers–England–Biography. 3. Society of Friends–Doctrines–History–17th century. I. Title.
BX7795.F7G85   1986   289.6'092'4   [B]   86-19548
ISBN 0-913408-91-3

Copyright Friends United Press 1986
    101 Quaker Hill Drive, Richmond, IN 47374

For my parents, Robert and June Gwyn.

Contents

A GUIDE TO CITATIONS

The number of references to George Fox's writings in this study demands that an abbreviated form of citation be used. This brief guide gives full citation to the abbreviations used.

NJ   George Fox, *Journal*, John Nickalls, ed. (Cambridge: University Press, 1952).

BJ   George Fox, *Journal*, Bicentenary Edition by Norman Penney, 2 vols. (London: Friends Tract Association, 1891).

CJ   George Fox, *Journal*, Norman Penney, ed., 2 vols. (Cambridge: University Press, 1911).

I-VIII   George Fox, *Works*, 8 vols. Philadelphia: Gould, 1831).

Fox's *Works* divide up by volume as follows:

Vols. I-II *Journal*, edited by Thomas Ellwood, first published in 1694.

Vol. III   *The Great Mystery . . .* — controversial works, first collected and published in 1659.

Vols. IV-VI *Gospel Truth Demonstrated* — doctrinal works first published as a collection in 1706.

Vols. VII-VIII *Epistles* — over 400 collected and first published in 1698.

These abbreviated citations, followed by colon and page number, give the exact location of materials quoted or referred to in the text of this study. All biblical quotations in the text of this study come from the Authorized (King James) Version, since that is the Bible used most by Fox and thereby contains wording most easily identifiable in his writings. This is most helpful, as Fox constantly quotes but rarely cites scriptural references.

For serious students of Fox and early Quakerism, a somewhat more exhaustive footnoting of data can be found in the original thesis version of this book, available through University Microfilms, Ann Arbor.

PREFACE

The past fifty years have witnessed a growing movement in the Society of Friends to rediscover the original message and intent of Quakerism. This effort has been stimulated by the gnawing sense among many that early Quaker writings manifest a powerful spirituality considerably beyond the scale experienced among Friends today. Neither the liberal-mystical nor the Protestant revisions of Quakerism have appeared able to account for the full theological framework of early Quakerism, much less match its vitality.

Scholarly attempts to reconstruct early Quakerism, particularly the founding vision of George Fox, have been spearheaded by Lewis Benson, a non-academic who has spent a lifetime carefully reading and correlating Fox's writings. This work in itself has been a major effort, since Fox was not a systematic writer in the usual sense, and many interpretations have suffered from incomplete, impressionistic analysis. But Benson has also added to this correlative labor a number of key theological insights into the central message of Fox's proclamation. His publications, which began appearing in the 1940s, have been among the most probing and controversial modern Quaker writings. Tragically, due in part to his lack of academic standing, these publications (a book, some articles and tracts) have not circulated beyond Quaker circles. Yet they have influenced a generation of Quaker scholars who share in varying degrees Benson's concern and conclusions.

After World War II a number of young American Friends were concerned for a more profound and resolute Quaker faith to stand up to global traumas such as the one they had just survived. T. Canby Jones, Hugh Barbour, Wilmer Cooper, Dean Freiday, and Arthur Roberts are included in this generation, all devoting major research efforts to early Quakerism, all except Freiday becoming academic leaders of Friends in Quaker colleges.

There are many important insights that have generated from this nucleus of scholars over the years. These are buried away in unpublished doctoral theses and conference papers and scattered through various and sundry issues of *Quaker Religious Thought*, *Friends Quarterly*, and Friends Faith and Life volumes. They represent a rich resource that remains obscure even among Friends today, and unknown to others.

The present study by no means claims to summarize all this body of literature. It does represent, however, gleanings by one from a newer generation, as well as insights and concerns coming from a somewhat different perspective. My own background in biblical studies was the basis for mind-reeling experiences when first reading Fox's writings. What I particularly noticed was Fox's fluid and pervasive use of the language of apocalyptic, especially from Revelation. Some conversation on this subject in 1977 led to the invitation from Wilmer Cooper and Dean Freiday to write an article on Fox's apocalyptic outlook for the Faith and Life Movement. The research that began there has culminated with this book.

One of the most intriguing findings in my research has been to see the way in which Fox's theology anticipates some of the recent trends in modern biblical research. Lewis Benson has already identified an important example of this in Fox's recovery of a prophetic Christology, the perspective which New Testament research has shown to be key to the earliest Christian proclamation. What this study more fully shows is that Fox's message unfolds within the horizon of the *eschaton*, the ultimate destiny of the world. Fox's entire outlook from personal spiritual experience, to the role of ministry and worship in the Church, to social and economic questions, is always involved with the cosmic drama of salvation history. This consistently eschatological approach is today recognized by New Testament scholarship as the outlook of the early Church. Fox vitally recaptures the apocalyptic spirituality of New Testament Christianity.

Of course, "Primitive Christianity revived" is a notion long and vigorously dismissed by modern scholarship. Critical research has shown a variety of emphases within the New Testament Church. Moreover, it is difficult to compare religious phenomena coming from vastly divergent times and places. Yet if apocalyptic is "the mother of Christian theology," as Ernst Käsemann has powerfully argued, then can we so easily avoid comparing Fox's radical emphasis with those found in the New Testament? To what other historic example can we compare it as appropriately?

In this study I am greatly indebted to the life work, the personal counsel, and the encouragement of Lewis Benson, Dean

Freiday, and T. Canby Jones. Access to Lewis Benson's index of Fox's writings has also been a considerable help in identifying and correlating thematic materials in Fox's works. Several individuals from the New Foundation Fellowship, particularly John Curtis, have added helpful advice and encouragement. I have also been greatly aided by my long friendship and dialogue with Richard Sturm, a student of New Testament apocalyptic. The Berkeley Friends Church has been of help as I revised the original thesis version into book form. Barbara Mays has offered important suggestions in finalization. And throughout, I have been sustained by the patient encouragement of my wife, Dorian Petri.

Finally, I am compelled by a deepening sense of what is at stake in this line of study. If a previous generation of Quaker scholars was moved by World War II to search for deeper roots, then I am part of a generation even more urgently pressed by the spectre of an impending holocaust, rather than a past one. The apocalypse of the Word is the only power in the world more powerful than the atomic, ecological, and/or genetic apocalypses we now face. It is the only power that can stand above the forces at work in the world today, bringing them to the judgment bar of God, subjecting them to his wisdom. Let us repent and turn to this alternative apocalypse.

INTRODUCTION

In the vast history of Christian life and thought, the Quaker founder George Fox is a unique figure. Living in the great age of the Puritan revolution in England, he was part of a society obsessed with the Reformation spirit of "primitive Christianity revived." Yet, in a period in which so many original thinkers and actors emerged, no other figure assumed the heroic stature and style of apostolic witness that Fox attained. A man without any formal theological education, who shunned academia all his life, he was cast out of "steeplehouses," beaten, stoned, and imprisoned on numerous occasions for the gospel he preached. It was not the most outrageous gospel to be preached in that period, but it was the message that elicited the most vehement and systematic persecution of those who proclaimed it. Its scandal arose not only from its surprising claims to salvation and its threat to the established Church order, but also from the flagrant intractability with which Fox and the other early Friends preached it in words and acts.

The impact of Fox and the movement he founded in seventeenth century England has led historian George M. Trevelyan to conclude that "George Fox made at least the most original contribution to the history of religion of any Englishman."[1] Similarly, Church historian Williston Walker deems Fox "one of the few religious geniuses of English history."[2]

The violent reprisals by various forms of Church establishment which beset the early Quaker movement from 1649 until Toleration in 1689 were only the more extreme form of controversy that raged between Quakers and Protestants during these years. The nature and extent of differences between the Quakers and their Protestant milieu have been the issue of historical and theological debate in the twentieth century. The two dominant modern interpretations of the Quaker message have been the mystical reading by Rufus M. Jones and the Protestant reading by Geoffrey Nuttall and Hugh Barbour.

MYSTICAL

Rufus M. Jones remains probably the best known Quaker religious thinker of this century. Though his influence at large can be seen in American religious figures such as Harry Emerson Fosdick, it is his interpretation of early Quakerism we will examine here. In the opening decades of this century, Jones published a number of major works which gave a bold, new interpretation to Fox and the early Friends. Inspired by the rise of religious liberalism, psychology, and his own philosophical inclinations, Jones portrayed Fox's message as a highly evolved mysticism, following in the tradition of the great Continental mystics and spiritualists. He pressed this line of interpretation forcefully, despite the fact that he could not substantiate any familiarity on Fox's part with that mystical tradition. He could only speculate at "parallelism with celestial currents."[3] Jones defined mysticism as "life itself at the highest inward unity and its most consummate attainment of Reality."[4] He placed mysticism at the heart of all religions that emphasize the primacy of personal experience.

Jones posited *mysticism* as the life-center of early Quakerism. To this core he added *prophetism* as an important secondary aspect; Quakers "employed the common stock of ideas and enthusiasms preserved in the creative literature of prophecy and revelation." There is little doubt "that this prophetical and apocalyptic element vastly helped to produce the mental and emotional climate and atmosphere of the movement . . . ."[5] It is clear that Jones saw the prophetic aspect simply as the affectual and stylistic mode of Quaker mysticism. This becomes more obvious when we find *moralism* as Jones' third aspect of early Quakerism. This other secondary aspect serves as a corrective to the tendency of prophetism to be "dreamy, visionary, and seething with ill-directed enthusiasm." The moral concern of Fox was "that society here on earth might take on a likeness to the Kingdom of Heaven."[6]

Jones placed Fox in a long line of spiritual reformers in Christian history, beginning with the Gnostic and Montanist groups of the second century. He characterized them as "devoted Humanists":

> They shared with enthusiasm the rediscovery of those treasures which human Reason had produced, and they rose to a more virile confidence in the sphere and capacity of Reason than had prevailed in Christian circles since the day of the early Greek Fathers. They took a variety of roads to their conclusion, but in one way or another they all proclaimed that deep in the central

nature of man — an inalienable part of Reason — there was a Light, a Word, an Image of God, something permanent, reliable, universal, and unsundered from God himself.[7]

Jones conceived of Fox as advancing a concept of rationality as a divine aspect of human nature. Hence, he assigned to Fox an optimistic view of the human condition, in which the person's innermost core is eternally good and unfallen. Given this impression of Fox's thought, Jones naturally concluded that early Friends were in conflict with Puritanism because they simply "lived and thought in another world of ideas."[8]

The mystical interpretation of Fox's message may be seen as an attempt to come to terms with Fox's universalist aspect. Jones' tripartite conception of early Quakerism posits a mystical core of spiritual experience to which one's language of description is only a secondary husk. Reading Fox closely, however, shows that while Fox believes in a universal spiritual experience that may remain unnamed, this light very definitely has a name — Jesus Christ — and that the language of the Bible is essential to understanding this experience. Quaker scholar T. Canby Jones concludes from his extensive study, "Incessantly, inevitably, and unalterably George Fox identifies and defines the Light as Christ."[9] Moreover, Fox is quite clear that moral imperative is essential to the experience of Christ's light. Morality cannot be made a secondary aspect for Fox; Christ's light is moral, or it is not his light.

Jones' sense of the universal is tied to an understanding of human reason as a divine, saving faculty. But we shall see repeatedly in this study that Fox understands the light as inward but fundamentally alien to human nature. Far from being optimistic about human capacity, Fox sees our nature as utterly dark; human reason may be creative, but it is ultimately unable to save. When we understand this, we see that the early Quaker conflict with Puritanism was hardly the chance collision of two different thought-worlds Jones imagined, but a struggle within the *same* world.

The liberal interpretation of Quakerism by Rufus Jones is similar to the liberal approach to the New Testament pioneered by Rudolf Bultmann and others. Bultmann attempted to "demythologize" the Jewish theological language and assumptions permeating the New Testament message in order to isolate a vital existential core of universal meaning. Again like Jones, Bultmann tended to strip away *theology*, and understanding of God, as a secondary husk, in favor of *anthropology*, an understanding of humanity on its own terms, as the essential truth.[10] The cosmic horizon of New Testament proclamation became swallowed up in an "intrapsychic event."[11] In supposing that the heart of Jesus' message had nothing essentially to do with the Jewish religion around him, Bultmann and other liberal interpreters arrived at a core message that had a lot to do with their own modern assumptions.

The philosophical liberalism of Rufus Jones' mystical interpretation of Quakerism therefore contains the same problem that the liberal theological interpretation of the New Testament created. It ignores the structural integrity of the message itself, finding a "buried treasure" at the core which, in fact, has been projected there by the investigator. There is too much in Fox's writings that Jones had to ignore in order to reach his conclusions. Fox's approach may perhaps be accurately called mystical, but not by the definition Jones gave to that word.

PROTESTANT

The next major trend in the interpretation of early Quakerism sprang mainly from historical research into seventeenth century Puritanism. As the spectrum of Puritan movements of the 1640s and 50s came to be better known, it became clear that the social, political, and theological traits of Quakerism did not burst upon the scene completely out of nowhere. Fox and early Friends were recognized to be influenced by and addressing a thought world of radical, or "spiritual," Puritanism that had already spawned many of the concepts and practices that would be crystallized in Quakerism. This led to the conclusion that Quakerism is one manifestation of the broader Reformation movement because of its several points of similarity to Puritanism, in particular, and to the fundamental orientations of John Calvin and Martin Luther, in general.

The first decisive study in this historical analysis came with Geoffrey Nuttall's *The Holy Spirit in Puritan Faith and Experience* (1946). It is a convincing effort "to present Quakerism in its historical context."[12] Taking a number of radical Puritan themes, he shows the flow in Puritan thought toward the conclusion of Fox and other early Quaker writers in each case. Nuttall's approach helps us understand the way Fox's preaching spoke to many pressing spiritual concerns of the day, as well as suggesting that these concerns shaped Fox's own thought.

Nuttall posits a "fundamental difference" between Quakers and Puritans, but downplays it, concluding that Quakers "in the exclusive sense are not Puritans but the Puritans' fiercest foes, but who yet repeat, extend, and fuse so much of what is held by the radical, Separatist party within Puritanism, that they cannot be denied the name . . . ."[13] The main difference that Nuttall finds in Quaker thinking is that he feels they err theologically (see Chapter 4 on the Puritan-Quaker debate about Christ's light). Here lies the problem with Nuttall's analysis. He judges Quakerism from a Puritan theological agenda, rather than appraising it on its own terms. His important contribution is in showing areas of thematic continuity between radical Puritans and Friends; nevertheless, he fails to recognize and credit the inner integrity of Quakerism independent of Calvinism. By making the Holy Spirit the chief theme of comparison, Nuttall misses the fact that *Fox's central concern is with Christ the Word, present by his Spirit*. This concern creates a fundamental shift in Fox's theological categories, one that is not easily detected by showing continuities in language.[14]

The chief extension of this historical relating of Quakerism to English Protestantism has been made by Hugh Barbour, a leading historian of Quakerism today. His *The Quakers in Puritan England* (1964) is probably the most influential contribution in the area of early Quaker history since W. C. Braithwaite's massive study. Barbour's analysis is mainly socio-historical, though it also contains a wealth of theological insights, focusing on Quakerism's first decade. Extending Nuttall's work, he narrates the birth of Quakerism in the fertile matrix of spiritual Puritanism where prayer, preaching, singing, and daily life were increasingly subjected to the Spirit's leading.

The main thesis on the origins of Quakerism emerging from Barbour's book is that

> . . . .clearly Quakerism was not a mere reaction against Puritanism but much more a movement into untouched territory. In the North (where Quakerism first appeared) the frontier character made this an 'awakening' among the unchurched, not unlike the Great Awakening under Jonathan Edwards or the Kentucky camp meetings of the American Second Awakening.[15]

Barbour does not carelessly lump the early Quaker message, with its peculiar emphases, together with a generic Puritanism. He gives a sensitive reading to several points that differentiate Quakerism from the contemporary movements. But ultimately, Barbour finds Quakers to be simply a bold mutation within the Puritan species of the Protestant genus. He views early Quakers as a Puritan revival movement with a few new twists of its own.

Barbour can flatly state, "Historically and theologically, Friends are Protestants."[16] He finds Quakerism to operate too much within the Protestant emphases of personal experience and justification by faith to be classified otherwise. "To sum up, Quakerism can historically be called the ultimate form of radical Protestantism, and doctrinally a development and extension of Reformation thought...."[17]

The contributions of Nuttall and Barbour have provided a much-needed corrective to the liberal assumptions of Rufus Jones' mystical reading of Fox. Far from being incidental to Quakerism, the language early Friends used can be seen as partaking in an evolving theological debate, as research into the Puritanism of the day has shown. This historical analysis has contributed to our understanding of early Quakerism in much the same way history-of-religions research has aided our grasp of the New Testament message in this century.

Nevertheless, historical analysis can easily fall prey to the problem of *reductionism*; themes shared by different movements may be emphasized at the expense of their originality. Seeking points of analogy, we may join together two different phenomena without respecting the real organizing principles of either one. The Old Testament has at times been overly generalized with its ancient Near Eastern religious counterparts. Research into Hellenistic religions has led some to see Paul as a Gnostic. And as we have already suggested with regard to Nuttall's work, the Protestant interpretation views early Quakerism too much through a Reformation theological framework. Certainly Fox shares with the Reformers a strong emphasis on experience and saving faith. Yet these points of emphasis find their place within a framework; the Christian experience unfolds within the context of Christ's return, instead of scripture's record. Lewis Benson has characterized this shift in framework as the "Copernican revolution" of Quakerism.[18]

The Protestant interpretation of early Quakerism has dominated Church historical scholarship in recent decades. Yet while it corrected Jones' view of Quakerism operating in an alien thought-world, it has overdrawn its image of the Quaker-Puritan debate as a filial squabble within Protestantism.

AN ALTERNATIVE APPROACH

Attempting afresh to place early Quakerism properly within Church history, let us now turn to another rubric, one suggested by Albert Schweitzer in his historic *Quest of the Historical Jesus.* Schweitzer sadly comments that

> the whole history of Christianity down to the present day, that is to say, the real inner history of it, is based on the delay of the Parousia, the non-occurrence of the Parousia, the abandonment of eschatology, the progress and completion of the "De-eschatologising" of religion which has been connected therewith.[19]

In his study of the gospels, Schweitzer finds Jesus' message to be consistently eschatological in its outlook. That is, it thoroughly shared in the popular Jewish beliefs in a coming Messiah, the kingdom of God, the suffering and glorification of God's elect, and the resurrection of the dead. These themes characterize the Jewish apocalyptic thought of the day and infuse the life and teachings of Jesus, as well as the early Church's proclamation of him. Jewish apocalyptic looked forward to a coming climax in history, a time when the world as it was known would pass away, ushering in a new age of God's righteousness. The early Church shared in this expectation, specifically awaiting the fulfillment of the great triumph of God revealed in the cross of Jesus. This fulfillment would come by the *parousia*, the risen Lord's return in glory to assume his reign on earth.

Therefore, in the quotation above, Schweitzer suggests that the entire history of the Church may be interpreted as its response in various ways to the delay or non-occurrence of this return of Christ. He also suggests that this response has been one of progressive abandonment of eschatology, end-time theology, as the pivot point of Christian thought. It is his judgment that in this abandonment the Church has lost the inner integrity and vital power of New Testament Christianity.

That abandonment may be seen, beginning by the second century, in a number of directions taken by the Church. The growing perception that the parousia had been delayed threw the Church into a state we might call *anti-crisis*. There were two responses to this anti-crisis. One was to abandon the expectation of historical fulfillment, to revision Christ as a teacher of timeless, metaphysical truths, more world-transcending than world-transforming. Such a view fit more comfortably into the Greco-Roman world, where teachers of wisdom were better accepted than a Coming Lord. Yet other Christians saw this approach as an abandonment of the promises of scripture and the teachings of Jesus and the apostles. These teachings, the emerging New Testament canon, were used by "successors" to the apostles as the authority for rejecting such deviation. The Church must be preserved in good doctrine and order until the Lord's return. In this open-ended context, the fervent expectation and clear priorities of the early Church naturally gave way to an interim ethic of institutionalism. No longer living in the "end-time," the Church accommodated itself to "the meantime," where the kingdom of God may become simply an internal reality of the heart, a promise of a distant future, or the institution of the Church itself.

In lieu of Christ's return, a human rule has been seen as necessary for the interpretation of scripture, the promulgation of Church doctrine, and the oversight of the Church. This institutionalizing trend has "de-eschatologised" the Church even as the hope of the parousia has been retained. During periods of social and institutional stability, the eschatological hope has often become more vague; sometimes metaphysics has gained influence. At other times of social and political upheaval, the sense of the "last times" has been revived and the expectation of the Christ's return increased, as we shall see in seventeenth century England. Yet in either case, we find one assumption constant: until Christ does return, there is no reason to expect his eschatological righteousness to be preached or fulfilled on earth. Hence, the interim ethic of the Church. As Schweitzer implies, these tragic realities predominate to this day.

Accepting this rubric of Church history, we must define and appraise George Fox's message and the early Quaker movement it generated first of all as a response to "the delay of the parousia." Modern interpreters have not addressed the subject by this criterion. Rufus Jones understood Fox as a mystic who tapped the wellspring of all great religions. By this interpretation he connected early Quakerism with the metaphysical tendency in Christian history. Nuttall and Barbour place Fox within the realm of radical Puritanism, where increasing emphasis was laid upon the guidance of the Holy Spirit. Nevertheless, the authority of scripture was maintained, along with a future expectation of the parousia.

Lewis Benson[20] has shown that the core of Fox's message is found in his repeated proclamation that "Jesus Christ is come to teach his people himself." Clearly, this is a bold statement on the issue of the parousia. Fox's preaching represents a historic return to the consistent eschatology of Jesus and the New Testament Church. Fox portrays every aspect of the Christian experience within an apocalyptic horizon, from personal experience and its relation to scripture, to Christian worship, ministry, and Church order, to the Church's relation to the state and the ultimate consummation of history. Yet the apocalypse in personal experience remains the focus, even in the widest vistas of Fox's vision.

Ernst Käsemann, who has done more than any other modern New Testament interpreter to further our understanding of early Chrisitan apocalyptic, makes the following observation on the relation of the cosmic horizon to personal experience in early Christian thought:

> . . . salvation history must not take precedence over justification. It is its sphere. But justification remains the centre, the beginning and end of salvation history. Otherwise the cross would inevitably lose its central position and then everything would be distorted — anthropology and ecclesiology, as well as Christology and soteriology.[21]

Fox's understanding indeed places justification in right relation to salvation history, leading him to bold positions in all the areas cited by Käsemann — positions that set him apart from the Puritan and wider Protestant realms.

Justification and sanctification become one continuous work of God in Fox's preaching that "Jesus Christ is come to teach his people himself." There is neither a retreat to metaphysics nor a resort to the interim ethic and government of the institutional Church. Christ is come by his Spirit to judge, to empower, to war against Satan, and to rule among his people. The kingdom of God is revealed concretely on earth now. Fox comes to these conclusions without falling into the trap of spiritual enthusiasm or privatism. Unlike Paul's opponents at Corinth and Philippi, Fox by no means underestimates the problem of sin, but witnesses to the greater power of the risen Lord to save and gather his people. The cross relentlessly maintains its central position in Fox's writings.

In preaching Christ's return as a presently unfolding reality, Fox recovers the consistent eschatology of the New Testament faith, shattering the perceived problem of a "delay" or "non-occurrence" of the parousia. He does this as he witnesses to the second advent of Christ in the same terms that the gospels use to witness to the first advent. The *problem* in both cases is with the expectation and perception of the people, together with the vested interests of human authority. The "messianic secret," the scandal that Jesus was not recognized as Messiah by the Jews, is relived in the drama of Christian disbelief in his return and his present power to save *from* sin, rather than *in* sin. In his first advent, Christ was revealed in a carpenter's son from Nazareth; in his second advent, he is revealed in a universally bestowed light. In both cases, his commonness is a stumbling block to the pious.

Fox's preaching that "Christ is come to teach his people himself" therefore connects the hope of the parousia with the question of Christian knowledge. In other words, *apocalypse* and *revelation* are reunited in the basic sense of the Greek word *apokalupsis* as it is used in the New Testament. For example, the Apocalypse of John is the revelation of the end given him by Christ. Apocalypse as revelation itself leads us to conclude that Christian apocalyptic is most basically a matter of present experience, rather than speculation upon the future, as scholars have often assumed. Current New Testament scholarship, centering on the Pauline literature, is moving toward these conclusions. The content of the Christian revelation is eschatological: the risen Lord reveals the realities of the end-time — the last judgment, the righteousness of God, new creation — *now*.

The two verbs in Fox's central proclamation, "come" and "teach" thus form a unity. They are two aspects of the same divine act. And again, the teaching of Jesus in his second coming affirms his teaching in his earthly ministry. The earliest Christian proclamation about Jesus understood him to be a prophet and teacher of Israel.[22] The gospels portray him as the successor and fulfillment of all the prophets of Israel, especially Moses. And the Church in Christ is a prophetic community, speaking and acting in the Spirit of Jesus.[23]

While modern scholars generally assume that the prophetic Christology (along with the consistent eschatology) died with the apostolic generation,[24] we nevertheless see with Fox a clear return to prophetic Christology. Lewis Benson again deserves credit for rediscovering this fundamental orientation of Fox's Christology.[25] Not only did Fox preach Christ foremost as a heavenly Prophet-like-Moses, but the implications he drew for worship, ministry, and Church order established the early Quaker movement as a prophetic community much like that described in the New Testament. Early Friends concluded that communion with the risen Lord must be substantially the same as that enjoyed by the first disciples — a fellowship in which he *teaches* his friends.

PART ONE

**THE HISTORICAL BACKGROUND AND DEVELOPMENT
OF EARLY QUAKERISM**

1. THE PURITAN REVOLUTION

> *I was moved to open my mouth and lift up my voice aloud in the mighty power of the Lord, and to tell them the mighty day of the Lord was coming upon all deceitful merchandise and ways, and to call them all to repentance and a turning to the Lord God, and his spirit within them, for it to teach them, and tremble before the mighty God of Heaven and earth, for his mighty day was coming; and so passed through the streets. And many people took my part and several were convinced. And when I came to the town's end, I got upon a stump and spoke to the people, and so the people began to fight, some for me and some against me . . . .*[1]

This account by George Fox of a market day in Kendal, 1652, describes the kind of reception he and his fellow Quaker preachers often had. They preached a message that agitated and polarized entire communities, precipitating profound faith in some hearers and violent alienation in others. British historian Christopher Hill, who from a Marxist perspective has written extensively on the seventeenth century, ponders this phenomenon:

Reading Fox's *Journal* one at once becomes aware of a gap between the events described and the apparent reasons for them. *Why* did such vast crowds gather to hear Fox? Why and how were so many convinced? Why were priests, some magistrates, and some of the 'rabble' so enraged?[2]

Hill, like most modern historians on that period, fails to find "any great theological novelty" in Fox's message, nothing that had not already been expressed in some manner by the radical Puritans of the day. It must be said that Hill's best contributions to our understanding of the Puritan revolution come from his social and economic insights as a Marxist historian, rather than as a theologian. Nevertheless, Hill shows a commendable sensitivity to the theological themes of the day and their interplay with social and economic factors. And though I come to different conclusions about the originality and significance of Fox and early Quakerism, I do make ample use of Hill's important contributions regarding the historical forces preceding and surrounding the Quaker phenomenon.

In *Puritanism and Revolution*, Hill makes a helpful assessment of the task of understanding the dynamic forces at play in the rise of Puritanism:

> The connections of religion, science, politics, and economics are infinite and infinitely subtle. Religion was the idiom in which the men of the seventeenth century thought. One does not have to accept the idiom, or take it at its face value, to see that it cannot be ignored or rejected as a simple reflex of economic needs. Any adequate interpretation on the English revolution must give full place to questions of religion and church government, must help us to grasp the political and social implications of theological heresy. . . . What we need today, I suggest, is a return to these contemporary interpretations, integrated with the results of recent research into industrial history and modern studies of the relation between Puritanism and the rise of capitalism. . . . Any event so complex as a revolution must be seen as a whole.[3]

Two historical chapters will focus on the relationship between the religious, social, and economic developments leading up to the emergence of Quakerism in the 1650s, as well as the way in which Quakerism responded to these developments. The key issue among these categories which will dominate my investigation will be that of *eschatology* — the belief in the end-times, the return of Christ, the coming of the kingdom of God. End-time language and expectation shaped and gave a particular energy to the socio-political struggles of both Puritans and Quakers. In the case of Puritanism, this line of thought tended to be mainly a speculative, political ideology, based upon apocalyptic books of the Bible, such as Daniel and Revelation. Texts were employed in order to identify certain political figures with the antichrist, to calculate the end of the world, or to make messianic claims for political agendas. Such speculation mobilized great political and military energies.

On the other hand, Quaker preaching, while sharing some of these characteristics, will be seen to lay primary emphasis upon apocalypse in its literal sense of revelation. Geo-political speculation gave way to a knowledge of Christ's return in personal experience. This approach created much less political ideology (Hill's chief disappointment with Quakerism), yet it generated a movement with dynamic social and economic reordering and a powerful political witness that far outdistanced the Puritan efforts. What we find in Fox's preaching are the same hopes shared by his Puritan contemporaries, yet a new basis for these hopes in a radically personal spirituality. It is an experience of apocalypse, like that described in John 3:19 — "And this is the judgment, that the light has come into the world. . . ."

Finally, these differences in understanding are closely related to fundamentally differing concepts of the Word of God. The Puritan insistence upon the Word as scripture goes hand in hand with its speculative predictions of the end based upon proof texts. The Quaker insistence upon the Word as Christ's spiritual revelation, however, inspires a more organic understanding of apocalyptic literature and places apocalypse within the realm of personal experience. The first two chapters focus on this question historically; the rest of the study will open the issue theologically.

THE RISE OF PURITANISM

The Puritan revolution, culminating in the establishment of the Commonwealth in the 1640s and terminating with the Restoration of the monarchy in 1660, represents the convergence of many different religious, economic, and political forces. A variety of impulses and interests came together under the Puritan banner. Opposition to these forces by monarchy and Church hierarchy forged them into a dynamic and creative unity. Though the Quaker movement arose only in the last decade of this revolution, the 1650s, our understanding of Quakerism will depend upon our grasp of the century of English history that preceded it.

The foundational event that set the forces of revolution in motion was the break with Rome and the establishment of the Church of England under the authority of Henry VIII in 1534. The Henrician Reformation was essentially an act of state which intended modest changes in Church doctrine and order. Of course, it is generally agreed that this act was precipitated not by Henry's religious zeal so much as by his rebellion against Rome's encroachment upon his royal matrimonial affairs. But his own personal freedom was not the only strategic goal that Henry sought to achieve. He also effected a dramatic consolidation of economic and political power under the crown. Not only did he make himself Supreme Governor of the Church, replacing Rome's authority, but he also took away from the Church considerable economic and political assets, placing them directly within his own secular control.

Monasteries and other Church properties were dissolved; some became properties of the crown while others were either given or sold directly to propertied laymen. Most of these recipients were of the lesser gentry — local subjects favored by Henry over the old medieval aristocracy. Among these newly ascendant figures were ready entrepreneurs with new ideas for economic venture and development. This distribution into entrepreneurial hands provided a major catalyst for England's economic advance. The repercussions of a fresh burst of capital into the economy spread in wider circles over the sixteenth century. As Hill points out, it was to help fuel the capitalistic groundswell in England, which was developing in the clothing and mining industries, as well as in agriculture.[4]

Moreover, though the crown originally retained many of the Church's properties for itself, these also gradually entered the economy as Henry, and later Elizabeth, had to liquidate them to finance military operations. Thus, both directly and indirectly, capitalistic growth was boosted by the dissolution of Church properties.

Henry's handling of the Church properties was a pivotal event — one with implications that would go much further than he dreamed. His original intent apparently was to consolidate his own monarchical power. In the short term the strategy worked quite well. But the long-term effect was to create a growing, independent, propertied class with few direct obligations to the crown. It inspired a tide of enterprise which had little regard for idle and inefficient wealth. A process was thereby begun which eventually would lead to the overthrow of the monarchy.

The Church suffered severe losses in its political and social powers as well. In time, these would converge explosively with the economic change we have just described. Abbots were removed from the House of Lords, reversing Church power there from an absolute majority to a minority. Concomitant with the loss in properties was a great curtailment of the Church's system of patronage in jobs for laymen as well as clergy.

The religious and social power of the Church diminished as confession, penance, and the sale of indulgences were abolished. The destruction of Church iconography weakened the awe-inspiring qualities of the Church. Finally, Henry's authorization of an English translation of the Bible struck the key blow to the traditional religious authority of the Church. The Church of England assumed a generally Protestant stance on authority as it rejected the Roman formulation of scripture and tradition. The Word of God in scripture became the sole doctrinal authority. Yet here we discover the essential paradox of the English Reformation. As Dean Freiday points out, though Henry replaced the Pope when he assumed the *governance* of the Church under the crown, he did not assume magisterial authority in matters on *doctrine.*[5]

English Protestantism invited men and women to read the Bible themselves without the doctrinal litigation of Church tradition. Yet at the same time it maintained a conservative royal control over Church liturgy and government. The official stance which developed to express this tension was that while scripture stood as the sole authority in matters of doctrine, secondary matters of liturgy and order could be managed in any form that did not explicitly contradict the New Testament witness. Thus, scripture and Church tradition were replaced, one might say, by scripture and royal discretion. If England could have worked out this approach in isolation, it might have been imposed more easily. But, as we shall see, Reformation thought on the Con-tinent was to make this settlement appear sadly lacking to England's more impassioned reformers. A tension generated within the Church of England between doctrine and order was to pit the Word against the crown. This tension was eventually to wrest the crown from atop the Church in much the same way that the tension between free enterprise and traditional royal economic authority was to lead to the overthrow of the crown's state supremacy.

Edward VI's brief reign continued Henry's new formulation. Mary's violent reign attempted to reimpose Rome's authority over the English Church. When Elizabeth ascended to the throne in 1558, the framework of the English Reformation had to be constructed all over again. Elizabeth's religious leanings were definitely Protestant, but she faced much political uncertainty. Perhaps because it was difficult to know how much Roman Catholic opposition might exist in the nation, she chose a fairly conservative course regarding the Church.[6]

In early 1559 Parliament passed two acts which basically reestablished the shape of English Protestantism as it was before Mary's interruption. The Act of Supremacy placed Elizabeth as the Supreme Governor of the Church and required all clergy, like magistrates and civil servants, to take an Oath of Supremacy. The second item was the Act of Uniformity, which established a new Prayer Book. Further, practices regarding Church decorations and clerical vestments were ordered to be the same as those prescribed under Edward VI. The Queen and her Commissioners were to dictate all major aspects of Church life and worship.

Many expected this cautious initial settlement to be modified and refined in a more Protestant direction shortly thereafter. But Elizabeth stood resolutely in this formulation throughout her reign. Hill speculates that the court soon recognized that a diminishing profile of the Church was potentially destabilizing to the social order. Beginning with Elizabeth, and becoming much more explicit with James I and Charles I, we can see the growing perception that the interests of the Church and crown would rise or fall together.[7] This led to an increasing resolve to maintain the traditional image and stature of the Church against the wider implications of Protestant reform, no matter how justifiable according to scripture.

Meanwhile, the more radical currents of the Reformation on the Continent, particularly the Calvinist watershed, were streaming into England. Many Protestants exiled under Mary's reign settled in Switzerland and saw Calvin's programmatic reforms of Church and state first hand. A small English Protestant community thrived in Geneva, where an English translation of the Bible was printed in 1560, under the leadership of William Whittingham. This translation, referred to as the Geneva Bible, became commonly available in England. It contained marginal notes which supplied the reader with Calvin's interpretations. This Bible, and those who brought it to England, began during Elizabeth's reign to exert a more radical influence.

Anabaptist thought also filtered into England, through Holland. Though this flow is harder to trace, John Punshon[8] has supplied enough evidence to show that Anabaptism introduced into England radical ideas — separation of Church and state, rejection of infant baptism, reliance upon the Spirit — that would surface later in radical Puritanism.

These new doctrines spread rapidly through an English Protestantism which felt itself unbearably tantalized by a Reformation that was continually compromised by royal conservatism. Calvinism assumed the dimensions of a revolutionary ideology for those who longed for a thorough-going transformation of England into a godly society. Calvin (as well as Luther) had placed the Reformation in an apocalyptic horizon by identifying the papacy as antichrist. Calvinists formulated textual proofs as well as numerical proofs (based upon calculations on the number 666) to support this identification. Protestants understood themselves as engaged in an international alliance to vanquish the beast and break its grip on the Christian world. For a time, even Elizabeth's cautious government found this rhetoric to be useful in focusing patriotic resolve against the twin enemies of France and Spain.[9]

Yet, as English Protestants looked around themselves in their own Church order, they detected what they believed to be the "rags" or "tail" of antichrist still operative in the liturgical and episcopal structures of the Church of England. They began to call for the removal of these antichristian offenses. Their demand was rooted in the Calvinist insistence upon scripture as the sole authority for all aspects of Church life and practice. As a result, some clergy refused to follow the full dictates of the Prayer Book or to wear the prescribed vestments. These were dismissed by Elizabeth from their appointments. With their dismissal, the seeds of English Separatism were sown.

The birth of the Puritan party centered in the towns of England, mostly outside the radius of the court's more thorough scrutiny. Here thrived an intense devotion to Bible reading and biblical preaching, shaped mostly by Calvinist interpretation. Preaching formed the spearhead of the movement — in direct contradiction to Elizabeth's directive that a reading from the Book of Homilies must suffice for most Church occasions. Calvinist preaching of the Word could not tolerate such a subordination to liturgical uniformity.

Peter Toon notes that while early Puritanism is often described as a ministerial movement, the pastors played only the most visible role. Their ability to advance their message owed much to the support of sympathetic laymen among the magistrates, merchants, and aristocrats throughout the country. These politically and economically powerful figures shared the passion for uncompromised reform.[10] Some of these were members of the newly ascendant propertied class whose capitalistic style owed nothing to the traditionalism represented by the court, but owed much to the dissolution of the old Church power. They supported the discharged or otherwise separated ministers in private chaplaincies and lectureships, which were active and popular preaching ministries outside the direct control of the state Church.

The growth of the Puritan party was greatly advanced in the last quarter of the sixteenth century as Cambridge, and, to a lesser extent, Oxford, began to supply a new generation of ministers dedicated as never before in England to the preaching of the Word. Most of these entered official Church appointments and sought to push the Puritan reforms as far as possible without confronting the higher authorities within the Church.

Another key to the proliferation of Puritan theology was in the growth of "exercises for prophesying," which were held regularly in the universities and market towns. Here several preachers would come together to preach, one after another, on a given text. Hebrew and Greek philology, history, and classical rhetoric often entered into these exercises, giving a scholastic aspect as well. Large crowds attended these meetings and the spread of Puritan views thereby reached wide segments of the society.

Puritan clergy not only preached to their congregations, but they also catechized them in Puritan doctrine. They exhorted followers to a godly life of hard work, moral rigor, and Bible reading. Their appeals to an efficient and scrupulous life went hand in hand with the industrious ambition of the new capitalism.

The Puritan party sought to replace the episcopal hierarchy of the Church with a Presbyterian government, derived from Beza and other Calvinists on the Continent. The growing Puritan conviction that no authentic reform could take place without a reform in Church order made this appeal an increasingly all-or-nothing issue. When the Queen and Church leaders opposed even minor revisions proposed in Parliament, the polarization between Puritans and the state Church became more serious. Eventually, the movement despaired of passing its agenda for reforms, and the Presbyterian initiative was dropped. Puritans continued to grow throughout the country, but no more efforts were made to persuade the Elizabethan government after the 1580s.

When James I, who had been raised a Presbyterian in Scotland, ascended to the throne in 1603, there was a renewed feeling of political hope. Appeals were made immediately to the new King. James was soon to disappoint the Puritans, however. Some minor liturgical changes were made, and a new translation of the Bible, which appeared in 1611, was authorized. But Chruch hierarchy remained untouched. Instead, James devoted much energy to the rhetoric of a king's divine right, a hardline stance in the face of growing Puritan strength in both the Church and Parliament: "the state of monarchy is the supremest thing on earth; for kings are not only God's lieutenants on earth, but even by God himself they are called gods."[11] As God's lieutenant, James did not feel compelled to take orders on Church governance from God's Word, as delivered by his own subjects.

Under James, new Church canons were passed, aiming to force Puritan influences out of the Church; and in 1605, approximately one hundred Puritan ministers were turned out of their appointments as a result. Parliament, embodying the social, religious, and economic forces of Puritanism, experienced growing frustration with the King, feeling that it should have more authority in these matters. Yet Parliament was still far from ready to challenge royal sovereignty. Issues lapsed into a stalemate for the remainder of James' reign.

In 1625, James was succeeded by Charles I. Charles was probably not as gifted a ruler as Elizabeth and James, who had consistently held the Puritans at bay, rebuffing their proposals and maintaining unquestioned supremacy, if not authority. But Charles also inherited a throne that had steadily lost centralized control over the nation's economics and politics. The Puritan revolution was coming to maturity, and an inexorable shift of power from court to country was taking place. Nevertheless, Charles failed to deal creatively or sympathetically with the realities of a new propertied class and its growing clamor for religious and economic reform.

Hill suggests that Charles and his advisors made the mistake of seeing the Puritan hostility toward his religious policies as a cynical mask for underlying dissatisfaction with his economic policies.[12] But it was cynicism on the part of Charles that the Puritans felt was evident on almost every front. The King weakened a potentially burgeoning economy as he continued to favor inept monopolists from the ranks of the aristocracy, denying calls for free trade to bring more able industrialists to the fore. Charles furthermore pursued a foreign policy that did not align England with the Protestant forces and nations against the growing threat of attacks by Catholic forces on the Continent. Finally, with his chief minister over Church affairs, Archbishop Laud, Charles intransigently withstood the demands for reform. Clergy refusing to use the Prayer Book or to wear the prescribed vestments continued to be removed from their posts. Leading Puritan critics were fined, whipped, and mutilated. With the spectre of religious persecution now fully revealed, the line between court and country was decisively drawn.

Not wishing to deal with the growing opposition in Parliament, Charles dissolved it in 1629 and did not call another one for eleven years. Shut off from political maneuver, alienated by the harshness of Laud, Puritans began to despair of the amendability of the present system. The language of reform began increasingly to give way to that of apocalypse. The identification of antichrist with the foreign forces of Rome during the Elizabethan era shifted under the Stuart kings to a domestic critique of prelacy (i.e., hierarchical Church government) in England. Antichrist's relics were now seen in the whole structure of the Church of England, particularly in the exercise of civil authority by bishops and the practice of excommunication, but extending even to the tithe system of Church support. While critiques of prelacy went back as far in England as Wycliffe (1320?-1384) and the Lollards, they now operated within a political and religious movement whose momentum could not be stopped.

In the 1630s the ranks of those Puritans who still struggled to conform to the episcopal system and change it from within were steadily thinned. The Church of England was increasingly viewed as antichrist's stranglehold upon England, and Charles certainly did not appear to be the godly prince fit to lead the nation out of this captivity.

One major alternative for Separatists during the unhopeful 1630s was to leave the country. Some went to Holland and elsewhere in Europe. But the most daring migrated to America, a wilderness where a more radically fresh start could be made. The Puritan experiment in Massachusetts revealed the agenda that would dominate the Commonwealth of England in the 1640s and '50s. The goal was not a religious liberty but a Calvinist theocratic state. The model of Church government in this case was Congregationalism. Godly leaders were chosen to govern the colony according to God's Word as revealed in the Old and New Testaments and to uphold the Congregational order. During the 1630s, some ten thousand Puritans sailed to Massachusetts. For those with the Congregational vision, it was a true Promised Land. For those who sought religious toleration, it became simply the old bondage under a new banner. Four Quakers would be hanged in Boston between 1659 and 1661.

As the 1630s came to a close, the social, economic, and religious forces set in motion by Henry VIII a century before had come to maturity. The settlement that for Henry had been a shrewd feat of royal aggrandizement became for Charles a politically untenable position. Hill summarizes these developments thus:

> In all spheres, if we extend our vision to the middle of the [seventeenth] century, the long-term outcome of [Henry's] Reformation was the opposite of that intended by the Machiavelians who introduced it. Charles I's Secretary of State, the near-papist Windebanke, pointed out to the representative of the Pope in England the historical irony of the situation. "Henry VIII committed such sacrilege by profaning so many ecclesiastical benefices in order to give their goods to those who, being so rewarded, might stand firmly for the king in the lower house; and now the king's greatest enemies are those who are enriched by those benefices . . . . O the great judgments of God!"[13]

In this overview of the English Reformation and the century of developments that followed it, we may see how the traditional socio-economic position of the Church was undercut and destabilized. We may see at the same time that the Henrician and Elizabethan settlements applied a royal conservatism which attempted to restabilize Church order in the face of growing popular outcry for a Calvinist reform according to scriptural authority.

The dynamics of these and later developments bear fruitful comparison to those in Judaism within the late pre-Christian and early Christian era. The rise of Puritanism has clear social and religious affinities to the emergence of Pharisaic Judaism in the second century before Christ. Since the time of the Persian domination of Palestine, the internal civil and religious government of Jews in Judea was consolidated under the High Priest. This fusion of civil and religious authority under one leadership sometimes subjected religious policy to political pragmatism, especially when it came to appeasing the regional overlords.

At the same time, however, a strong popular movement arose, emphasizing the study and observance of the Torah. This movement gave rise to the Pharisaic party, made up mainly of the mercantile class in the cities and towns, as opposed to the Sadducean party, which represented the aristocratic elite of Jerusalem, more socially and politically influential with the High Priest.

The Pharisees exhorted their people to a godly life of Torah reading and moral circumspection. The legal requirements of the Torah were interpreted and applied to a variety of circumstances by the Scribes. The Pharisees were often critical of the political pragmatism exhibited by the High Priest and the Sadducees in relation to the Greek and Roman oppressors of the times. They constantly strove, with occasional success, to reform the political and religious life of the nation according to the Torah and their own traditions of interpretation. For now let us simply note that both Puritans and Pharisees were part of middle-class reform movements which upheld a written, codified Word of God, with a body of their own interpretation, as an authority for spiritual life, against a compromised religious and political leadership.

THE CIVIL WAR AND THE COMMONWEALTH: 1640-52

Charles' suspension of Parliament might have lasted longer had he not needed Parliament's authority to raise money. His calling it into session in 1640 marks, in effect, the beginning of the English Civil War, since by this time the Puritan party was so strong and rebellious that Charles was not, and would never be, able to control it. Hill summarizes the overthrow of Charles as a revolt of the taxpayers.[14] The propertied class, including much of the aristocracy, had lost faith in the leadership of Charles and was ready to place rule in the hands of its own elected representatives.

Late in 1640, Puritan leaders presented Parliament with the "Root and Branch Petition." This document listed the many evils Puritans saw in the Episcopal Church government, particularly the civil powers wielded by bishops. It besought Parliament to abolish this government "with all its dependencies, roots and branches . . . and [that] the government according to God's Word may be rightly placed among us . . . ." By late 1641, Parliament was able to draft and pass a petition, a "Grand Remonstrance." Though it assured the King that Parliament had no desire to abandon the enforced uniformity of a state Church, it did seek a reform according to God's Word, in order to "unburden the consciences of men of needless and superstitious ceremonies, suppress innovations and take away the monuments of idolatry." Charles flatly denied this petition. Further petitions and demonstrations by the citizenry ensued. The situation degenerated until, in September, 1642, Charles' military forces clashed with those of Parliament and war began.

The Civil War was not to be readily won. But in the meantime, Parliament set in motion a process for reforming the Church. In June, 1643, the Westminster Assembly of Divines was created, made up of both clergy and laymen, to reform the doctrines of the Church of England. Reforms of Church order presumably would come later. Potential achievements of this group, however, were soon to be altered by political events.

Parliament began to fear that it could not win its war with Charles and felt compelled to bring the already sympathetic Scottish forces to its aid. But the Scots would not aid Parliament without a civil and religious pact. In September, 1643, the Solemn League and Covenant was accepted. Among its provisions was the agreement that the Church of England would undertake a reformation of doctrine, worship, and government "according to the Word of God, and the Example of the best Reformed Churches." To the Scots and to the powerful Presbyterian force in Parliament, this obviously meant the adoption of a Presbyterian Church order.

Suddenly, the transformation of England's Church doctrine and government was Presbyterian by definition. It remained for the Westminster Assembly, which was dominated by Presbyterians, in any case, to work out its own expression of this settlement so that the new order could be established.

This act of desperation by Parliament may be seen as a key factor in the Commonwealth's later inability to resolve its religious and political conflicts. A move to the Presbyterian model back in the 1580s, when it was first proposed, might have captured the momentum of the Puritan movement in its early stages and produced a fairly united English Presbyterianism. But after half a century of religious dissent and Separatism, other more radical models of Church government were widely supported — all claiming to be based upon the Word of God in scripture. Congregationalism was a thriving movement by this time, and a broad array of sectarian activity was beginning to unfold. Some radical Puritans denounced the very idea of a state Church. Thus the Parliamentary settlement, like the Henrician and Elizabethan ones before it, was to be seen as a compromise of, rather than a total adherence to, the Word of God. It was to inspire similar dissent, but on a broader scale. None of these settlements brought the Church in England to rest solidly upon the Word of God.

Prelacy was not dismantled completely until 1646 when Parliament hesitantly installed some parts of the Presbyterian form of government. The Westminster Assembly's Confession and catechisms were not given approval until 1648. By this time there was strong Independent (Congregational) opposition, led by Oliver Cromwell and the New Model Army, to the Presbyterian domination of Parliament. The New Model Army, based upon the Puritan ideal of ranking men according to ability rather than social standing, was an intensely spiritual and politically radical force. It delivered the key victories against the royalist forces in 1645-6. It was the New Model Army and its supporters that had Charles executed in 1649, over the protests of more moderate Puritans. By the end of the 1640s, the nation was effectively controlled by the Army under Cromwell's leadership.

But the division between Parliament and the Army was only one aspect of the splintering that was taking place in the Puritan movement. With the end of the monarchy came a suspension of censorship, which resulted in an explosion of tracts, expressing a wide variety of religious and political views. The tone of these writings was often highly apocalyptic. It was widely believed that the Lord was doing a truly new thing in England, that the very kingdom of God might soon be established there, to spread abroad over the earth. At first, an almost messianic hope was identified with Parliament as the body which would bring the rule of saints at last to the land. Emigration to America had dropped off sharply in 1640 as a sign of this expectation. But as the Presbyterian faction began to assert relatively conservative control, more radical spirits looked to the New Model Army or to the growing sectarian movements for the coming deliverance. Before long, the Presbyterians themselves were identified with antichrist, just as the papists and prelates had been before.

Now the impulses for reform were reaching a fever pitch. A much more severe critique of the Church developed, even among prominent figures associated with Parliament.[15] By 1650 Cromwell ventured that any distinction between clergy and laity was antichristian. Poet John Milton asserted that antichrist could be found in the institution of "hireling" ministry itself, which amounted to buying and selling the Word of God.

Even as the Westminster Assembly was formulating its official Confession, catechisms, and Directory of Public Worship, its very assumptions were being attacked by radical Independents and sectarians, such as the Baptists. It was objected that set prayers and recitations were not true worship. Only the Spirit could lead men and women to worship God properly; a prescribed liturgy only "quenched the Spirit." Just as Elizabeth had tried to suppress the provocative biblical preaching of the early Puritans, now the Presbyterians in their turn were rebuffed for their efforts to establish uniform public worship; a more spontaneous style, led by the Spirit, was beginning to be favored.[16]

The plethora of radical sects which sprang up at this time around the emphasis on the Spirit is closely related to the rise in the seventeenth century of science, experiential philosophy, and individualism. The vividness of personal experience, which any man or woman could have, was of course, the life-giving impulse of all Reformation thought. But that pulse was exhilaratingly quickened by a stress upon the Holy Spirit that Luther and Calvin had never fully embraced. Luther's early writings on the Holy Spirit were considerably toned down after the sobering experiences of the Peasants' Revolt. Calvin wrote freely of the Spirit but maintained it within the framework of enriching faith and the assurance of scriptural authority. The successors of both men tended to limit attention more to the Word in scripture itself, and up to this point, Puritans had followed in their footsteps.

But, ironically, just as England was free at last to establish its long-awaited Church order "according to God's Word," that "touchstone" turned to sand. The Presbyterian approach that was imposed upon England was only one model that could be constructed from the scant New Testament references to Church order. Puritanism was splintered at its moment of victory — over the very Word of God that had been its unifying standard for decades. The Spirit which inspired the writers of scripture, now began to take on a spontaneous, hypostatized authority of its own in worship and daily life. For the more radical minds, "according to the Word" gave way to "in the Spirit" as the new rallying cry.

The Holy Spirit came to be a principle of religious *pluralism* in the 1640s and '50s. This pluralism was already embodied in the Army's broad spectrum of religious viewpoints, which had not bothered Cromwell even from the start. Indeed, Cromwell and the Army had encouraged a policy of tolerance beginning in 1650 when the Act of Uniformity was abolished and replaced by a more loosely conceived act against blasphemy. Though Cromwell was never able to enact a formal policy of toleration, his ability to enforce an effectual one was key to the rise of many sects, and of the Quakers.

In these developments we can see the flowering of what has been called radical, or spiritual, Puritanism. Radical Puritanism, fired by the momentous events of the war and the suspension of censorship, operated on a set of premises different from those of the traditional Puritan coalition. Whereas the Puritan call for Church reform had traditionally assumed a uniformity of religion under state control, Independents and Baptists were beginning to conceive of a separation of Church and state authority. Moreover, as we saw, the old Puritan alliance had socio-economic foundations in the rise of a new propertied middle class and worked for an economic system of free enterprise and competition favoring creative entrepreneurs with capital. The Puritan revolution was the victory of this alliance. Radical Puritans, on the other hand, noticed that this revolution had not addressed the vast segment of the *poor* in society, who were no better off than before. They reasoned that if the purpose of the Civil War was to establish God's kingdom among his people, then Parliament should institute reforms to serve God's interest in *all* his people.

The socio-economic insights of radical Puritanism were embodied mainly by the Leveller party. Levellers advocated a wider suffrage to include all free men in the land. They also demanded an end to the enclosure (and thus control) of common lands by the wealthy, which shut out the poor from an important resource. They worked for the establishment of farm tenant rights. More extreme Levellers, who became known as Diggers, illegally formed communes on common lands. Levellers were the first among the Puritans to question the basic assumptions of property rights.

Inspired by the accounts in the Book of Acts of the common treasury of the apostles, Levellers reasoned that a rule of the saints in England should instigate a levelling of material wealth. Their arguments, while more a matter of economic theory and political ideology, were supported by selected biblical texts and envisioned "Jesus Christ as head Leveller."[17] Leading figures, Gerrard Winstanley and John Lilburne, were also influenced by the new spirituality of Puritanism, often making decisions by attempting to sense the guidance of the Spirit.

During the 1640s Levellers enjoyed strong ties with the Independents and the Army, helping to form a radical coalition against Parliament. But as power shifted to the Independents, this coalition fell apart. Levellers were alienated when Independents failed to adopt any substantial part of their democratic reforms. A number of Leveller leaders were arrested in 1649, marking the end of this movement as a powerful political force.

Observing, in retrospect, the unfolding of the Puritan revolution, we can see in the Commonwealth period a general movement to the left. Yet even as this process took place, there was a shattering effect, leaving the elements of original Puritan unity strewn across a religious and political landscape beginning with the Presbyterians, then the Independents, the Levellers and the spiritual sects. Parties used scripture forcefully against political power but could not create unity with scripture when given that power.

At the extreme end of this spectrum were two groups particularly important for our understanding of Quakerism —the Ranters and the Seekers. The Ranters' name suggests their expressionistic style. They were antinomian libertines who delighted in swearing, drinking, bawdy singing, smoking tobacco, and promiscuity. Deducing from the Bible that God is the author of both good and evil, they assumed an indifference to sin. Their uproarious meetings were often held in local taverns. Nevertheless, it must also be said that Ranter writings were among the most original and insightful of the period. In the late 1640s, their nihilism caught the growing sense of futility in England and attracted thousands, especially among the young.

The Ranters were the only group which the tolerant Cromwell would not uphold. They might easily be disregarded as the lunatic fringe of Puritanism if their views had not often cogently summed up the direction of radical and spiritual Puritanism. As we noted before, the pluralism which Puritan spiritualism championed against the coercion of state religion was rapidly converging with the individualism already advanced by humanism and experiential philosophy. The Baptist Henry Denne speculated on a divine light within everyone.[18] The anarchic spirit of Ranterism took hold of this concept with relish. Jacob Bauthumley, for instance, denied the authority of scripture, insisting that the individual be guided by the mind of God within. Joseph Salmon insisted that Christ is incarnated in the individual — and that antichrist is incarnated, as well, wherever this truth is denied.[19]

The development of religious thinking as expressed by these varied groups is essential for our understanding of the ideas that led up to Quakerism. It is also needed for interpreting the breakdown of the Puritan movement, which began around 1650. We find the political force of Puritanism splintered into infighting among factions whose aspirations ranged from reduced monarchy to a form of proto-communism. At the same time, we see the apocalyptic horizon collapse as the view of evil in society shifted from prelacy to Presbyterianism, to state religion, and finally expressed itself in individual depravity. Lastly, we observe the Word's authority in scripture relativized by the authority of the Holy Spirit, which was in turn blurred by a principle of revelation variously understood as divine spirit, reason, and incarnation.

Christopher Hill is correct in seeing this process as the decline of Puritanism's revolutionary potency.[20] With the vision of antichrist within the individual, the uniquely powerful apocalyptic drive that had fused Puritan religion and politics was swallowed up at last by the Calvinist doctrine of human depravity. Levellers and other radical Puritans could be stopped effectively in their campaigns for messianic reform simply by pointing to the continued existence of sin. "Paradise can be regained only in heaven, and meanwhile sin justifies inequality and social subordination. 'If paradise were to be replanted on earth,' wrote a bishop in 1653, 'God had never expelled man (from) paradise.' "[21] Faced with this theological dilemma which was inescapable within the bounds of Calvinism, radical Puritans resorted either to the nihilism of the Ranters, or to the Spirit's leadings — neither of which was producing a dynamic unity among them.

With the beginning of the 1650s, the stagnation of Puritanism became increasingly apparent. Oliver Cromwell's rise to Protector of the nation found him hard pressed simply to maintain the modest reforms already gained in the badly divided Commonwealth. He would soon become reviled by both the left and the right — even identified with antichrist. In 1650-51 many Ranter leaders were arrested and imprisoned under the new Blasphemy Act in an effort to stem the tide of anarchy. By 1652 the Puritan movement was in disarray. The feeling of disillusion at that point was wearily expressed by William Erbury toward the end of his life. He concluded that all the churches "say that they are in Gospel order, and are not, but do live in Babylon. And there are not they only, but all the scattered saints, this day to dwell, and I also with them, waiting for deliverance."[22] John Webster, an associate of Erbury, wrote that it would be better to "sit down and wait in silence than be beholding to the pretended light and direction of deceivable guides."[23]

Similarly, the Ranter leader Joseph Salmon, his high spirits cooled by a brief imprisonment (and recantation — Ranters were a provocative but not heroic lot), wrote these words before departing for Barbados, never to be heard from again:

> The World travails perpetually, every one is swollen full, big with particularity of interest . . . labouring to bring forth some one thing, some another, and all bring forth nothing but wind and confusion. . . . I am now at rest at the silent deeps of eternity, sunk into the abyss of silence, and (having shot this perious gulf) am safely arrived into the bosom of love, the land of rest. . . . My great desire . . . is to see and say nothing.[24]

The state of radical Puritanism by 1652 is best embodied by a group known as the Seekers. The Seeker phenomenon was not a sect — in fact, it defined itself in opposition to sects by stressing more what it had *not* found than what it had found. It was made up of thousands who had fitfully passed from one movement to another, finding a fleeting satisfaction, but no lasting peace or unity. Unlike the Ranters, the Seekers still diligently searched for the path of true righteousness. They denied not only the state Church in its episcopal and Presbyterian orders, but also the hireling ministry and sacraments. They began to meet in silence, praying aloud or witnessing as moved by the Spirit.[25] Though the spiritual life of the Seekers was rich, and many of their leaders were extremely gifted, they felt that they had come to the end of a long and painful road of false gatherings. Together they would wait in patience, "Expecting a farther Manifestation."[26]

This theme of silence which characterized the twilight moment of radical Puritanism was soon to take on a transformed meaning in Quakerism.

2. THE LIFE AND TIMES OF GEORGE FOX

You have known the manner of my life, the best part of thirty years, since I went forth, and forsook all things; I sought not myself. I sought you and his glory that sent me; and when I turned you to him, that is able to save you, I left you to him: and my travels have been great, in hungers and colds, when there were few, for the first six or seven years, that I often lay in woods and commons in the night; that many times it was a by-word, that I would not come into houses, and lie in their beds. And the prisons have been made my home a great part of the time, and in danger of my life, and in jeopardy daily.[1]

Amid the tumult of the Puritan revolution, George Fox grew up in the Midlands of England. Born in July, 1624, in the little village of Drayton-in-the-Clay, Leicestershire, he was the son of upright parents with Puritan leanings. He was an unusually reserved and serious child who by the age of eleven "knew pureness and righteousness," being taught by the Lord "to act faithfully in two ways, inwardly to God and outwardly to man."[2] He was profoundly disturbed by a wantonness he saw in young and old alike, in their "loving foul ways and devouring the creation."[3] He apparently received only a basic education and was apprenticed by his parents to a shoemaker during his teens. His work often included shepherding, which was well-suited to his reflective and solitary nature.

In September, 1643, at age nineteen, he left his home to begin a long period of wandering which was to extend into nearly an entire lifetime of itinerant ministry. He travelled mainly in the North, sometimes settling in a town for a while, but even then remaining generally aloof. Often he would walk in the fields at night, painfully burdened by intense spiritual questions. He sought answers to these questions through extensive study of the Bible and conversations with Puritan ministers and "professors" (a term used by Fox for any person who professed the Christian faith). But none of his mentors could supply answers commensurate with the depth of his questions. In fact, during a period spent back in his home village, Fox discovered his own pastor (an able Presbyterian, twenty years his senior) appropriating his insights into the Sunday sermons.

Fox had a consuming thirst for righteousness that could not be quenched by an assurance of pardon. The righteousness Fox sought was more than a release from guilt. By perhaps any Puritan standard, he maintained a godly life of honesty, sobriety, hard work, and devotion to the Bible. Fox records no feelings of guilt in his spiritual dilemma. But he did feel a temptation to sin and an overpowering sense of despair for all his moral scrupulosity. His description of his problem sometimes sounds much like that which Paul describes in Romans 7:21-24 — "wretched man that I am! Who will deliver me from this body of death?"

Fox lost respect for those who urged him to find joy in such a life, calling them "miserable comforters." He left the company of more orthodox Puritans to seek out the dissenting groups, where he found more kindred spirits. Yet "I saw there was none among them all that could speak to my condition." It was at this point, in 1647,

> when all my hopes in them and in all men were gone, so that I had nothing outwardly to help me, nor could tell what to do, then, Oh then, I heard a voice which said, "There is one, even Christ Jesus, that can speak to thy condition," and when I heard it my heart did leap for joy.[4]

This experience revealed to Fox that the voice of moral demand he already knew was the voice of one who had shared his condition, who could lead and empower to victory. This moment did not mark the end of Fox's spiritual torment. At times his temptation to despair was even greater than before. But, "My desire after the Lord grew stronger, and zeal in the pure knowledge of God and of Christ alone, without the help of any man, book, or writing."[5]

His experience continued to intensify — sublime visions and insights alternating with severe depressions. He was given frightening insights into all kinds of sinful conditions, all having origins within. "And I cried to the Lord, saying, 'Why should I be thus, seeing that I was never addicted to commit those evils?' And the Lord answered that it was needful that I should have a sense of all conditions, how else should I speak to all conditions; and in this I saw the infinite love of God."[6]

During 1647 Fox gradually began to overcome his temptations to despair as his experience of Christ's teaching increased and as he felt himself to live in the power of it. He was overcome by a "great work of the Lord" for almost fourteen days, in which his countenance was changed and he felt the gift of discernment given him — a power that would astonish and disarm many in years to come. He felt himself emerging from spiritual bondage in the power of Christ.

In 1648 Fox experienced the culmination of his conversion process:

> Now I was come up in spirit through the flaming sword into the paradise of God. All things were new, and all the creation gave another smell unto me than before, beyond what words can utter. I knew nothing but pureness, and innocency, and righteousness, being renewed up into the image of God by Christ Jesus, so that I say I was come up to the state of Adam which he was in before he fell.[7]

By this time the essential outlines of Fox's theological vision were complete. He was sharing his understanding of the gospel with others, and people came from near and far to see this remarkable young man. He counts his "convincements" of others as going back as far as 1646.[8]

Fox recounts this story of his early years as if he knew nothing of the Civil War raging all about him — not even of the currents of radical Puritanism which flowed so strongly in the North. He cites no influences, other than the Lord's own teaching, in the formulation of his gospel message, though there are definite areas of overlap with Baptist, Independent, and Seeker contemporaries. It seems clear that his viewpoint must have been informed in part by conversation with these groups. Rufus Jones psychologizes this phenomenon by speculating that Fox had heard certain ideas expressed by Baptists and Seekers, but that they stayed submerged at a subconscious level until suddenly they surfaced as insights seemingly from another world.[9] Similarly, Hugh Barbour, in noting that Fox admits no sources, reasons that in the Puritan hotbed "the newness of experience hid the familiarity of the phrases they used and made each finder a new prophet."[10] However, it seems likely that the lack of "footnotes" in Fox's writings arises from that fact that he considered all ideas to be "notional" until grounded in experience. Thus, when Fox states that "the Lord showed me" that true ministers do not need to be "bred-up" at Oxford or Cambridge,[11] for example, he is not unaware of the Baptist testimony to the same truth. But when this truth had been manifested in his own spiritual development, it began to play an active role in his own vision and ministry. Until that point, Fox considered such ideas as notions, not worth mentioning.[12]

It was shortly after Fox's experience of sanctification in the "paradise of God" that he, at age 24, heard God's call,

> to go abroad into the world, which was like a briery, thorny wilderness, and when I came in the Lord's mighty power with the word of life into the world, the world swelled and made a great noise like the great raging of the sea. Priests and professors, magistrates and people, were all like a sea, when I came to proclaim the day of the Lord amongst them and to preach repentance to them.[13]

Fox goes on to describe his commission to ministry in four pages outlining the theological and social testimonies which would be programmatic for his message. These range from turning people generally from darkness to the light of Christ's immediate teaching, to the specific refusal of "hat honor" (removal of the hat) when addressing social superiors. As W. C. Braithwaite concludes, this sense of commission led Fox to consider himself not the founder of a new sect but the prophet of a new age.[14]

Fox understood himself to be a "preacher of righteousness," after the New Testament description of Noah (2 Pet. 2:5) with the full cataclysmic implications that go along with that Old Testament figure. He began preaching in market places, fairs, law courts and public houses, to "cry for justice" and to denounce vain pastimes and fashions. This witness, while dramatic, was probably little different from that of many itinerant Puritan preachers. Even his dramatic entries into "steeplehouses" to argue with the preachers were already practiced by the Fifth Monarchists, a millenarian offshoot of the Baptists who will be mentioned further below. But Fox pursued these activities with a perspective that gave them a new significance.

Fox records his first arrest for this practice at Nottingham in 1649. Seeing a large steeplehouse on a Sunday morning, he heard the Lord command him, "Thou must go cry against yonder great idol and against the worshipers therein." He listened as the "priest" (Fox's term for any professional minister) stood above the people, preaching on 2 Peter 1:19 ("We have also a more sure word of prophecy . . ."). The preacher gave the standard Protestant interpretation that this Word is scripture, the touchstone and judge of all doctrines, to end controversy. Despite a law strictly forbidding the interruption of a sermon, Fox involuntarily cried out, "Oh no, it is not the scriptures." He testified that the "day star" (vs 19d) is Christ and that his Spirit is the touchstone for doctrines, leading to all Truth. He was imprisoned only briefly in Nottingham.[15]

Fox continued preaching around the region until the next year, 1650, when he was arrested at Derby. He was committed to prison there under the newly passed Blasphemy Act. He records the key interchanges at his trial:

> At last they asked me whether I was sanctified. I said, "Sanctified? yes," for I was in the Paradise of God. They said, had I no sin? "Sin?" said I, "Christ my Saviour hath taken away my sin, and in him there is no sin." They asked me how we knew that Christ did abide in us. I said, "By his Spirit that he has given us." They temptingly asked if any of us were Christ. I answered, "Nay, we are nothing, Christ is all." They said, "if a man steal is it no sin?" I answered, "All unrighteousness is sin."

Fox concludes wryly, "And so they committed me as a blasphemer and as a man who had no sin . . . ."[16] Judge Bennett of Derby was the first person Fox remembers calling him and his associates "Quakers" — as a response to their bidding him tremble at the Word of God. (They had first referred to themselves as "Children of Light" in 1648, a name already shared by some Seekers. The name "Friends" arose only later.)

George Fox's sentence at Derby was originally to have been six months, plenty of time to sober a Ranter, which the authorities who tried Fox probably thought him to be, given his puzzling attitude toward sin. About the time he was to be released, he was offered a captaincy in the New Model Army, a testament to the radical appeal of his message and his powers of leadership. "But I told them I lived in the virtue of that life and power that took away the occasion of all wars, and I knew from whence all wars did rise, from the lust according to James' doctrine" (James 4:1). The soldiers countered that they offered the position out of love and kindness; "and I told them if that were their love and kindness I trampled it under my feet."[17] Angered by his contempt, they cast him into a dungeon, where he was to spend another six months.

Fox was released in late 1651 and managed to stay out of prison for over a year. During this period, his preaching continued to intensify and the Quaker movement was born. Hill points out that Fox was able to work freely at this time probably because the North was under military control from 1651 to 1653, and both the Army and the radical justices who were in power were sympathetic at least to the general direction, if not the peculiar message, of Fox and his followers.[18] In the last months of 1651, Fox's preaching led to the convincements of several radical Puritans who would become key figures in the Quaker movement. These included Richard Farnsworth, William Dewsbury, and James Nayler.

Fox did not linger long with a particular group. Near Beverley, for instance, he spoke to a congregation during their worship service. They eagerly asked him to come and preach to them again later in the week, "And I directed them to their teacher Christ Jesus, and so passed away."[19] At times local clergy would take issue with his teachings, though apparently few could match him in debate. His vast knowledge of the Bible, together with his disarming powers of spiritual discernment, were so unnerving that opponents either fell silent or "flew into a rage." His entrances into towns and villages were becoming notorious, as he rode or walked through the streets, wearing his large hat and plain leather suit, preaching the day of the Lord:

Yea, the Lord's everlasting power was over the world and did
reach to the hearts of people, and made both priests and professors tremble. It shook the earthly and airy spirit, in which they
held their profession of religion and worship, so that it was a
dreadful thing unto them, when it was told them "The man in
leathern breaches is come."[20]

Fox increasingly made it his habit to enter the steeplehouses
and gather people out from them. He attacked these Church
buildings as idols because they were wrongly called "the
Church" or "the house of God" and were maintained by the
coercive tithe system. Similarly, Fox criticized the clergy for
their dependence upon tithe support, calling them merchandizers
of the gospel, in contrast to Christ's free teaching. A typical confrontation of this kind took place at Pickering:

The steeplehouse was exceeding much painted, and I told [the
priest] and the people that the painted beast had a painted
house and opened to him the ground of all those houses and
their superstition and their ways, and the end of the apostles
going into the temple and synagogues, which God had
commanded, which was not to hold them up but to bring them
to Christ the substance. So was my end in coming there, not to
hold up these temples, priests, and tithes, which God had never
commanded, but to bring them off all these things to Christ the
substance; and so showed them the true worship which Christ
had set up . . . .[21]

These testimonies, which struck to the very foundations of the
socio-economic status of the Church and ministry, were the most
antagonistically received. Such encounters in the steeplehouses
of northern England often ended violently. Fox was beaten with
staves, fists, branches, clods, and even the Bible. He was stoned,
thrown down steps, over hedges, and into the streets, and
knocked unconscious. Sometimes the local minister instigated
these assaults. Fox's descriptions of these encounters remind us
of nothing so much as Paul's confrontations in the synagogues.
Indeed, Fox understood his steeplehouse entries as following in
the example of Paul and the other apostles.

As these assaults increased in 1652, Fox's message began to
strike home with more people, and the threat to the established
Church was acutely perceived as local steeplehouses were
sometimes emptied of attenders by Fox's preaching. The process

set in motion by Henry VIII with the destabilizing of Church property had now come to its radical culmination in the message of George Fox.

By the summer of 1652, Fox had reached and gathered hundreds in diverse communities in the North, where they now met together under the Lord's free teaching. But the real coalescence of the movement took place that June as Fox connected with large Seeker gatherings in Westmorland. Travelling toward that district, he was moved to climb up a high hill, called Pendle Hill, where he could see much of the surrounding countryside. There the Lord showed him the places where people were to be gathered. That night, Fox had a vision of a great people in white raiment by the side of a river, coming to the Lord.

A few days later, there was a large, general convincement near Sedbergh, at the border between Yorkshire and Westmorland, by the River Rowthey. Fox understood this to be the fulfillment of his vision. The next Firstday (Sunday) he came to Firbank Chapel, where a large gathering of Seekers was taking place. Fox did not interrupt or criticize the preaching of Francis Howgill and John Audland, who were already sympathetic to his message. In the afternoon Fox climbed the nearby hill, heeding the command of the Lord that he should go to the rock in the mountain, even as Christ had done. Over a thousand people gathered around him that afternoon as he "declared freely and largely God's everlasting Truth and word of life about three hours." The summary is worth quoting fully here, as it gives the overall revolutionary program of his message:

> I was made to open to the people that the steeplehouse and that ground on which it stood were no more holy than that mountain, and those temples and "dreadful houses of God," (as they called them) were not set up by the command of God nor Christ; nor their priests as Aaron's priesthood; nor their tithes as theirs was. But Christ was come, who ended the temple, and the priests, and the tithes, and Christ said, "Learn of me," and God said, "This is my beloved son, hear ye him." For the Lord had sent me with his everlasting gospel to preach and his word of life to bring them off those temples, tithes, priests and rudiments of the world, that had gotten up since the apostles' days, and had been set up by such who had erred from the spirit and power the apostles were in; so that they might all come to know Christ their teacher, their counsellor, their shepherd to feed them, and their bishop to oversee them and

their prophet to open to them, and to know their bodies to be the temples of God and Christ for them to dwell in.

And so I opened the prophets and the figures and shadows and turned them to Christ the substance, and then opened the parables of Christ and the things that had been hid from the beginning, and showed them the estate of the Epistles how they were written to the elect; and the state of the apostasy that has been since the apostles' days, and how the priests have got the scriptures and are not in that spirit which gave them forth; who make a trade of their words and have put them into chapter and verse; and how that teachers and priests now are found in the steps of both the false prophets, chief priests, scribes, and Pharisees, such as both the prophets, Christ, and his apostles cried against, and so are judged by the prophets' Christ's and the apostles' spirit; and all that were in it could not own them. And so turning the people to the spirit of God, and from the darkness to the light that they might believe in it and become Children of the light, and turning them from the power of Satan which they had been under to God, and that with the spirit of Truth they might be led into all the Truth of the prophets', Christ's, and the apostles' words.[22]

Fox's message presented to these Seekers a radical and integrative critique of the Church, and a coherent alternative, based upon a prophetic understanding of Christ's immediate teaching, revealing, and ordering power within the believer, the true temple of God. He held this understanding up against not only all existing forms of Christianity, but against the entire bulk of Church history since the apostolic period.

There was a large convincement at Firbank Fell, with the able Seeker leaders brought into the ministry of the Quaker message. Fox went on to Preston Patrick Chapel, where there was another general convincement of Seekers. From that point on, the group stopped meeting at the chapel and met in homes instead. Fox moved on later that month to Swarthmoor, where he had a powerful effect upon Margaret Fell, wife of the local justice, Thomas Fell. Their home, Swarthmoor Hall, would become the center of operations for the Quaker movement over the next years, due in part to the legal shelter provided by Judge Fell during the 1650s. Fell never actually joined with the Quakers, though his wife was profoundly convinced and went on to become one of the key leaders of the movement. Eleven years after Thomas Fell's death, Margaret Fell would marry George Fox in 1669.

The intense activities of this one month were pivotal for the Quaker movement. Not only were many hundreds convinced, but among them were several gifted radical Puritan leaders who would exponentially increase the outreach of the Quaker gospel throughout England. Their systematic efforts brought the message to London and the rest of the South during the next years.

THE APOCALYPTIC OUTLOOK

Fox's message was a flash of new light upon the gathering gloom of radical Puritanism. It addressed and confirmed many of the important themes of Puritanism, while placing them in a new framework. That framework was built upon the foundation of Fox's central statement that "Christ is come to teach his people himself."²³ This bold proclamation implied three assertions which spoke powerfully to spiritual Puritanism from a new perspective.

First, it asserted that the vivid apocalyptic expectations of the people were now being fulfilled; *Christ had come* to lead his faithful in new paths, thus setting up a new order and government. This announcement of a present spiritual return of Christ, placed emphasis upon *apokalupsis* in its basic sense of *revelation,* transcending the Puritan inclination toward speculation on dates, indentification of figures in Revelation, etc. This experiential focus became the basis for the Quaker outlook at history in general, as we shall see in succeeding chapters.

Secondly, this work by Christ superseded all existing Church orders, governments, teachers, and ministers, which could only stand in the way of the full exercise of his messianic offices. Fox viewed the general tenor of Church government and support since the apostolic age as 1600 years of apostasy, the government and oppression by antichrist. The official temples and ministers of Christendom, which were not ordained in the New Testament, were thus an idolatrous offense which must give way to the true temples of God, the bodies of his faithful, and their true prophet, bishop, counsellor, and priest, Jesus Christ.

The third assertion was that though Christ's teaching and government were by means of his Spirit, the emphasis was upon *Christ himself*, the creating and redeeming Word of God. From this perspective, the immediate and spontaneous authority of the Spirit was not presented as a temporal adjunct to an overall doctrinal authority of the Word as scripture. Instead, the Word and Spirit were fused in Christ's immediate and inward leadership of his people in their daily lives and in their understanding of his gospel. Fox testified that he was taught the gospel *directly* by the Lord, just as Paul claimed to have received the gospel by revelation, rather than by tradition (Gal. 1:11f). Therefore, Fox denied scripture to be the *Word* of God and touchstone of doctrine, but instead affirmed it to be the *words* which God inspired the prophets and apostles to write, the *record* of the Word's dealings in the world.

Thus, a startlingly new formulation of Church government "according to the Word of God" was presented in the message of Fox — one which stood decisively apart from the Reformation watershed of Puritan thought.

In one respect, the Quaker message represented the culmination of the interiorizing and spiritualizing process which had developed in radical Puritanism in the 1640s. Meanwhile its apocalyptic claims and social implications revived and reunified the reforming impetus of the Commonwealth, but in a new way. Quakerism's apocalyptic sensibility involved experience and revelation, more than speculation and ideology. This made its thrust more prophetic, with dramatic implications for preaching and Church order. Fox called men and women to a new *unity* based upon religious experience and social praxis, rather than *coalitions* based upon biblically-derived ideals and shared interests. Further, his "lion's den" style of confrontation in the steeplehouses inspired not reflective thought about Church structure, but a sense of crisis and decision which demanded action. Sometimes the action was violently negative; other times, entire communities were brought into the new movement. The Quaker phenomenon was born of apocalyptic moments of that kind.

The evangelical thrust of Quakerism was enlivening to disillusioned Puritan radicals. If they had begun to despair of politically reforming England of its antichristian Church government, they could at least rid *their* lives of it. They could deny their support to this system by refusing to attend its worship or pay for its establishment. Lewis Benson's conclusion that the early Quaker movement was one of Church *renewal* rather than reform[24] is not an overstatement. Out of this renewal an alternative social order was taking shape, one which displayed in practice some of the changes Puritans had tried to create politically.

THE ECONOMIC OUTLOOK

When George Fox preached, his hearers felt they recognized echoes of radical Puritanism. When he was arrested at Carlisle in 1653 the mob cried, "Down with these round-headed rogues."[25] The next year he was again arrested, on the false suspicion that he was plotting against the government. While Fox's economic critiques centered usually upon the status of the Church, he also addressed the wider economic issues of the society. In 1653 he quoted Isaiah against the enclosure of common lands: ". . . you that set your nests on high, join house to house, field to field, till there be no place for the poor, woe is your portion" (Isa. 5:8). He reminded all oppressors, "exalt not yourselves above your fellow creatures, for ye are all of one mould, and blood . . . ." And to those at ease he warned, "the time is coming when the poor despised ones shall sit down with Abraham, Isaac, and Jacob, and a cry will be among you, and a howling . . . ."[26] Quakers attracted many Levellers, including leader John Lilburne in 1655. Fox was not the leading Quaker writer on economic subjects and seldom addressed them directly. But his few statements clearly reveal his basic orientation. In 1658 he wrote to the Protector and Parliament with several social concerns. He urged the government not to allow people to go begging, adding the argument that poverty often led to stealing. He suggested that it be the responsibility of the rich either to provide for the necessities of the poor or to employ them.[27] The next year Fox wrote again to Parliament with more explicit recommendations. He proposed that all great houses, abbeys, steeplehouses, and even Whitehall should be turned into alms houses, and that monastic and glebe lands should be used to support the poor, with manorial fines turned over for this use as well. He urged that the poor, blind, and lame be provided for, "so that there be not a beggar in England."[28] Again we see Fox's central concern to dismantle the established Church structures in order to provide for the true temples of God. It is clear that in such a massive land reform and transfer of wealth Fox envisioned a social revolution that would reach to the poorest segments of society.

But again, while Quaker economic reform proposals revived the concerns of the Levellers, they also succeeded in transcending the realm of theory. The new economic order was already being realized within the Quaker community. Special Quaker bodies were organized on the local level to explore the needs particularly of poor Friends, but also other poor in the community. Aid was given from whatever sources were available. At a nation-wide General Meeting of Friends at Skipton in 1660, some local justices and militia came to break up the gathering. But when Friends showed them the records of their work in poor relief (particularly among Friends, desiring to keep all their adherents without any obligation to parish relief), the justices were deeply moved, admitting that Friends were doing the work they themselves would otherwise have to do. In epistles to Friends, Fox counselled that legacies given to local meetings should be used to help set up apprentices in the trades; he also urged them to provide care for the unstable and infirm and to set up their widows and young men in gainful employment.

It has been suggested that the Quaker emphasis upon a reordering of social and economic structures was inspired in part by the fact that the early Quaker movement was populated by large numbers from the lower classes.[29] The evidence for this assertion has been reviewed and disputed by R. T. Vann.[30] Vann finds a large representation of the middle class, as well as a notable sprinkling of the gentry, in the first decade of Quakerism. The evidence, however, is scant, based upon legal and financial records in which the poor might not be represented fully. Besides, it is difficult to distinguish middle and lower classes based upon terms like "yeoman" and "husbandman." Whatever the relative proportions in the early Quaker ranks were, it is clear from the wide range of representation that wealthy and poor alike were welcomed into the movement. All were brought into a dramatic sense of new order — one that did not involve a systematic redistribution of wealth among Friends, but aimed to meet the needs of all.

THE SOCIAL OUTLOOK

If rich and poor alike were welcomed into the Quaker movement, it was not due to an elevated opinion regarding the poor, but a humbling view of *all*, as Hugh Barbour points out.[31] Though Friends made bold claims about the power of God working in them, the glory was distinctly God's. The role of God's obedient creature was to be meek and low, trembling before the awesome power of God's living Word as the human will gave way to the divine. Consequently, Quaker testimonies sought to maintain this consciousness of creatureliness in the individual Friend, as well as to inspire it in others. Friends seemed less troubled by wealth in itself than by the social elevation and hubris that came with it. At the same time, poverty carried not only the tragedy of human deprivation, but the temptation to envy.

One of the most immediately obvious of these social testimonies was the plain dress of Quakers. This, of course, was in line with the Puritan tradition of plainness in attire, but was more radically carried out. Rich and poor Friends alike wore unadorned clothing in subdued colors. Fox wrote often to Friends against following the vain fashions of the world.

Other testimonies were a more direct affront to the world. Friends refused to take off their hats or to "bow and scrape" before the rich and powerful. Instead, they might warn them of the day of the Lord — a more profound act of concern. Similarly, they refused to use "you" toward an individual, insisting upon "thee" and "thou." By this time in England, this archaic form was used mainly toward a social inferior and was considered a social slight toward any respectable person. These testimonies created constant friction between Quakers and their contemporaries, often causing difficulties for Friends, particularly when appearing before judges.

> But Christ saith, "How can ye believe, who receive honour from one another, and seek not the honour that cometh from God only?" [John 5:44] . . . Oh, the rage and scorn, the heat and fury that arose! Oh, the blows, punchings, beatings, and imprisonments that we underwent for not putting off our hats to men! . . . And though it was but a small thing in the eye of man, yet a wonderful confusion it brought among all professors and priests.[32]

Typical of this confusion is a statement by a critic named Fuller, who speculated in 1655 that unless they were repressed, "such as now introduce Thou and Thee will (if they can) expell Mine and Thine, dissolving all property into confusion."[33] Though this statement misconstrues the economic aims of the Quaker movement, it does rightly capture the social demand of its gospel.

Probably the most profound social re-ordering within early Quakerism was the move toward equality of women. From the very beginning, women played a major role in the preaching of the Quaker message. Elizabeth Hooten, formerly a Baptist, is the first person Fox names as having been convinced by his message. She went on to be an important Quaker evangelist until her death in Jamaica on a missionary journey with Fox in 1672. Margaret Fell's leadership was central to Quakerism, both before and after Fox's death. While some women Quaker preachers, like Fell, came from more elevated social and economic backgrounds, a surprising number of them were from the lower ranks, often having worked as domestic servants.[34] The roles played by women as leaders and speakers for the Quaker movement were a source of reproach from critics, and were not always well accepted within the movement itself. We will examine the role of women further when we look at Quaker organization in the 1660s.

The social heterodoxy displayed by early Quakers led many Puritans to equate them with the antinomian Ranters. John Bunyan wrote in 1656 that Quakers held the same opinions that Ranters had already held long before, "only the Ranters made them threadbare in the alehouse, and the Quakers have set a new gloss upon them again, by an outward legal righteousness."[35] Indeed, it does appear that many Ranters entered the Quaker movement in the 1650s. Fox records several incidents where groups of Ranters were convinced. A judge told Fox in 1652 that if it had not been for the Quakers, the nation might have been overrun by Ranters. Fox, in fact, would not completely condemn the Ranters. He felt that they had once had great meetings but had not waited upon the Lord to feel his presence and power to gather them. Thus, they had "spoken themselves dry and had spent their portions and not lived in that which they spake . . . ."[36] One Ranter characteristic that irritated Fox greatly was their use of flattery and exalted language toward one another — a direct contradiction of the Quaker stress upon humility.

As Fox's critique of the Ranters suggests, Friends not only experienced Christ's leading them out of the social structures of the world, but they also submitted to his guidance in attaining a new, end-time sense of reordering. Thus, the testimonies and practices which arose were informed not so much by theories about society and the nature of men and women, but by their experience of Christ's ministry among them, empowering rich and poor, high and low, man and woman. This sense of discovery, as Hugh Barbour points out, made these testimonies more evangelical *campaigns* than moral *codes*.[37] They were a witness to Christ that pricked the conscience of those who came into contact with Quakers. And the steadfastness with which Friends maintained them, despite hardships and persecutions, had the powerful effect of convincing many of the Quaker message.

The profile of the early Quaker community and their fluid approach to social standing and economic needs are much like that of the early Church. In both cases, men and women who experienced discomfort with the wider social order found new freedom and mutuality in the faithful community — even though their new life placed them in greater conflict with society. Both groups *anticipated* a new world order, in terms of both expecting it and enacting it.

THE LAMB'S WAR

The Quaker preaching campaign of the 1650s seriously threatened the established ecclesiastical, social, and economic order in England. It was succeeding where radical Puritanism had failed, mainly because it had escaped the quandary of Puritanism's theological assumptions. It did so in the following ways.

First, in identifying the Word as Christ's immanent teaching and leadership, rather than as scripture, Quakerism was able to formulate a Church order which recaptured the spirit of New Testament Christianity, instead of attempting to revive the historical artifact of its dead letter. This approach at the same time gave Fox and early Friends a fresh reading of scripture and new insights into the example of the New Testament Church.

Second, Quakerism rejected the Calvinist insistence upon the inescapability of sin this side of the grave. Christ's teaching as the ultimate authority meant for Quakers an infallible guide that, if obeyed, could lead into the same perfection that Adam and Eve knew under God's teaching in Eden. Thus, Fox could feel himself come into the garden paradise. The overcoming of sin implied God's kingdom overcoming social injustice as well.

Thus, the argument that continued sin makes the establishment of God's kingdom on earth impossible may have levelled the Levellers, but it did not shake the Quakers. Early Friends refused to allow God's freshly revealed righteousness to lapse into a personal piety; their message was a *call* and a *claim* to both personal righteousness and social justice.

Finally, as radical Puritans had begun to argue for a separation of Church and state (against the traditional theocratic vision of Calvinism), Quakerism took this separation as an assumption. Fox's radical vision of Christ's saving and gathering power led him to see the Church — a renewed Church — as the focus of God's kingdom breaking forth on earth. Seeing that this is Christ's power, and not the state's, Quakers did not propose that their religion become the state religion of England, but simply appealed for the freedom to practice and propagate their faith. The Quaker view of the relationship between Church and state was thus *prophetic* rather than *political*. The Church's effect upon the state was to spread in evangelizing the society, in demonstrating the new order within its own ranks, and in witnessing to the government for more just laws and practices. We will examine these aspects of the early Quaker movement in greater depth in our final chapter.

Thus, a revolutionary Quaker campaign, radically different from the tenets of Puritanism, was advanced upon English society. The Quakers called this campaign the *Lamb's War*: ". . . and now is Christ come who will make war in righteousness and destroy with the sword of his mouth all these inventions that have been set up since the days of the apostles . . . ."[38] This is a battle fought both within and without:

> The word of the Lord God to all my brethren, babes, and soldiers, that are in the spiritual warfare of our Lord Jesus Christ. Arm yourselves, like men of war, that ye may know what to stand against. Spare not, pity not that which is for the sword (of the spirit), plague and famine, and set up truth, and confound deceit, which stains the earth, and cumbers the ground . . . . And wait in the light which comes from Jesus, to be clothed in his zeal, to stand against all them who act contrary to the light; which are sayers, but not doers.[39]

Due to the systematic nature of Quaker preaching and witnessing, there may not have been a single parish in England untouched by the Quaker challenge by 1660. As the Civil War raged through the 1640s, pursuing a Puritan vision of the kingdom of God through violent means, the Lamb's War extended through the 1650s, based upon different assumptions, utilizing different means. Quaker missionaries, many of them women, also set out to bring the message of Friends to America, Rome, Africa, the Middle East, and even China during this time. Inspired by the geometric growth of the movement in England, some Friends expected the Lamb's War to achieve world conquest within a generation.[40]

CRISIS OF 1659

The Quaker movement reached a decisive turning point in the year 1659.[41] Oliver Cromwell died in 1658 and was succeeded as Protector by his son, Richard. The political situation by this time had degenerated hopelessly into factionalism. Richard Cromwell found his position untenable and resigned in May, 1659. The Rump Parliament, led by Republican Sir Henry Vane, was left to deal with this stalemate by itself.

Vane was a religiously and politically radical Puritan in an eclectic style. He envisioned a Commonwealth led by a coalition of Baptists, Quakers, and Fifth Monarchists — a new and radicalized formulation of the government of saints. Under his leadership, representatives from Parliament approached Quakers in May about this new coalition. They were asked to make lists of corrupt and persecuting judges throughout England, along with recommendations for replacements. It was assumed that Quakers and Quaker sympathizers would be suggested. Friends had no antagonism toward such an idea; leaders had encouraged Friends during the 1650s to take office and be patterns and examples of righteousness to others.[42] With the help of the extensive Quaker networks of communication, the lists were quickly assembled. They revealed a strong preference for firm Commonwealth supporters and included several Quaker names. There was also a strong plea made for the abolition of tithes, which were not only a theological abomination to Friends, but also the occasion for many fines and imprisonments.

By July George Fox issued his most socially radical and politically explicit tract, *To the Parliament of England: Fifty-nine Particulars for the Regulating of Things.*[43] presenting an extensive program ranging from land reform to the abolition of tithes and religious persecution. The issue of tithes was central to Friends and would be decisive for any Quaker involvement in a governmental coalition. Therefore, when Parliament deferred action on the abolition of tithes in July, Friends were bitterly disappointed. July seems to have been the turning point for all groups involved. Vane's political momentum began to fade and the Army's support flagged at this time.

By August the Quaker leadership was painfully caught in a dilemma. There was much at stake for the Quaker movement. After two decades of Puritan upheaval, now becoming chaos, there was a growing sentiment in England for a restored monarchy. The reform impetus in general, and the Quaker movement in particular, would certainly suffer from a restored monarchy and state Church. Yet Friends would be decisively compromised by entering a coalition that was neither politically viable nor theologically true to their principles. Fox entered a severe depression at this time, a period of despair which lasted for ten weeks. In the endless Puritan in-fighting, he reports, "... I saw how the powers were plucking each other to pieces. And I saw how many men were destroying the simplicity and betraying the Truth . . . . I was burdened and almost choked with their hypocrisy and treachery and falseness."[44]

In August, a Royalist uprising was met and crushed by Parliamentary Forces. Some Quakers were involved in this military action. Fox openly condemned all military and insurrectional activity by Friends and was evidently able to stop this trend.

As the Rump Parliament degenerated, the Army grew impatient and took over Westminster in October. The Committee for Safety, the ruling junta, again led by Vane, made proposals to Friends at this time, even offering Fox the rank of colonel in the Army. But by this time, Fox had emerged from his inner turmoil with a strong sense of direction. He apparently had a clear leading that Friends should not meddle in these last throes of the Commonwealth. He began to set forth the position of Friends in relation to this imminent change in a brief epistle written in October:

> The Lord is king over all the earth, and Christ hath all power in heaven and in the earth; and he is King of kings and Lord of lords, let him rule and reign in all your hearts by faith, and exalt him in the land, and in your assemblies.[45]

By December, Quakers issued an official statement of complete neutrality. James Maclear reasons that Fox and the other Quaker leaders saw that a Quaker involvement in an eleventh-hour Commonwealth government would only increase the wrath against them when monarchy was restored. This pragmatic consideration may well have been part of their reasoning.

But more to the point in a highly prophetic mind like Fox's would have been the issue of the Lamb's War. A political undertaking would have to be justified in terms of the very stringent demands of the holy war tradition of the Bible. This would mean that the weapons of conflict must remain purely spiritual, according to Ephesians 6:11-17, without resort to the carnal sword. It would also mean never returning to the spiritual Egypt from which Christ had delivered them (see Deut. 17:16; Jer. 42:7-22; Ezek. 17:11-21) to make alliances compromising to his revealed Truth. This consideration would have been crucial in the eventual Quaker rejection of a coalition role, and this rejection was precipitated by Parliament's failure to abolish tithes. Fox was a prophetic absolutist, not a political negotiator.

This contention would appear to be supported by a meeting between Fox and Henry Vane in 1658. Vane had been anxious to meet Fox for some time, presumably not only out of religious interest, but also with future political possibilities in mind. Fox's account of the meeting[46] shows that he immediately sought to clarify theological issues with Vane. The conversation centered upon the primacy of experience and the Word of God. Vane was not able to come to agreement with Fox and the encounter broke off with a bad feeling. This aggressive search for a common religious foundation had also been typical of Fox's few encounters with Oliver Cromwell.[47] (Their first meetings were positive and emotional; but their latter ones were filled with more contention, owing partly to Fox's frustration with Cromwell's leadership.)

Writing during the Restoration, at a time of great persecution of Friends, Fox is silent in his *Journal* about the entire matter of Vane's proposals to Quakers in 1659. But it seems reasonable to conclude that when he heard of the proposals made in May, his initial response, though cautious, revealed his hopes for the Commonwealth and his fear of the monarchical alternative. But, by July, the prospects appeared too compromising to Quakers, presenting too great a conflict with the principles of the Lamb's War. Fox may have recalled the crippling position the Commonwealth had found itself in when it entered into the Solemn League and Covenant with the Scots in order to defeat the Royalist forces. In any case, the severity of Fox's depression testifies to the considerable value he placed upon the Commonwealth experiment and the deep disappointment that the Lamb's War could not join with it. The stance with which he emerged similarly testifies to his singular hope in a renewed Church in the face of what must have been a great political temptation.

The closing days of 1659 and early 1660 saw Fox's efforts devoted to shoring up the confused ranks of the movement, bringing the more rebellious elements back in line and bracing for the onslaught of the Restoration.

At this momentous juncture we find Quakerism to be a burgeoning movement. Braithwaite estimates that by 1660 there were probably thirty to forty thousand Quaker men, women, and children out of an English population of five million.[48] While these numbers are not enormous, they make the impact of the Quaker phenomenon all the more telling. Working singly or in groups, Friends maintained a relentless attack upon the established Chruch in England, interrupting services, going naked through the streets for a sign (see Isa. 20:2ff.), refusing to pay tithe assessments. An intense storm of controversial literature raged between Quakers and their critics. About twenty anti-Quaker tracts were published per year during the 1650s, and Friends were very careful to see that each published attack was answered in print. In 1659 Fox published a compendium of his own responses and counterattacks, provocatively titled, *The Great Mystery of the Great Whore Unfolded; and Antichrist's Kingdom Revealed unto Destruction.*

All the more notable is the hardship which the Quaker witness often exacted. The practice of waiting upon the Lord and coming under Christ's teaching was a slow and often painful process of self-critical awareness and denial of worldly fashions. The Quaker life was often as materially austere and plain as it was spiritually rich and colorful. For their refusal to doff their hats, swear oaths, or pay tithes, and for their preaching offensives launched in steeplehouses and marketplaces, they were fined, whipped, branded, dunked, put in stocks, and imprisoned. Though none was sentenced to death in England, several had died by 1660 from exposure to flagrantly bad prison conditions.

It is estimated that some three thousand Quakers suffered various forms of persecutions during the Commonwealth period.[49]

The stark profile of the early Quaker sometimes could work advantageously, however. Fox notes that initially Quaker shopkeepers were shunned for their beliefs and practices. But because of their refusal to barter, insisting upon the "yea and nay" of the one-price system, people found that they could send their children to a Quaker shop and not be cheated. This made many Friends thrive so that some feared another wave of economic revolution in the nation.[50] But overall, these gains were far outweighed by fines, confiscations, and imprisonments. Sometimes the mobs were as dangerous as the authorities. Meetings were often harrassed, with Friends occasionally receiving bodily injury. Fox writes of a Friend's house where meetings were regularly held; glass could not be kept in the windows due to attacks from throngs.

FIRST-CENTURY PARALLELS

As we have already seen, Fox was keenly aware of the first-century synagogue dynamic evoked by Quaker confrontations in the steeplehouses. He understood the Quaker insistence upon the inward teaching of Christ to be a recovery of the first-century Christian understanding of the Word and the risen Christ's spiritual leadership. Likewise, he viewed the Puritan insistence upon scripture as the Word to be "in the footsteps of the Pharisees," given the latter's insistence upon the Torah's authority. For Fox, Christ's fulfilling and ending of the law implied an inward sense of God's will that not only confirms but also surpasses any codified ethic derived from scripture.

The comparison of the Puritan-Quaker debate of the 1650s to what we know of the Jewish-Christian controversy of the first century is compelling. In the first chapter, we pointed to some parallels between the rise of Pharisaic Judaism and the Puritan revolution. It is important to mention again that like Puritanism, Pharisaism was mainly a middle-class movement, dominated by merchants in Jerusalem and the outlying towns. The Pharisaic movement was as distant, even alienated, from the peasantry as it was from the Sadducean aristocracy. Though the Pharisaic party never attempted to achieve dominance over its opponents through civil war, events eventually did conspire to make it the decisive force in Judaism. The Jewish revolt, culminating in the destruction of the Temple in C.E. 70, ended the effective role of the Jewish priesthood and the Sadducees. Pharisaism, in the form of rabbinic Judaism, emerged as the unifying force in Judaism during the C.E. 80s.

Meanwhile, Christianity had arisen as a prophetic movement whose dynamism had challenged Pharisaic piety from the start. Its leadership and following were drawn in great part from the peasantry, though other segments of Jewish society were represented as well. In its development up to the C.E. 80s, Christianity flourished both within and without the realm of Judaism. Those Jewish Christians who remained in the synagogue community were engaged in an intensifying debate, in which the rival theological claims for the Torah and Christ escalated.

J. Louis Martyn has written extensively on the Jewish-Christian debate of the first century, particularly after C.E. 80, as reflected in the Gospel of John.[51] Sometime in the mid-'80s, the Eighteen Benedictions of the synagogue liturgy were amended by the rabbis in an effort to weed out the Nazarenes (Christians) and the Minim (sectarians). Among the new Benedictions was a malediction against these two groups. The secret Jewish Christian in the synagogue congregation would either have to pronounce a curse upon himself or fall conspicuously silent. At a time when Judaism was attempting to shore up its ranks, this liturgy was probably useful for drawing a line between Jewish orthodoxy and Christian heresy.

We find a striking parallel to this phenomenon in the Puritan-Quaker controversy of the 1650s. In 1657, on a missionary journey through Scotland, George Fox discovered a Presbyterian liturgy formulated against Quakers:

And they gathered great assemblies of priests together and drew up articles to be read in their parishes in the steeplehouses and that all the people should say Amen to them, which are as followeth in part:

First: Cursed is he that saith every man hath a light within him sufficient to lead him to salvation and let all the people say, Amen.

Second: Cursed is he that saith faith is without sin and let all the people say, Amen.

Third: Cursed is he that denieth the sabbath day and let all the
people say, Amen.[52]

These maledictions were each aimed against well-known
Quaker positions, including doing business on Sunday. Like the
Jewish Christians reluctant to leave the synagogue, their social
and religious home, Quakers who lingered in the Church of
Scotland were soon forced to declare themselves either in or out.
The consequences of that decision could be drastic. In the
Scottish town of Heads, Fox discovered that the Presbyterian
clergy had excommunicated known Friends and ordered loyal
parishioners not to conduct business with Quakers. This
sanction created severe deprivation for some Friends. Fortunately, Fox was able to convince (convert) the local judge, who
brought these practices to a halt. Often the network of
communication and relief work among Quaker communities was
effective in getting aid to suffering Friends around the country or
even overseas. This practice is reminiscent of Paul's collection
among the churches to aid the Church at Jerusalem.

The friction between Puritans and Quakers during the 1650s
created social, economic, and physical hardships for Quakers,
inspiring virulent polemics against the Puritans much like those
against "the Jews," found especially in the Gospel of John. In
both cases, these polemics must be seen in the broader
perspective allowed us by time. They express the painful birth
pangs of a vigorous new religious movement emerging from the
midst of a great old one. The message of the younger, originally
intended as a fulfillment and expansion of the elder's tradition, is
rejected as such and takes on a new life of its own — but not
without some parting shots.

But once again, like the Jewish-Christian conflicts of the first
century, the conflicts between Quakers and Puritans were soon
to be eclipsed by a much harsher, more imperial form of
repression. The Restoration was to place Quaker and Puritan
alike under a withering blast of religious persecution.

THE RESTORATION AND THE QUAKER STUGGLE FOR SURVIVAL: 1660-1675

In May, 1660 the son of the beheaded Charles I was crowned
Charles II. The attitude of the new monarch toward his father's
enemies was basically forgiving, though he did see to it that
eleven key figures in the execution of his father, including Henry

Vane, were hanged, drawn, and quartered. Many in England were relieved to return to monarchy and episcopacy after two decades of Puritan factionalism and military rule. Besides, the terms of the Restoration considerably reduced the powers of both the crown and the Church. Hence, the Puritan revolution had been able to achieve a lasting political accomplishment. But in an ironic way this proved to work against religious radicals; the new King spoke in favor of religious toleration, but he did not wield the political power to grant it. This power soon proved to be in the hands of the Cavalier Parliament, dominated by firm Royalists who disliked and distrusted Puritans or any other group which would not conform to the Church of England.

Quakers hastily sought an audience with the King. Richard Hubberthorne met with Charles only five days after the coronation and gained a promise from him that Quakers would not be molested so long as they lived peaceably. The King freed seven hundred Quakers still in prison from the Commonwealth days. There was discussion of giving Friends liberty of worship and perhaps even exemption from tithes.

But while these considerations were still pending, Quakers received a major setback. Early in January, 1661 the Fifth Monarchists staged an insurrectional attempt in London, in an apparent attempt to prepare the way for an imminent physical return of Christ. The insurrection was quickly put down, but there was fear that groups other than the Fifth Monarchists alone had been involved in the plot. People connected Friends with the Fifth Monarchists probably because both had spoken of an imminent age of fulfillment. Immediately, Quakers throughout England were rounded up and jailed — some forty-two hundred in all, including all the adult Quaker males in some areas. Fox himself was arrested, but only briefly held.

In a few days, Fox and eleven other Friends were able to meet and draft a declaration to the King, entitled "A Declaration from the harmless and innocent People of God, called Quakers, against all plotters and fighters in the world."[53] This was the first categorical statement to the world of the Quaker commitment to non-violence. In it, they testified to their own experience of Christ's leadings to peaceful action, cited scriptural support for these leadings, and appealed to their history of non-violence. They utterly denied all plotting and indicated their willing submission to civil authority, no matter how many times it might persecute them. They could not be counted on to fight with "carnal weapons" for God's kingdom, much less for any worldly kingdom. This document was instrumental in the subsequent issuing of a royal proclamation freeing all Quakers.

Though this position is essentially the same that Quakers might have formulated in the 1650s if a similar crisis had occurred,[54] the tone implies a new political reality. George Fox had spoken challengingly to Oliver Cromwell and Henry Vane when he had encountered them. He had even bid Cromwell to lay his crown at Jesus' feet.[55] It seems probable that Fox had held out some hope, at least temporarily, that these tolerant and religiously earnest Puritan leaders might be able to help the Quakers, and that the tidal wave of the Lamb's War might float their governments toward a new ordering of society.

But with the Restoration, the Quaker attitude toward the government immediately took a new course. It appears as if no point of serious political engagement with the new government presented itself to Friends, except the appeal for toleration of this notorious group which stood so much in antithesis to the premises of the reconstituted Church of England. In this Royalist period of retrenchment in the old values of social and religious hierarchy, Quakers were dangerously conspicuous in their plain clothes, plain language, and message of apocalypse.

If this dilemma was not clear to Friends by the time the Fifth Monarchist debacle was over, it quickly became apparent as the 1660s unfolded. Under constant suspicion and disdain from Parliament and local justices, Friends could be imprisoned at any time simply by being tendered the Oaths of Allegiance and Supremacy. Quakers, as well as Baptists, followed the clear imperative of Jesus (Matt. 5:34) and James (James 5:12) to "swear not at all." They offered freely to declare their loyalty; but this was unacceptable, of course, to persecutors. The refuser could be imprisoned until the next Quarterly Sessions, when the Oaths would again be tendered. Upon second refusal, the fourteenth century penalty of *praemunire* could be exacted, which meant loss of estate to the crown, suspension of rights, and an indefinite imprisonment.[56]

Braithwaite persuasively compares this form of persecution with that suffered by early Christians under the Flavian Emperors of Rome. At that time, Christians were forced either to offer wine and incense before a statue of Caesar, thus joining the Caesar cult, or face the penalty of death. Like early Christians, early Friends saw the issue of Christ's ultimate lordship at stake.

Quaker Isaac Penington explained that swearing was allowed to fallen men under the Mosaic Law, but is forbidden to those renewed by Christ:

> That which the Law called swearing, the Gospel calls confessing, which confession, in the life, in the truth, in the renewed principle, is the weight and substance of that whereof the oath was but a shadow . . . . entering into the Law-bond is a laying of the Gospel-bond by.[57]

Just as the Caesar cult turned the worship of Christ into a lie, so the giving of the Oath of Allegiance or Supremacy would be a treason against and subversion of the power of Christ within.

The demand of the Oaths proved the easiest way to harrass or imprison Quakers, though Parliament soon passed more specific acts expressly designed to stamp them out. In early 1662, the Quaker Act was passed. It penalized any person who insisted "that the taking of an oath in any case whatsoever (although before a lawful magistrate) is altogether unlawful and contrary to the word of God." It penalized any who tried to persuade others to this effect. It penalized Quakers for gathering in groups of five or more under the pretense of worship not authorized by law. Penalties consisted of fines and imprisonments. The passage of this Act was immediately followed by brutal attacks upon meetings and subsequent mass imprisonments. By October, thirteen hundred Friends were again in prison.[58]

Fox had already been imprisoned for five months in the latter half of 1660, even before the Fifth Monarchist uprising, on suspicion of plotting against the King. This was the fifth imprisonment of his life. In September, 1662 he was arrested in Leicestershire under the Quaker Act and refused to take the Oath. Fortunately, the charges against him were so poorly laid that he was freed after only one month. In early January of 1664 he was again arrested at Swarthmoor for meetings held contrary to the Act. Appearing at the Lancaster Sessions, he was imprisoned for refusing the Oaths. He spent the next year in the Lancaster jail where he suffered illness from exposure during the cold winter. The following summer he was transferred to Scarborough Castle. Finally, in September, 1666, he was freed upon an order from the King, after approximately twenty months of detention.[59]

Other Friends were less fortunate, however. The persecutions in London were especially severe and the prison conditions were terrible. Quaker leaders were detained even when others were finally set free. By the spring of 1663 key leaders John Audland, Thomas Aldam, Edward Burrough, John Camm, and Richard Hubberthorne were dead. Most others were in prison. This greatly curtailed the ministry within Friends meetings, as well as the thrust of their evangelical outreach. Yet the numbers of Quakers continued to grow rapidly,[60] perhaps due to the striking resolution of the Quaker witness.

Vann shows that the socio-economic profile of Friends declined during this period, due to *praemunire*, fines, and loss of income during imprisonments. It became more threatening for eldest sons, for example, to become Friends since *praemunire* could wipe out an entire inheritance. Persons of social standing and political potential could never hope to gain office as Quakers, so the representation from among the gentry diminished.[61] The great exception to that rule, of course, was William Penn, son of the First Lord of the Admiralty, who became a Quaker in 1667.

In July, 1664, the Conventicle Act was passed, inspired by fears of a Puritan rebellion. This new act was essentially the same as the Quaker act but was broadened to affect all nonconforming groups. This proved to be a hardship for a number of Puritan fellowships, though, as even the anti-Quaker critic Richard Baxter noted:

> . . . here the fanatics called Quakers did greatly relieve the sober people for a time: for they were so resolute, and gloried in their constancy and sufferings, that they assembled openly . . . and were dragged away daily to the common Gaol, and yet desisted not, but the rest came the next day nevertheless, so that the Gaol at Newgate was filled with them. Abundance of them died in prison, yet they continued their assemblies still! . . . Yea, many turned Quakers, because the Quakers kept their meetings openly and went to prison for it cheerfully.[62]

Thus, despite the broadened intent of the Conventicle Act, Quakers continued to bear the brunt of Parliament's phobia regarding nonconformists. Fox disdainfully noted the way Presbyterians and Independents, who had tried in the 1650s to force Quakers to practice *their* form of religion, hid their own practice of it now. He criticized them for meeting secretly in homes, having tables set with food as a ruse in case the authorities came to investigate.[63] This practice, called "house-creeping," was rejected by Quakers and Baptists.

When Fox was freed from Scarborough Castle, he found the Quaker movement in disarray. The combined forces of growing numbers, stress from hardship, and the maturing of the movement led Fox to undertake a major new program among Friends — the organization of meetings into *gospel order*. Obedience to Christ's ordering had been a great concern from the beginning. The system of regular meetings to do the Lord's business had begun in the 1650s. These included local, regional, and national gatherings. These meetings were engaged in recording and assuaging the suffering of Friends, as well as keeping order among Friends.

But this system had not yet been fully realized around the country. With the extreme hardships being borne by Friends and the toll that was being taken upon the Quaker leadership, a more extensive effort at organization was required. Moreover, up to this point, all these meetings had been conducted among male Quakers only. In 1667 it was "opened" to Fox that in Christ's restoration of all things (Matt. 17:11; Mark 9:11) to the perfect order that existed before the Fall, men and women must again become "help-meets" (Gen. 2:18) to one another. He was moved to set up parallel men's and women's monthly and quarterly meetings throughout all the nation and to advise Friends elsewhere to do the same. Their purpose, as Fox describes it, was "to admonish, and exhort such as walked disorderly or carelessly, and not according to the Truth; and to take care of God's glory."[64] Thus, in a period when Friends were being thrown into prison by the thousands for meeting illegally, Fox set about to establish more meetings of Friends. Just as the Lamb's War was the Quaker answer to the Puritans' Civil War, so the setting up of men's and women's meetings during the Restoration period advanced a different restoration — one that was not retrenchment but the realization of God's new order of the gospel. This "counter-restoration," as we might call it, reveals Fox's genius for articulating the counter-cultural demand of the gospel.

Still so weak from his imprisonment that he could barely ride a horse, Fox began in London with his intensive national campaign to establish these meetings. His initiative seemed like a radical departure to some Quakers, especially those whose Ranter backgrounds made them prefer the anarchy and expressionism that the movement had sometimes allowed. Indeed, Vann asserts that many leading figures from the earlier days dropped out of the movement over this issue.[65] But the turnover in leadership during this period probably had as much to do with the lethal effects of persecution, which have already been noted. By the end of 1669 Francis Howgill, one of the last great Quaker preachers from the 1650s, had died in prison. This factor, combined with the bold and unilateral quality of Fox's organizational initiative, made 1667 the point at which Fox emerged as the overwhelmingly leading figure in the Quaker movement. Nayler's charismatic preaching and Burrough's brilliant and tireless work in London had made them the only figures comparable to Fox. Both were long dead by 1667.

Nevertheless, Fox's efforts did meet with substantial resistance. Especially disturbing to many was the independent power given to women. In his *Journal* Fox relates being confronted by a dissident in 1673, as opposition was coming to a head. The man asked him if God hadn't commanded that a man must rule over his wife (Gen. 3:16). Further, he asserted that it was an abuse to the established male eldership to set up women's meetings. Fox replied that such eldership was of the Fall, not the restoration by Christ.[66] Opposition culminated at this time with the Wilkinson-Story Separation, which led some local and national leaders to split from the movement.

To some, Fox's organizing plan may have seemed different in tone from the expansive days of the Commonwealth. But it flowed naturally from the gospel he had preached for twenty years. Business was carried out in the same prophetic manner that worship followed, waiting upon the Lord for guidance. The same light that showed Friends their sins and their savior, and which had inspired the fiery gospel preaching of the Quakers, would also lead them into the order of Christ's gospel for their lives and work together. Fox's attacks upon the established Church were not the rebellion of an individualist against the constraints of corporate faith, but the outcry of a person with an alternative vision of what corporate faith can be. At the conclusion of his *Journal* he reviews the beginnings of the movement as the Truth's springing up "to us *so as to be a people to be the Lord.*" What is important to recognize is that this system of monthly, quarterly, and yearly men's and women's meetings was *not* the Church government itself, but the discipline by which Christ the head was allowed to rule the body of his Church according to his Spirit. We will give further attention to gospel order in our later chapters.

In 1669, Fox made a successful missionary journey to Ireland,

where many were convinced. Later that same year, he married
Margaret Fell. At that time, the first Conventicle Act expired.
Parliament passed a second Conventicle Act in May, 1670. Fox
was arrested at meeting the First-day after the Act went into
effect, but was released without a fine by a friendly judge. The
new Act was aimed not at imprisoning dissenters but at financially
ruining them with fines.[68] It was useful in maintaining the
disruption and harrassment of meetings and the personal hardship upon Friends.

Physically exhausted from his itinerating and spiritually
overwhelmed by a decade of relentless persecutions, Fox fell
gravely ill, in terms which he describes both spiritually and
physically. This illness, lasting from autumn 1670 to spring 1671,
included a temporary loss of sight and hearing, and was a time of
great travail and exotic visions.

In August, 1671, Fox left England with twelve other Quaker
preachers for a missionary journey to the West Indies and
America. They were able to bolster the struggling frontier meetings and bring in new converts as well. Fox rode hard and slept
out at night, as he had done in his younger days. Of special interest to him was conversation with the American Indians. His
belief in the universal saving light of Christ which could be
answered regardless of a knowledge of the gospel made these
encounters different from any he could have had in England.
While these conversations usually involved a witness to the gospel message,[69] they also included attempts to compare spiritual
experience.[70]

After nearly two years of travel, which had taken them from
Barbados to Rhode Island, the group left America, arriving back
in England in June, 1673. Fox was immediately beset with the
challenges of the Wilkinson-Story controversy over women and
Church order. But he was not able to deal with this for very long,
as he was arrested in December under the Conventicle Act after a
meeting in Worcestershire. He spent all of 1674 in prison and
received the sentence of *praemunire* during this time.

Fox grew very ill in prison, and it appeared that he might not
survive the winter of 1674-5. The King was willing to release Fox
under a pardon, but Fox would not accept a pardon, insisting
upon his innocence of any wrongdoing. A lawyer named
Corbett eventually was able to argue successfully that imprisonment under *praemunire* was illegal, and Fox was set free in
February of 1675. This concluded the last of his eight imprison-

ments, which totalled nearly six years out of the twenty-five since he was first imprisoned at Derby. He received no more major harrassments from the civil authorities after this time.

Quakers in general, however, were still very much persecuted after 1675. Yet in spite of staggering losses in the leadership among Friends and the toll it took on evangelical activity, the Quaker movement was much larger and more solidly established by this time than it had been in 1660. Much of this growth was surely due to the steadfastness of these fanatics; the example of the Quakers spoke more eloquently than words.

The consolidation of the movement into a coherent, single body, however, must be largely credited to Fox's initiative and relentless efforts. His work during this period showed an inspiration for organization that counterbalanced his mercurial gifts for iconoclasm and insight into individual experience. In this effort he transformed what might have been a short-lived spiritual revival into a standing witness that has survived three centuries.

GEORGE FOX'S LATER YEARS, 1675-1691

Soon after his release from prison in February, 1675, at age 50, Fox retired to Swarthmoor for over a year. During this time he slowly recovered strength and spent time with his wife and step-children. But his time was hardly idle. His major project was the dictation of his *Journal*; he also carried on a great deal of correspondence, much of it in efforts to heal the Wilkinson-Story rift, and reviewed and organized the quarter century of Quaker correspondence that had been collected at Swarthmoor.

In the spring of 1676 he began travelling again, visiting meetings and preaching at length, though he was not able to ride as tirelessly as he once had. In the summer of 1677 Fox embarked on a three-month missionary trip to Holland and Germany, accompanied by other Quaker leaders, including Robert Barclay and William Penn. On this trip he visited the tiny and scattered groups of Friends on the continent, some of whom had been persecuted. He appealed to local authorities, pleading for toleration, while engaging in debates. In Amsterdam, religious freedom, combined with his wide reputation, allowed him to preach to large crowds. A shorter visit to Holland by Fox followed in 1684.

Except for these trips, Fox spent most of his last years in London, continually seeking to establish gospel ordering in

Friends meetings. One project was to bring Friends of a certain profession together to discuss the implications of Quakerism for their particular work.[71] The wider possibilities of gospel ordering continued to occupy his mind.

The persecution of Friends extended well into the 1680s. Fox continued to visit Friends in prison and urged authorities to use moderation. A major political campaign for tolerance was mounted by Friends at this time. As early as 1675, Friends had been urged to vote only for candidates who would sign an agreement to work for toleration, and Quakers were becoming a political force to contend with. They rented a room in a coffee-house near Parliament as an office to coordinate lobbying activities. Fox, Penn, and other prominent Friends made personal contacts with members of Parliament and testified at committee hearings. Friends across the nation were urged to write to their representatives on the issues of toleration.[72]

But no relief was achieved for Quakers until after Charles' death in 1685. James II was immediately beset with new Quaker lists of sufferings and appeals for toleration. In March, 1686, he issued a General Pardon and a warrant releasing some Friends from prison and cancelling fines for not going to church. In the following year the Declaration of Indulgence was issued, allowing religious meetings that were openly held, which did not include any speaking against the King.

Finally, under the new reign of William and Mary, the Toleration Act was passed in 1689, granting Friends and other nonconformists almost full liberty. Some problems took many more years to alleviate, however. The Affirmation Act of 1722 finally released Friends completely from the oppressive demand to take oaths. But it would not be until 1832 that Friends would be allowed to hold office.[73]

Because of their insistence upon meeting openly, if for no other reason, Friends suffered during the Restoration more than any other dissenting group. It is estimated that the total number of Quakers suffering imprisonments, fines, and other penalties and hardships during this period easily exceeded fifteen thousand. The number of deaths from persecution is estimated at more than 450. These figures include only those persecuted in England and Wales.[74]

George Fox lived long enough to see the end of this terrible siege. He died peacefully on January 13, 1691, at age 66, after having preached vigorously only two days before. Satisfied that the Lord finally required no more service from him, his last words were, "I am clear, I am fully clear."[75]

Though he had remained as active as possible up to the end, Fox had gradually removed himself from the center of Quaker activities during his last years. The only responsibility left to be passed on at his death was the work of foreign correspondence.[76] Consequently, the Church suffered no chaotic dislocations following his death.

Nathaniel Stephens, pastor to George Fox during his boyhood in Drayton, and later his opponent, said accurately of him, "there never was such a plant bred in England."[77]

PART TWO

THE MESSAGE OF GEORGE FOX

We must not have Christ Jesus, the Lord of life, put any more in the stable among the horses and asses, but he must now have the best chamber, the heart, and the rude, debauched spirit must be turned out.[1]

3. CHRIST'S WORK IN HUMAN EXPERIENCE

The kingdom of God, the promised reign of God on earth, was the dearest hope of the Puritan revolution. And, as the Commonwealth displaced the monarchical government and hierarchical Church in the 1640s, many expected the reign of God to precipitate with the "rule of saints" (the Parliament, but later seen as the New Model Army). The splintering which the Puritan movement experienced as it attained national power, however, frustrated and even mocked that hope; bitter in-fighting paralyzed Parliament and precipitated a military rule, rather than a millennial one.

By the 1650s the kingdom of God was a fading hope in England. Some desperate factions, like the Fifth Monarchists, plotted violent insurrection to induce the reign of Christ in the land. But others hedged their prophecies, making the latter days of God's glory contingent upon a world-wide defeat of the Church of Rome and its forces. Only then would there be a pouring out of the Spirit on all flesh (Joel 2:28).[2]

But by this same time there was a growing movement in the

North which had gained the derisive name "Quakers." George Fox, its central figure, preached that the kingdom of God *was now known* among those who had "come to the spirit of God, and to the spiritual birth by which the things of God are known" (John 3:3, 5, 8).[3]

When Fox began preaching this message, he had no academic credentials with which to command the attention or credence of his hearers. He had no affiliation with any existing Christian gathering to legitimate his message. What drew people to hear him — by the hundreds and eventually by the thousands — was perhaps not so much his treatment of Christian *doctrines* as such, as his ability to describe and make vivid the Christian *experience*. To be sure, there was a strong doctrinal dimension to his preaching and writing, which came into sharp focus in attacks upon Puritan teachings. But his doctrine grew less out of a scholarly treatment of biblical exegesis and Church traditions than from his own experience of Christ's saving work.

Thus, the gospel he preached was less *propositional* than *experiential*; it made alive the experience of Christ that hearers already knew to some extent, or else sought to know, and placed that experience in the wider context of an unfolding historical drama. This drama would be decided in their own lives, individual and corporate. In Fox's preaching, the most intimate personal struggles were tied to the most publicized national and global ones in a single cosmic conflict. His message cut through the speculative and doctrinal constructs of Puritan expectation in much the same way that Paul's preaching of the gospel transformed the salvation historical predictions of Jewish apocalyptic into an apocalyptic *experience* of the cross.[4]

The best way for us to begin to understand Fox's salvation message is to examine closely his own early experiences. Approaching Fox's message in this way will not only provide a helpful introductory overview, but it will also illustrate Fox's emphasis upon experience as the starting point of theology.

EARLY EXPERIENCE OF GEORGE FOX

As summarized in the second chapter, Fox spent his later adolescence in solitary wanderings, plagued by a temptation to despair. He was confused and disturbed by these feelings, and, though already a very moral and serious-minded young man, he was given to intense circumspection about his conduct. Sometimes spiritual "openings" would come and give him fleeting joy;

> yet great trouble and temptation came many times upon me, so that when it was day I wished for night, and when it was night I wished for day [Deut. 28:66] . . . . And frequently in the night [I] walked mournfully about by myself for I was a man of sorrows in the times of the first workings of the Lord upon me.[5]

Fox repeatedly sought the counsel of respected Puritan ministers, asking them what was the cause of temptation to despair. Some were more sympathetic than others, but "none could reach my condition."[6] He believed that he knew Christ's abandonment during this time, feeling that these mentors were "miserable comforters" (Job 16:2).

He gave up on the more orthodox ministers and began to seek out the radical "dissenting people," but none of them was able to address his dilemma either. Finally, after about three years in this condition,

> when all my hopes in them and in all men were gone, so that I had nothing outwardly to help me, nor could tell what to do, then, Oh then, I heard a voice which said, "there is one, even Christ Jesus that can speak to thy condition," and when I heard it my heart did leap for joy. Then the Lord did let me see why there was none upon the earth that could speak to my condition, namely, that I might give him all the glory; for all are concluded under sin, and shut up in unbelief as I had been, that Jesus Christ might have the pre-eminence [Col. 1:18] . . . . And this I knew experimentally.[7]

While he had known this inward teaching since childhood, it was not until this moment that he realized that this teacher alone, and no outward one, could answer his uncertainties and lead him to the peace of God's righteousness. From this point on, Fox was at last *settled* under the teaching of Jesus Christ, an entirely sufficient grace.

Slowly this experience began to break down the paralyzing temptation to despair:

> My desires after the Lord grew stronger, and zeal in the pure knowledge of God and of Christ, without the help of any man, book, or writing. For though I read the scriptures that spoke of

Christ and of God, yet I knew him not but by revelation [Gal. 1:12, 16], as he who hath the key did open, and as the Father of life drew me to his Son by his Spirit.[8]

Fox came to learn not only *about* Christ but *from* Christ himself — unmediated by the Bible or by preaching.

And the Lord did gently lead me along, and did let me see his love, which was endless and eternal, and surpasseth all the knowledge that men have in the natural state, or can get by history or books [1 Cor. 13]; and that love let me see myself as I was without him.[9]

Christ's revelation thus gave Fox an insight into himself, a self-critical awareness which discovered sin and insufficiency, even while strengthening him in this awareness with love.

But this was not the end of Fox's sorrows and temptations; still they raged within him. Yet Christ showed him how he, too, had been tempted and had overcome, and that Fox would overcome as well. He became increasingly uncomfortable around his Puritan contemporaries — his former mentors — who did not believe in the overcoming of temptation and sin, accommodating themselves to despair:

And I saw professors, priests, and people were whole and at ease in that condition which was my misery, and they loved that which I would have been rid of. But the Lord stayed my desires upon himself from whom my help came, and my care was cast upon him alone.[10]

Here we may see the seeds not only of Fox's strongly internal understanding of the spiritual process, but also of his Separatist vision for Friends.

A sense of triumph over sin began to emerge in Fox's experience, as he started to see consistently not only *himself* in his own sinfulness, but also *Christ* in his righteousness and love. He became aware of a *new will* rising up within:

Again, I heard a voice which did say, "Thou Serpent, thou does seek to destroy the life but canst not, for the sword which keepeth the tree of life shall destroy thee." So Christ, the Word of God, that bruiseth the head of the Serpent the destroyer, preserved me, my inward life did spring up in me, to answer all the opposing professors and priests, and did bring in scriptures to my memory to refute them with . . . And I saw death, how it had passed upon all men and oppressed the Seed in man and in me, and how I in the Seed came forth . . . .[11]

Coming into the power of the risen seed and the revelation of Christ's light, Fox was given clearer insight into the troubled condition he had been suffering:

> But oh, then did I see my troubles, trials, and temptations more than ever I had done! As the Light appeared, all appeared that is out of the Light, darkness, death, temptation, the unrighteous, the ungodly; all was manifest and seen in the Light.[12]

This light became a pure fire within him: "then I saw how he [the messenger of the covenant] sat as a refiner's fire and as the fuller's soap" (Mal. 3:2f). It became a purifying and discerning power within,

> by which I did discern my own thoughts, groans and sighs, and what it was that did veil me, and what it was that did open me. And that which could not abide in the patience nor endure the fire, in the Light I found to be groans of the flesh (that could not give up to the will of God), which had veiled me, and that could not be patient in all trials . . . and could not give up self to die by the Cross, the power of God, which the sword of the Spirit [Eph. 6:17] cuts down and which must die . . . . and I discerned the groans of the spirit, which did open me, and made intercession to God, in which spirit is the true waiting upon God, for the redemption of the body and of the whole creation [see Rom. 8:18-26].[13]

Thus Fox was able to discern two powers operative within himself — the fleshly power of his own thoughts and will, and the spiritual power of Christ's revelation and will.

Fox came to know an apocalyptic battle waged within himself between Christ's power and Satan's. With this battle, his own redemption and that of the creation hung in the balance. Fox witnessed a transformation being wrought within:

> The living light of Christ manifesteth all things; and the spiritual fire trieth all things, and severeth all things . . . . for he showed me that which can live in his holy refining fire, and that can live to God under his law . . . . And I saw the mountains burning up and the rubbish, and the rough and crooked ways and places made smooth and plain [Isa. 40:4] that the Lord might come

into his tabernacle. These things are to be found in a man's heart. But to speak of these things being within seemed strange to the rough and crooked and mountainous ones. Yet the Lord said, "O Earth, hear the word of the Lord" [Jer. 22:29]![14]

Still the temptations and sufferings continued, as Fox gained insight into not only his own previous condition, but the conditions of others as well:

The Lord showed me that the natures of those things which are hurtful without were within, in the hearts and minds of wicked men. The natures of dogs, swine vipers, of Sodom and Egypt, Pharoah, Cain, Ishmael, Esau, etc. Those natures I saw within, though people had been looking without.[15]

The final stages of Fox's sanctifying experience saw the sorrows and temptations give way at last to a sublime joy, particularly as he began to see not just the work of Satan but also the work of Christ going on in others:

I had a sense and discerning given me by the Lord, through which I saw plainly that when many people talked of God and of Christ, etc., the Serpent spake in them; but this was hard to be borne. Yet the work of the Lord went on in some, and my sorrows and troubles began to wear off and tears of joy dropped from me . . . . And I saw into that which was without end, and things which are hard to be uttered, and of the greatness and infiniteness of the love of God, which cannot be expressed by words.[16]

This sense of discernment appears to have been key to his overcoming temptations and depressions, since it helped him to distinguish Christ's voice from Satan's, both within and without. For example, in the next year (1648), he passed under a momentary temptation, hearing a deceiving voice within. The voice clouded and confused him; but

as I sat still under it and let it alone, a living hope rose up in me, and a true voice . . . . And immediately the cloud and temptation vanished away and life rose over it all. . . .[17]

The tempting voice had told him that "all things come by nature." But the second voice told him, "there is a living God who made all things." He found this voice to describe his experience truly — that a power totally beyond him, yet working within him, had saved him from ruin.

Finally, in the same year, Fox's spiritual pilgrimage came to its completion. He felt his understanding and his path to be so thoroughly cleansed and transformed that he could state,

> Now I was come up in spirit through the flaming sword into the paradise of God. All things were new, and all the creation gave another smell unto me than before, beyond what words can utter. I knew nothing but pureness and innocency, and righteousness, being renewed up into the image of God by Christ Jesus, so that I say I was come up into the state of Adam which he was in before he fell.[18]

Fox did not conceive of this state simply as a return to a primeval innocence, but as

> another or more steadfast state than Adam's in innocency, even unto a state in Christ Jesus, that should never fall . . . in which the admirable works of the creation, and the virtues therof, may be known, through the openings of that divine Word of wisdom and power by which they were made.[19]

With this remarkable vista of apocalyptic fulfillment we come to the conclusion of George Fox's formative spiritual development, one that launched him into the world with the gospel message decidedly different from that of his Puritan contemporaries. This message is based upon his experience and the implications he drew from it. His saving experience was not wrought by a *preached* Word; in fact, he found the Puritan ministers to be "miserable comforters" precisely because they sought to comfort him in and help him adjust to a sinful condition he could not accept.

Nor was it a *written* Word that opened the mystery of faith to him, even though he studied scripture assiduously and had great breakthroughs of interpretation during these early years. It was the *living* Word that reached Fox in his hopeless state — just as it stopped Paul in his tracks on the road to Damascus. This Word, this revealing light of Christ, slowly raised Fox from his near despair of righteousness. It led him to a new self-awareness, allowing him to see the insufficiency of his own strivings after righteousness. It gave him a new sense of inward commandment, leading him to a new righteousness, one beyond his own making. Crucial to this transformation was the experience of God's alluring love, creating in Fox a *desire* to know God's will and a *power* to obey it. This personal commitment to God's will rose up in place of an outwardly transmitted code of Christian moral obligation. Standing in the light of his inward teacher, joined to the victorious seed, Fox came to experience the divine command less in a strict *imperative* sense than as a *cohortative:* "thou shalt" became "let us!"

George Fox's experience must be seen as *apocalyptic* in that it combines several characteristics that are hallmarks of apocalyptic thought. These include: a sense of God's final judgment; an intense and cataclysmic warfare between the forces of good and evil; destruction and new beginning; fulfillment which resembles in some ways a primeval state; and a redemption that encompasses the wider created order. While most of his contemporaries looked to geo-political events for the much-expected apocalypse, George Fox found its beginnings revealed upon an inner land-scape.

Now that we have examined the salvation experience of Fox, we can consider the gospel message that he derived from it. We shall see that Fox, perhaps as originally as any other Christian thinker since Paul, drew his theological structures from the shape of his own experience of Christ. His relationship with Christ supplied a key to scripture and to his proclamation, "Christ is come to teach his people himself;" the apocalypse begins with the voice that says, "There is one, even Christ Jesus that can speak to thy condition."Christ'steaching reveals the end of the old order and the beginning of the new; those who are obedient to this teaching enter the new order. Thus, the goal of Fox's preaching is to turn "all that would know the way to the kingdom" to this apocalyptic revelation.

FOX'S PREACHING OF CHRIST'S SAVING WORK[20]

From the day George Fox heard the voice say to him, "there is one, even Christ Jesus, that can speak to thy condition," he understood the risen Lord's presence to be his sole hope of salvation. When he received the commission from the Lord to preach the gospel, he conceived of his task as one of bringing people into the same functional awareness that he had gained of Christ's revealing presence:

Now I was sent to turn people from darkness to light that they
might receive Christ Jesus, for as many as should receive him in
his light, I saw he would give power to become sons of God,
which I had obtained by receiving Christ.[21]

The consistent emphasis of Fox's preaching is the power of the
risen Christ within the believer. In the intensely Christian culture
to which he preached, a knowledge of the earthly life of Jesus
was assumed. It is Fox's insistence that no saving knowledge of
Jesus can come from the record of the New Testament. Only as
the light inwardly reveals Jesus to the believer is a saving
knowledge and power received. This understanding presents
Jesus less as an outward ideal to be emulated than the inward
incarnation of the new creature actualized in the obedient life of
the believer.

The Revelation of Condemnation. The initial and universal
function of the light Fox finds described in John 3:19-21: "And
this is the condemnation, that the light is come into the world. . . ."
Fox asserts:

"I am the light of the world [John 8:12], which doth enlighten
every man that cometh into the world" [John 1:9], saith Christ,
by whom it was made . . . . This is the light which shows you
the evil actions you have all acted . . . and all the ungodly
speeches you have spoken . . . . Now if you attend to this light,
it will let you see all you have done contrary to it; and loving it,
it will turn you from your evil deeds . . . to Christ.[22]

This light, not a part of human nature or the natural conscience,
nevertheless "keeps thee in tenderness of conscience toward
God and man, and will never let thee swear . . . it will let thee see
if thou does, thou must not go unpunished; and will never let
thee follow drunkenness or vain company . . . ."[23] Fox points out
that this reproving power of the light is also witnessed in the
Letter to Ephesians (5:13): "But all things that are reproved are
made manifest by the light: for whatsoever doth make manifest is
light."[24] Those who do not flee this inward reproof will find a
limitless source of critical revelation:

and dwelling in this light, there is no occasion at all for stumbling
[John 11:9f], for all things are discovered with the light: thou

> that lovest it, here is thy teacher; when thou are walking
> abroad, it is present with thee in thy bosom; thou needest not
> to say lo here, or lo there [Mark 13:21] . . . . It will discover in
> thee the body of sin, and thy corruptions, and fallen estate
> where thou are . . . .[25]

Where the light is loved and the voice of Christ heard, therefore, the conscience is increasingly exercised toward God, giving a heightened moral awareness; ". . . but where it is hated, and the voice not heard, the conscience is seared [1 Tim. 4:2] and the light is their condemnation . . . ."[26] Those who hate the light, hate Christ. They can never come to a knowledge of God except by this light.

Therefore, the light in the first instance acts as a revealer of sin, an inwardly known law. This law written upon the heart (Jer. 31:33), if heeded, can be more effective than an outward or codified law, as Paul attests (Rom. 2:14f, 29). Of this law, Fox states,

> The pure and perfect law of God is over the flesh to keep it and
> its works, which are not perfect, under, by the perfect law; and
> the law of God that is perfect answers the perfect principle of
> God in every one. And this law the Jews and prophets and John
> were to perform and do. None knows the giver of this law but
> by the spirit of God, neither can any truly read it or hear its
> voice but by the spirit of God.[27]

So we see that Fox takes very seriously Paul's critique of the outward letter of the law and his assertion of a universally revealed law that exposes sin. Combined with the apparent universalism of John 3:19-21, this interpretation leads Fox to speak of the "light of the law" (Prov. 6:23).

This is the inward teaching that Fox had known from his childhood, which caused him to examine his deeds with relentless scrutiny. Yet as long as he failed to put his entire trust in this inward teacher — as long as he instead sought his answer from outward teachers — he wallowed in temptation and despair. When at last he was settled under the teaching of Christ Jesus, speaking to his condition, he then began to *see himself* more clearly. Sensing in this reproving light the love of God, he found his "desires after the Lord" to increase. In other words, he *loved the light* and came to it, to have his deeds made manifest (John 3:21). But this by no means suddenly became a carefree experience; it sometimes intensified the tendencies toward despair:

The law of the Spirit crosseth the fleshly mind, spirit and will, which lives in disobedience, and doth not keep within the law of the Spirit. I saw this law was the pure love of God which was upon me, and which I must go through, though it troubled me while I was under it; for I could not be dead to the law but through the law [Gal. 2:19] which did judge and condemn that which is to be condemned. I saw many talked of the law, who had never known the law to be their schoolmaster [Gal. 3:24] . . . .[28]

The universal experience of the law is the first step toward salvation. In his preaching, Fox sought to bring his hearers and readers into a sense of inward reproof, this light of the law. It is significant in this regard that the hearer's turning to this light was called by early Friends *convincement*. In seventeenth century usage, the word denoted not only intellectual assent, but primarily *conviction*, the pronouncement of guilt.[29] Those who were turned to the light therefore experienced themselves convicted of their sins (see Titus 1:9; James 2:9; Jude 15). In this way, they were convinced not by the *preached* Word, but by the *inward* Word, to which Quaker preaching turned them.

Puritan leaders, while placing considerable stress upon the sinfulness of the human condition, feared that such a relentless focus on personal sin and judgment would drive individuals to despair and suicide. Therefore, they cast their hearers upon the merciful and forgiving love of God and the righteousness imputed to believers by Christ's sacrifice. This approach naturally grew out of the despair of overcoming sin in this life. Fox was convinced that the comfort of the Puritans was in fact despair and could only come at the expense of a seared conscience. Therefore, he levelled stern invectives against his contemporaries:

> And to you who tempt God, and say, the Lord give us a sight of our sins, priests and people, does not the light, which Christ hath enlightened you with, let you see your sins . . . ? . . . Oh vain man! yet thou canst say, God is merciful; he is merciful and just, and that shalt thou see, when destruction is upon thee; for thou canst say, God is merciful, yet liveth in thy wickedness, passing on thy time without the fear of God, sporting thyself in thy wickedness.[30]

Fox thus understands despair, a condition which may be either expansive or depressive in mood, as the fatal alienation from God. He summarizes that "the cause of desperation is going from the light, for that which leads to presume, will lead to despair . . . and that is that which wanders to and fro, up and down [Amos 8:12], and hunts abroad, and builds that which God confounds" [Gen. 11].[31] Therefore, any gospel that does not lead men and women to this inward reproof will presume to create its own righteousness, not God's. Despairing of God's transforming power, they will build false and changeable doctrines that must be confounded by God's judgment, like Babel's presumptuous stairway to heaven.

The Revelation of Righteousness. Fox did not preach the light's condemnation as the salvation of the believer, any more than he found this initial stage of grace to be completely redemptive in his own experience. But as he once told a soldier visiting him during his Derby imprisonment, "that which showed him his sins and troubled him for them, would show him his salvation; for he that shows a man his sin, is the same that takes it away."[32] He exhorts those who have found the light to endure its critical gaze in hope of the power that follows:

> . . . in the light that shows you all this, stand, neither go to the right hand, nor to the left [Josh. 1:7]; here patience is exercised, here is thy will subjected, here thou will see the mercies of God made manifest in death . . . here thou wilt find a saviour, and the election thou wilt come to know, and the reprobation, and what is cast from God, and what enters: he that can own me here, and receive my testimony into his heart, the immortal seed is born up, and his own will thrust forth . . . for the first step to peace [Luke 1:79] is to stand still in the light (which discovers things contrary to it) for power and strength to stand against that nature which the light discovers: here grace grows, here is God alone glorified and exalted, and the unknown truth, unknown to the world, made manifest, which draws up that which lies in prison [1 Pet. 3:19], and refresheth it in time, up to God, out of time, through time.[33]

Here we find the second apocalyptic event of grace described: if the individual perseveres in standing before the light of God's judgment throne, giving up the self, then Christ the revealer comes to be revealed. This is the pivotal point of salvation, as not only the will of the flesh and the power of sin are judged, but a *new will and power* are raised up in the seed, the new person in

Christ. Fox describes this in his own experience as "my inward mind joined to his good seed," and as an "inward life" springing up in him. This means nothing less than the old age and order ("time") giving way to the new.

Fox identifies Christ as the seed, who bruises the head of the serpent (Gen. 3:15; Rom. 16:20), signifying the victory over Satan and his power. In the seed, men and women are brought again into the image of God:

> So every one of us, that is come into the seed of God, that bruiseth the serpent's head, that led man from God, who is . . . the author of separation from God, and the original of sin, which led man from his dominion over the handiworks of God [Gen. 1:26f]; which the royal seed Christ destroys, and renews man again in the image of God, and brings him again to his dominion over the handiworks of God.[34]

Thus, the scope of this dawning redemption is seen to extend to the human relationship with the creation. This restoration of the primeval dominion over creation is another important apocalyptic theme, affirmed by Paul (Rom. 8:18-23).

Fox also understands the seed Christ to be the seed of Abraham, by which all the nations are to be blessed (Gen. 22:18). Therefore, as the seed is raised up in the believer, he or she comes to dwell in that which inherits the promises of God, as well as the kingdom of God. Fox affirms with Paul that this seed is not many but one (Gal. 3:16). The promises of God are bestowed upon Christ alone. Therefore, all who know this seed raised up within are in the unity of this one seed, whether they be male or female. Dwelling in the seed, the children of the seed come to feel and live in an everlasting unity, peace, love, and joy with one another:

> It is one power that raiseth up the seed; and your faith being out of words, in the power, ye are all one, and that seed is one; and ye are all one, if ye be ten thousand; which seed is . . . Christ, and he is the master . . . .[35]

So, as the individual comes to feel the seed raised up, that person comes into a new order — a new dominion over the creatures, and a new unity and harmony with others in the seed. This is possible because the *power* is found in the seed to resist temptation and to obey Christ's voice. Fox can describe this new reality graphically:

> . . . for having a light from the word by which all things were made, and keeping the word, the power is received against all temptation, and they shall not come nigh . . . . Art thou tempted to make away with thyself? so was Christ. Look not at the temptation, but look at Christ, and there thou wilt receive power.[36]

As this new will/power is received, then the new community, the true Church, may be gathered and revealed:

> The church in God, is not an imitation, gathered from the letter [contra Puritan scripturalism] nor is a high-flown people in their imagination [contra Ranter enthusiasm], but are they who are born again of the immortal seed, by the word of God [1 Pet. 1:23], which lives and endures forever [Isa. 40:8], which the world knows not [John 1:10].[37]

The incarnation of Christ, the seed, is the incarnation in a oneness of experience and obedience that gathers people out of many conditions — male and female, Jew and Gentile, slave and free (Gal. 3:28).

To summarize this aspect of Christian experience in Fox's teaching, the raising of the seed is the birth of faith in the believer. It is preceded by the encounter with the law. Giving one's self up to this light of the law and its judgment, one eventually comes to know faith raised up and the law passed away. But for Fox the believer does not partake of Christ's victory only in the sense of his or her sins being cancelled by Christ's atonement, replaced by an imputed righteousness. Indeed, while the battle has been decided, it has really only begun.

The War of Liberation. With the raising of God's ensign (Isa. 11:10; 18:3; 30:17; 31:9), the mortal conflict between Christ and Satan for lordship over the individual begins in earnest. The sanctifying process begins as the light, which at first only served to expose sin, now sets out to destroy it. Fox urges new Friends: "In that which convinced you wait, that you may have that removed [which] you are convinced of."[38] Fox repeatedly defines the light as "life in the word," a formula evidently derived from John 1:4. Therefore, the work of the light is now to bring the believer into the power and life of faith:

> All Friends and people, that is to be condemned in yourselves, which led you from Christ, from God, and from unity in the light; I say, that is condemned by the light, and must be executed and killed, and stoned with the living stone [Dan. 2:34], run through with the living sword [Heb. 4:12f; Eph. 6:17; Rev. 19:18f], and hammered down with the living hammer [Jer. 23:29] to pieces, and burnt up with the living fire [Jer. 23:29], and so made an end of. For that which leads into looseness, whimsies, imaginations, false visions, though it be condemned, yet, if not executed, it is in danger to rise again; and if it rise again, and get over you, it will be your ruler . . . . Therefore, let the execution be speedily done . . . .[39]

Thus, by the power of his Word, God "hews down the first birth, that he may establish the second, and raise up the second . . . ."[40]

The conflict between the seed born according to the Spirit and the seed born according to the flesh (see Gal. 4:24-31) is a battle waged upon a human battleground:

> For the Seed of God is a burdensome stone to the selfish, fleshly, earthly will which reigns in its own knowledge, and understanding, that must perish, and [so] its wisdom, that is devilish. And the Spirit of God is grieved and vexed and quenched with that which brings into the fleshly bondage, and that which wars against the spirit of God must be mortified by it . . . . Therefore keep in the daily cross [see 2 Cor. 15:31], the power of God, by which ye may witness all that to be crucified which in contrary to the will of God, and which shall not come into his kingdom.[41]

There can be no peace as long as two wills compete for supremacy within. There can be no peace without a singleness of the eye (Matt. 6:22) and a purity of the heart (Matt. 5:8). This fact demands a totality of conquest suggestive of the holy war tradition of Deuteronomy 13 and Ephesians 6:

> Spare not that which is for the sword, and for the fire; let all fleshly-mindedness be trodden under your feet. And standing in the power, ye will see the seed slaying the fat, and chaining and binding the unruly, and succoring all the lambs and babes.[42]

As Barbour[43] notes, the journals of many early Friends describe long and painful periods during whch they subjected themselves to this terrible inward warfare in the light. Like Fox, many were driven to the brink of despair by this conflict. Yet it was the Quaker belief that this is the only way to the kingdom. It is significant that in this regard Fox often refers to Christ's revelation as the *word of patience* (Rev. 3:10). This battle is what Quakers meant by *conversion* — the translation of all aspects of life into the reign of God. *Convincement,* therefore, is only the first step on a long path. Friends were constantly reminded that they must come to *possess* that which they *professed*.

Fox insisted to his Puritan contemporaries that Christ's work of *justifying* sinners cannot be separated by his *sanctifying* of them by his inward guidance: "Justification and sanctification are one, not distinguished the one from the other in their natures, but are one in nature . . . for Christ . . . is he that sanctifies and justifies."[44] The same Christ that died for all, enlightens all.[45]

Yet sanctification does not consist solely in the negative function of destroying evil. As the old life is hewn down, the new life is sustained and nourished by the milk of the Word (1 Pet. 2:2). This nourishment is known as one is settled under the teaching of Christ and his positive guidance:

> And so all people, seeing the devil hath made the world like a wilderness, and there are so many ways in it that they do not know which way to come out of it, nor which way to follow. Therefore, this is my answer to you all, take David's lamp and light [Ps. 119:105]. You may say, what is that? and where is it? I say it is with you, the word of God [Deut. 30:11-14; Rom. 10:5-8].[40]

> O therefore, feel the grace and truth in thy heart, that is come by Jesus Christ, that will teach thee how to live, and what to deny. It will establish thy heart, season thy words [Col. 4:6], and bring thy salvation; it will be a teacher unto thee at all times.[47]

In hearing and obeying this Word, one's path comes to be cleansed (Ps. 119:9), and that path itself becomes a shining light, shining more and more unto the perfect day (Prov. 4:18).[48] "And thine ears shall hear a word behind thee, saying, This is the way, walk ye in it . . ." (Isa. 30:21).[49] Hence, a new person is known to grow up within, in the power of Christ's revelation. In cautioning Friends against the vain fashions of the world, Fox exhorts them: "let your minds be above the costly and vain fashions of attire, but mind the hidden man of the heart, which is a meek and quiet spirit, which is of great price (Matt. 13:46) with the Lord."[50]

The Light's Gathering Power: Gospel Order. As the seed consolidates its reign by the revelation of the Word in the heart, God's righteousness comes to be known in a joyful *new order* established in the life of the individual, as testified by the Psalmist (Pss. 37:23; 119:133). This order, however, becomes significant in Quakerism not only as an individual phenomenon; the light has spoken to individuals and transformed lives in all ages and places, wherever it is obeyed — even in the Church of England, Fox would admit. The Quaker movement, in Fox's thinking, was individuals coming together in this experience to be a *people*, living in a new order of *community*. When he recounts the beginnings of Quakerism, Fox speaks of the Truth having sprung up "to us so as to be a people to the Lord."

In our historical chapter on Fox's life, we described some aspects of the reordering wrought among early Friends inspired by the teaching of the Word. Against the enthusiastic worship of the spiritual Puritans and the anarchistic lifestyle of the Ranters, Fox stresses the *order* of life in Christ. He cites the orderliness of the New Testament Church (1 Cor. 14:40; Col. 2:5) and proclaims that this order is being built again among the Quakers, upon Christ the rock and foundation (Isa. 28:16; Matt. 7:24f; 1 Cor. 13:10-13; Heb. 11:10),[51] a spiritual house built of living stones (1 Pet. 2:5).[52]

> So all Christ's subjects of his kingdom are known by their birth and clothing and live in the order of his gospel of love, life, light, grace, and truth; and no man comes into this kingdom and order, but by the light, grace, truth, faith, power, and spirit, and anointing, and word of life [1 John 1:1] within, through which you know Christ, and his everlasting kingdom, that stands in power, and righteousness, and joy in the holy ghost [Rom. 14:17].[53]

Fox names this structuring *gospel order*. As Benson stresses, the order Fox describes arises peculiarly from the gospel he preached. Thus, "what Fox is telling us is that gospel order is essentially a relationship between God's son and God's people.

'They that do obey the voice of the Lord and Christ Jesus . . . in this they know the order of Christ.' "[54] Therefore, the system of monthly, quarterly, and yearly men's and women's meetings set up by Fox in the name of gospel order was not in itself the gospel order. The system was rather intended as a discipline by which Friends could maintain a functional openness to Christ's own direct government. As Fox frequently asserts, the gospel order, like the gospel, is "not of man nor by man" (Gal. 1:1, 11f). This order is greater than any Church humanly devised:

> And every man and woman that be heirs of the gospel, they are heirs of this authority and the power of God which was before the devil . . . . So they come to inherit and possess . . . the power of God which will last for ever and outlast all the orders of the devil and that which is of men or by men.[55]

The Church is not an aggregation of individuals who happen to share a common set of beliefs about God. It is rather a tightly-knit unity, a collective force that is experienced wherever Christ is the head and ruler (1 Cor. 12); it is the cutting edge of the new creation.

Fox's understanding of the Church is one in which individuals are to experience *together* the same judging, purifying, and transforming power of Christ's light that each already knows within. In this corporate dimension, the power of Christ's revelation is manifoldly increased. The blindspots and areas of resistance to the light's critical eye in one Friend are to be addressed with loving ministry by another Friend. Fox urges the men's meetings to "be not negligent . . . to admonish or exhort, and reprove in the spirit of love and meekness."[56] He finds ample witness to exhortation and admonition in the New Testament without the need of clergy to administer it. He states that

> in the church of Christ, where he is the head, there is his gospel and his order and his government; there is his power felt in everyone's heart, and there are his offices of admonishing, rebuking, exhorting, reproving, amongst them that are convinced, and converted, by them that are in the power . . . they that would not have the people to be admonished . . . and yet go into sin and wickedness, those are out of the gospel order and government of Christ Jesus . . . . [57]

So this work is to be carried out by those who have been shown to be "in the power" or "seasoned in the truth," and must be pursued with the same tenacious conquest that is expected within the individual. "Take heed of foolish pity; and if you not be diligent against all profaneness, sin . . . then you let those things come upon you, which you should be atop of . . . ."[58] The apocalyptic sense of holy war thus spreads from within the individual to the community of faith.

But discipline is not the end goal of the Quaker community any more than judgment is the final result of the light in one who loves it. Out of this refining fire comes a solidarity that the world does not know. The government of Christ is not a coalition of shared personal interests, but a selfless unity in the one seed. "Now, all loving the light, here no self can stand, but it is judged with the light; and here all are in unity, and here so self-will can arise, no mastery; but all that is judged out."[59]

Against the numerous and short-lived gatherings that had characterized the radical Puritan sects of that time, Fox asserts that this fellowship is one everlasting fellowship, above all the fellowships of the world, a "fellowship of the mystery which from the beginning of the world hath been hid in God" (Eph. 3:9).[60]

So we see that the community of faith, the children of the light (John 12:36; Eph. 5:8), and of the kingdom (Matt. 13:38), come through an apocalyptic experience of judgment and transformation, separating wheat from chaff. They come to a personal and corporate sanctification, to a new life in Christ, the end of the world (Heb. 9:26-28).[61]

> Now here is the baptism of Christ by fire [Matt. 3:11]: this Holy Spirit to plunge down the foul spirit and power that has got into man, which fills him with chaff and corruption. This baptism destroys him and his work in man, and burns him up and his chaff with his fire [Matt. 3:12]. So man and woman have had this chaff in them, with which the god of the world hath fed them. Now every one must know the baptism with the Spirit before they can come up into the garden in Paradise again; every man and woman must know this without book, in their own particulars.[62]

Again we see that Fox understands Christ's work, both within individuals and in the gathered Church, to be an *immediate* experience of his power; it is in no way humanly or scripturally mediated.

Perfection. In the image of the ascent back to paradise, we see how original wholeness plays an important part in Fox's understanding of final fulfillment. This is typical of apocalyptic thought. Fox can distill salvation history into a history of three teachers.[63] The first teacher was God in his open conversation with man and woman in paradise, commanding them what to do and what not to do. The second teacher was the serpent, or Satan, who drew the man and woman into confusion and disobedience, whereby sin entered in and death reigns; his teaching continues in the world. The third teacher, the "gospel teacher," is Jesus Christ, who in his earthly ministry and risen lordship leads his people out of confusion and into obedience and order, restoring the perfection known in paradise.

Fox finds perfection well attested in the Old Testament (Gen. 6:9; 17:1; Deut. 18:13; Job 1:8; Ps. 37:37; Prov. 4:18) both before and after Moses, and in the gospels (Matt. 5:48; 19:21; Luke 6:40; John 17:23) and epistles (2 Cor. 7:1; 13:9, 11; Eph. 4:13; 1 Thess. 3:16; Col. 1:28; 4:12; Heb. 2:10; 5:9; 7:19; 12:23; James 2:22; 1 John 3:6; 4:17) of the New Testament. He sees the teaching of the Puritans as a direct apostasy from the biblical witness and the Quaker experience of Christ. He asserts that they preach salvation *in* sin, rather than *from* sin. He claims that there is no salvation from the wrath of God except in salvation from sin. He likens Puritan preaching to proclaiming freedom to slaves without removing their chains or setting them free.[64]

> Now mark, the apostle saith, "He hath quickened us, who were dead in sin and trespasses, and hath made us to sit together in in the heavenly places in Christ Jesus; that in the ages to come he might show forth his exceeding riches and kindness toward us [Eph. 2:4-8]." Now the ages are come . . . that the apostle's preaching is fulfilled . . . . So mark, in Christ Jesus, *us* the church, *us* the saints, *us* the believers and true christians, made us to sit together . . . . and they are not to sit there in Adam in the fall, nor in Adam before he fell, but in heavenly places in Christ Jesus [who was] before Adam fell. And there is the safe sitting, in Christ the living way, the word of God, the power of God, the light . . . .[65]

Christ's salvation is more than a return to Adam's state before the Fall. It establishes believers in "heavenly places" — a fulfillment which overcomes the ethical separation between God and people. It establishes believers *together* in a way less prone to fall as Adam did.

George Fox preached an overcoming power in Christ, against the assumed modesty with which Puritans often proclaimed their own sinfulness. "For they who are the friends of Christ [John 15:14] are in his power, atop the power of sin, and trample it under foot."[66] Some found Fox's preaching of perfection to be a claim to equality with God. Fox never claimed this, but replied, "he that sanctifieth and they that are sanctified are all of one in the Son . . . the sons of God and the Father and the Son are one of his flesh and of his bones . . . ." (Heb. 2:11; Eph. 5:30).[67]

By perfection, Fox makes it clear that he means the absence of sin or error. The systematic rooting out and destruction of sin by the light and the "taking possession" of the inheritance of the kingdom in gospel order are intended to create a total transformation.

At the same time, however, he understands that perfection is fulfilled only in the *measure* of light, faith, or grace which one receives (Rom. 12:2f; Eph. 4:7-13). Any striving outside the light, beyond one's measure, will achieve only a human righteousness — a righteousness of one's own (Rom. 10:3). Fox testifies, "the faith of God is the gift of God, and it is perfect in us in its measure and degree . . . . We say, faith is perfect in the least measure and degree, the righteousness of faith" (Rom. 10:6).[68] Thus, "so far as men are perfect,"[69] it is by the measure they have received from Christ. An Anglican priest once confronted Fox, challenging him to proclaim his own perfection. Perhaps wishing not to boast beyond his own measure (2 Cor. 10:13, 15), Fox writes, "I told him what I was, I was by the grace of God."[70]

Perfection became one of the most controversial issues of early Quakerism in Puritan England. Puritans held to a certain sanctifying power in daily devotion to the Bible, prayer, and moral circumspection, but stopped far short of claiming a perfection like that before the Fall.

Unfortunately, none of the prominent Puritan critics reviewed in this study seems to have had a clear impression of Fox's teaching. Perhaps they knew it only as it filtered through more enthusiastic Quaker minds. Or perhaps it was simply belittled in the manner typical of Puritan-Quaker repartee. At any rate, the Congregationalist John Owen complained that the Quaker inward light had no real power to mortify sin, and that Quakers suffered from a "pleasing dream of perfection."[71] In another instance, he compared Friends to the first century gnostic enthusiasts. He quipped that the Quaker light only took away the *difference* between good and evil, giving liberty without a sense of sin or fear of punishment. Similarly, Richard Baxter cited the claim to perfection as an example of Quaker pride, remarking that the devil himself has either less pride or less ignorance.[72] A strong practitioner of Puritan ethical modesty, Baxter was horrified by the claim to dwell in heaven and demanded to know why then Quakers didn't look more beatific or appear with angels. He was willing to allow a perfection of sincerity, a perfection of parts, or eminency, or high degree, but not a sinless perfection.[73] Fox answered Baxter's accusations with citations from Jesus, Paul, and John. He countered that in truth, the devil speaks through those who speak for *sin* (i.e., for sin's inescapability).[74]

It would appear that these Puritan critics were indeed unaware of the intense consciousness of sin and the arduous process of transformation that lay behind the Quaker claim to perfection. It would also appear that they had little idea of the extreme dependence upon God's presence and power demanded by Quaker perfectionism. This is the despair that Fox detected in his environment as a young man, and from which he knew himself to be delivered.

Discernment in the Light. In the process of transformation in the light, the believer gains a growing sense of *discernment*, an interpretation of scripture and of experience. Fox characterizes sin and the Fall as a condition of "drowsy dreams and delusions;" he portrays sanctification as an awakening to righteousness.[75] "And that which letteth thee to see thy hardness, darkness, thoughts, and temptations, and the tempter, and thy confusion, deadness, and thy wants is the light, and power, and spirit of God in thee . . . ."[76] Confusion of mind and confusion of behavior are of a piece, and Fox equates confusion with sin (James 3:16). He frequently writes of God as a God of order and peace, over against the god of confusion, the god of the world (1 Cor. 14:33).

In the same vein, he refers to the natural languages of the nations, created at Babel (Gen. 11:9), as waters (the biblical image of chaos), under the power of evil (Rev. 17:1, 15). He opposes these to the *original* language, the Word of God, which leads out of confusion and evil. The Word of God not only orders and gives coherence to the mind and actions of the individual, it also gathers and gives coherence to God's *people*. The fleeting and sectarian gatherings of the Puritans, gathered by the natural *letter* of scripture, are only *imitations* of the Church.

> But dwelling in the light, all sects, and opinions, and religions are discovered, and stand naked before the Lord (and before all who are of God, and are seen with the eternal eye) . . . . Now dwelling in the power, in the eternal light, all sects and opinions come to be judged and overturned, and seen to be chaff that is to be burned, with that which cannot be quenched; for the light is but one, which is Christ . . . it leads you out of sects, out of forms, out of the beauty of the world, to live in the life and power . . . you come to be disciples of Christ and servants of truth . . . .[77]

Thus, *discernment* is identified with *judgment*, in which the believer sees the apocalyptic *separation* of the wheat from the chaff, of the emerging age and order which shall endure from the old age and order passing away. In Christ, "all things are naked and opened unto the eyes . . ." (Heb. 4:13). The apocalypse, or revelation, of Christ is the sight of the "eternal eye" given to those who love the light.

Fox frequently speaks of servanthood, submission, or *subjection* to Christ, the Spirit, truth, etc. For Fox, this means a subjection in the first and most basic sense of allowing Christ to be the *subject*, letting oneself be addressed as the *object* by him. This is at the heart of Fox's language of death of self and the raising of the seed as a new will:

> . . . as people come into subjection to the spirit of God and grow up in the image and power of the Almighty, they may receive the Word of wisdom that opens all things, and come to know the hidden unity of the Eternal Being.[78]

The light brings one to the *mind* of Christ; "it is present to teach thee, and judge thy wandering mind, which would wander abroad, and thy high thoughts and imaginations, and makes them subject; for following thy own thoughts thou art quickly lost."[79] Subjection to the light is not a matter of knowledge only. Fox warns Friends against a mere *gnosis*, noting that "many may have precious openings; but I desire that all may be comprehended in that thing which doth open to them; and that they may all keep in the daily cross . . . ."[80] By *comprehended*, Fox means here *to be overcome* as well as understood, as the

King James Bible translates John 1:5 — "And the light shineth in darkness; and the darkness comprehended it not."

In subjection,

> ye stand and live in that which scatters the clouds, and keeps your eye clear to the Lord God; by which you see him (in measure) with a good understanding, through all the evil powers and spirits which work in the darkness against him . . . .[81]

This clarity is maintained by *obedience*. When the motions of the light are not followed, the clouds and darkness of confusion will return.

With the gift of discernment, one comes to discern between the devil's voice and God's and to recognize the serpent speaking through others. At this point, one has come to see *over* the devil who darkens.

Thus, discernment is given by Christ who has the *key* (Isa. 22:22; Luke 11:52; Rev. 3:7) to open the meaning of the scriptures and all experience. This key "brings you to see and read one another, as epistles written in one another's hearts [2 Cor. 3:2], where in unity, love, and peace, ye will come to dwell . . . ."[82] By this key, the Word of wisdom (1 Cor. 12:8) opens up the handiworks of God's creation and shows their uses.

Fox understands the hearing and obeying of Christ's voice as the only path of life. All other paths lead to confusion and death.

> And he that heareth not the voice of the son of God doth not live, but is in death . . . . And the hour is come that they which have been in graves, have heard the voice of the son of God and do live . . . [John 5:24f].[83]

Hearing and obeying the Word of God is the true life in the Word — a living possession, not a dead "talk" or profession.

> And now you have an everlasting preacher, whom God hath anointed to preach . . . and everlasting prophet that God hath raised up, who is to be heard [Deut. 18:18]; all the living hear him, but the dead but talk of his fame.[84]

This life in the Word is nothing less than life in Christ: "The Son of God hath been talked of, but now he is come and possessed."[85]

The light in every man which doth enlighten every man, doth
teach the way to the kingdom of God, and no other way it
teacheth but the kingdom . . . [it] gives them the sense of trans-
gression, and an understanding of reproof . . . and that it is
which lets all men see the Most High reigning, and shall make
every tongue confess to the glory of God . . . .[86]

As the light gives insight into good and evil, a sense of God's
power within to do good, and an understanding of how to order
the creatures, the believer responds in an obedience which arti-
culates God's new order and declares Christ's victorious lordship to the world. This continuing revelation is a continuing
apocalypse in which the "daily cross" must be borne by the
faithful as together they fend off the incursions of the world's old
order, cultivating God's garden amidst the wilderness of confusion.

The light, the spiritual presence and power of Christ in the
world, is a paradox; it is both universally bestowed as an
unnamed revelation "in every man that comes into the world,"
yet it is unambiguously identified with Jesus of Nazareth. Understanding this mystery is essential to grasping Fox's message and
placing it in relation to Puritanism.

> *Yea, I say, all the men that come into the world, in Europe,
> Asia, Africa, and America, Christ enlighteneth every one of
> them . . . that with this light they might see him, the great
> mountain that fills the whole earth [Dan. 2:35], exalted above
> all the hills and mountains [Mic. 4:1] . . . .*[1]

4. FOX AND THE PURITAN CRITICS ON THE UNIVERSAL LIGHT OF CHRIST

As we have already begun to see, *the light* is Fox's most frequent term for the active presence of Christ. But as is also
apparent from the quotations of the preceding chapter, Fox uses
a wide variety of biblical terms interchangeably for this same
presence.

One of his most frequent terms in this regard is *that of God in
every one*,[2] a formulation apparently derived from the universal
note sounded by Paul in Romans 1:19 — "that which may be
known of God is manifest in them." Following Paul's thought in
Romans 1-2, he finds those without a knowledge of the gospel
"without excuse" for sin; they have a law written upon their
hearts (Rom. 2:15).

Fox also speaks simply of *Christ within,* based upon texts such
as Colossians 1:27[3] and 2 Corinthians 13:5.[4] *The Holy Spirit* is
also frequent in Fox's references to Christ's presence, emphasizing the Spirit as the means by which Christ is known.[5] It is clear
that while Protestantism normally speaks of the Spirit as an

interim help in Christ's absence, Fox views it as the mode of Christ's return.

Also frequent are terms like the *Word of God within* or *in the heart* (Deut. 30:14; Rom. 10:8),[6] or the *ingrafted Word* (James 1:21).[7] Fox also draws upon the Johannine tradition (John 1:1-9; 5:33; 1 John 2:14) for this usage.[8] He speaks evocatively of Christ's presence as a *witness* (1 John 5:10).[9] This term is important to Fox's understanding of preaching, as we shall see later. *Anointing* (1 John 2:27) and *grace* (Titus 2:11f) are emphasized in the sustained sense of God's teaching within.[10] Other terms frequently used synonymously by Fox include *truth* (2 Cor. 11:10; 2 John 2),[11] *covenant* (Isa. 42:6),[12] *measure* (Rom. 12:3),[13] and *cross* (Mark 8:34; Gal. 6:14).[14]

While Fox uses this variety of terms fluidly and creatively, the *light* remains his favorite term, both for its connection with John's assertion of universal revelation (John 1:9) and for its vivid evocation of revelation. He stresses relentlessly that Christ enlightens all, regardless of a knowledge of the gospel:

> I say with this divine light, the life in Christ, they may see Christ, the mountain [Dan. 2:35], in their own country, which fills the whole earth, for the light shines in their hearts to give the knowledge of the glory of God in the face of Christ Jesus [2 Cor. 4:6] . . . and here, in this mountain, the Lord will teach them his ways; and so the knowledge of the Lord shall cover the earth as the waters cover the sea [Hab. 2:14].[15]

Fox understands this light to be the covenant of light to the nations prophesied by Isaiah (42:6):

> He that sees the new covenant, Christ Jesus, to Jews and Gentiles, the covenant of light . . . and the blood of it, he that sees this, his eye is opened, and he is a believer . . . and no one comes to life, but he who comes to the light which Christ hath enlightened him withal.[16]

As we can see, Fox employs texts from both the Old and New Testaments to witness to this universal light. But, consistent with his overall message, Fox bases his teaching first of all upon his own experience. In the year of his calling to the ministry, "The Lord God hath opened to me by his invisible power how that every man was enlightened by the divine light of Christ; and I saw it shine through all . . . ."[17] It was from this experience that he drew a fresh interpretation of scripture.

Not surprisingly, Fox's assertion of this broad biblical witness to a universal saving presence of Christ was repeatedly attacked by contemporary Puritan leaders. Their objection was founded upon two assumptions drawn from Calvinist doctrine: first, the doctrine of *predestination*, by which God's grace efficiently goes out only to those whom God wills to, and shall, save; and second, the affirmation that the *Bible* is the Word of God, essential for salvation, through the reading or study of the gospel. The doctrine of the Bible as the saving Word meshes with that of predestination in the belief that individuals (mainly Europeans in the seventeenth century) encounter this Word by God's *providence*.

Therefore, in Fox's preaching Puritans heard what they felt to be two heresies: first they detected the belief commonly called Arminianism which states that God wills to save *all* people, even though not all will respond; second, they heard a strong challenge to the unique authority and saving power of the Bible.

Richard Baxter, one of the great Puritan pastors, levelled several attacks upon the Quakers in the 1650s. He wrote affirmatively of an inward light sufficient to reveal one's sins, leaving one without excuse for them (Rom. 1:20). But he insisted that this light is natural and not sufficient to salvation. He suggested that *many* lights are needed to give a person saving light. He made an analogy of this operation by which Christ is the sun, scripture is the external light flowing from the sun, man's reason is the eye, an inward light, and the Holy Spirit puts them (the gospel and reason) together to produce the illumination of the soul.[18]

The Baptist John Bunyan directed similar criticism against the Quaker conception of the light in his first published work.[19] Like Baxter, he charged that the Quakers' light is merely the natural light of human conscience, able to reprove sin and show that there is a God by the things created (Rom. 1:20), but not revealing the savior. Again like Baxter, Bunyan reasoned that a universally bestowed saving light would make Christ's incarnation, atoning death for sin, sending of the Spirit and the writing of scripture unnecessary.

The most extensive and incisive Puritan criticism, however, came from the Congregationalist John Owen, Vice-Chancellor of Oxford University and close advisor to Cromwell. Owen viewed

Quakerism as the "latter day madness" of the gnostics and Valentinians.[20] The Quaker phenomenon was no different from Satan's attacks upon the early Church, substituting a perfecting light and knowledge for the person of Christ. Owen agreed with Baxter and Bunyan that the Quaker inward light belittled the Jesus Christ of history. The Spirit promised by Christ is to glorify Christ. But the spirit of the Quaker glorifies itself.

In 1658 Owen feared that Quakers and other "fanatics" might gain influence at Oxford. He responded to this perceived threat with a treatise for the community, written in Latin and entitled *Pro Sacris Scripturis Adversus Hujus Temporis Fanaticos.*[21] Most of this work anticipates his later and more extensive writing on his favorite theme, the integrity and textual purity of scripture as the Word of God.[22] But the fourth Exercise of the treatise, "De Lumine Interno," addresses the issue at hand in this chapter. It represents probably the fullest Puritan statement on the light and the most careful critique of the Quaker position.[23]

Owen sees the internal light of the individual as reason, usually involved with the mind, though it can include the emotions as well. Every rational creature is endowed with this faculty of knowing (Sec. VIII). This light of rationality is typically engaged with mundane matters, but has some limited discernment of spiritual affairs, too (Sec. IX). It was given to the first man in paradise so that he might be obedient to the Word that communicated God's will. It was sufficient for that purpose, but in man's disobedience, he was punished by the loss of most of this light (Sec. X). In the condition of sin, blindness confuses the mind so that it cannot perceive God's glory or ultimate purpose. Even if this light had not been lost, it still would not be sufficient to save from the sinful condition of humanity, so as to help one know and worship God properly. He cites John 1:5; 1 Corinthians 2:14, and Ephesians 4:18 and 5:8 in support of this view of the human condition.

Salvation comes from Christ, the light of men. Christ reveals God and has abundantly done so by steps. First, he revealed God by his Spirit through the prophets (1 Pet. 1:11), like a dim light. Then, at last, he announced the Good News in his own person during his earthly ministry. After his resurrection, he poured out his Spirit upon the apostles, and they were empowered to write the New Testament, to share the light of knowledge itself for the sake of all who wish to obey it. Thus, Christ's light shines from scripture, reaching men by God's providence (Sec. XI). The light of scripture, combined with the action of the Holy Spirit, awakens the dead from among sinners, opening the eyes of the blind and giving the mind a knowledge of God's truth (Sec. XII). But Christ illuminates and inspires only certain chosen ones (Sec. XIII).

Without this light, one is left with only the faint sparks of the aforementioned primeval light of rationality. This allows one to discern morally between good and evil, perceiving one's obligations regarding the judgment of God. This faint light can be cultivated by contemplating the works of God in creation and providence, which are manifestations of his deity. It gives enough indication of God's existence and enough moral sensibility so as to leave one without excuse for sin (see Rom. 1:18ff) (Sec. XIV).

Owen deduces that it is this faint "blinking light" that the Quakers claim is able to save without the scriptures, even calling it Christ himself (Sec. XVI). Like Baxter and Bunyan, he demands that these "fanatics" explain, therefore, the importance of the Holy Spirit, scripture, and preaching (Sec. XX). He summarizes that "the Christ of the fanatics is the spirit of the world, mixed with everything, which is the all, and truly nothing" (Sec. XXI).

Owen finishes his treatment of the inward light by examining a favorite text of the Quakers, John 1:9, which he notes has been the topic of "great and horrible yelling." First, Owen departs from the Authorized Version translation of the verse, stating that Christ does not enlighten all men coming into the world, but that Christ, coming into the world, enlightens all men. He insists that by this more proper translation of the Greek, we are to understand that Christ never enlightened the *majority* of men — namely, all those who lived *before* the incarnation. Therefore, in the incarnation, Christ led men out of darkness. This illumination continues through the work of scripture and the Holy Spirit. However, even with this major qualification, Owen further asserts that the enlightening of "all men" does not mean *each and every* one, but only *some* — all those whom Christ wishes to save (Sec. XXV). Owen brings his argument to a close by stating somewhat ironically that the purpose of the natural light is to help man discern that all creation is filled with God, displaying his eternal power, divinity, and concern for his creatures, "so that all men everywhere ought to search after him much more . . ." (Sec. XXVI). Why he feels they should bother to do so, given his views on scripture and predestination, is left unclear.

It is interesting to note that the modern interpretations of early Quakerism as a radical Puritanism apply much the same critique to Fox's views. Not surprisingly, it is precisely on this question of a universal light that Quakerism is diagnosed as a *flawed* Puritanism.[24]

FOX'S RESPONSE

Since he did not read Latin, George Fox never answered Owen in print.[25] But we can find statements by Fox which address most of the questions Owen, Baxter, and Bunyan raised. First of all, Fox did not share the background in philosophical tradition that Owen, and to a lesser extent Baxter, employed. He tends more toward the simple biblical view of the light of God *versus* the darkness of the world. His view of human nature is summarily unhopeful, viewing it as utterly dark. Echoing Proverbs 20:27, he affirms that "the spirit in man is the candle of the Lord," a darkness to be lighted by the Lord (Ps. 18:28).[26] Hence, there is not even a faint glimmer of what might be called a primeval, natural light in the human condition as far as Fox is concerned. Fox places no stock in rationality, stating that the mind can only wander fruitlessly in regard to salvation.[27] The only created lights in Fox's view are those of the sun, moon, and stars.

Fox repeatedly affirms election and reprobation, but argues that the elect seed, to which the promise is given, is but one — Jesus Christ (Gal. 3:16). As many as walk in the light and teaching of Christ are in the election. He rejects the Calvinist conception of predestination, claiming that it places the fault for sin upon God. God warned Cain and Balaam, and promised Cain that if he did well, he would be accepted. The fault for their sin and rebellion was upon themselves. Further, Christ died for the sins of the whole world, the ungodly as well as the godly (Rom. 4:5). He enlightens every one and wills that all might believe (Rom. 5:6; 2 Cor. 5:15). Only those (like his Puritan critics, he warns) who hate the light shall be reprobated.[28]

Moreover, Fox rejects the standard Puritan belief that the prophets and apostles, as writers of scripture, received an *extraordinary* inspiration, in contrast to an *ordinary* inspiration in subsequent times. His repeated claim for the Quaker movement is that it is in the *same* Spirit and power that the prophets and apostles were in.[29] In Fox's view, the Holy Spirit and the Word have the same inseparable unity as breath and the voice. His descriptive language of the Spirit and the Word is often very much like that of the prophets, where the Spirit and the Word of the Lord come together in one experience (see Isa. 59:21; Ezek. 2:2; 11:5), the same phenomenon as described at Pentecost, the pivotal apostolic experience (Acts 2:4).

It is Fox's belief that this Word of God, unmediated by scripture, enlightens every one, and that the Holy Spirit, according to the prophecy of Joel, is poured out upon all flesh, even where the scriptures are not known nor the gospel preached. On his trip to America, Fox was able to explore this belief through conversations with the Indians. His question to them was simple — did they know something within them which reproved them when they did wrong? He concluded that all know this experience, and that it is the work of Christ's light:

> Now Jews, and the Turks, and heathen, and Indians, that do not nor will not profess and own Christ in the flesh, to be the Saviour; if one come to speak to them of their evil deeds and words, and ask them if there is something in them that tells them, they should not speak and do so, or so wickedly? (for the light of Christ troubles and condemns them if they do evil), here they will confess to the light of Christ though they know not what it is . . . .[30]

It should be recognized that Fox does not seem to allow here that the internal sense of condemnation may in many cases arise from the socially-conditioned conscience that all individuals develop. But he is clear that the conscience itself is a human, natural capacity and not a saving grace. His argument is that beyond the workings of the natural conscience, the light of Christ can and does inform men and women as to good and evil. This universal sense of good and evil, this experience of an inward judgment, Fox interprets by the Gospel of John and Romans 1-2 to be the light of Christ, while Baxter, Bunyan, and Owen are all agreed that it is a natural created light of conscience, insufficient for salvation.

Here we come to the heart of the matter: while Fox insists that this experience is the work of Christ's light, he sees it only as the *initial stage* of the light's action, and certainly not sufficient for salvation. The light's judgment is the work of the law written upon the heart (Rom. 2:15), exposing sin. Those who love this light and stand in it, though it troubles them, can thereby give themselves up to it. Through this law they become dead to the law and alive to God (Gal. 2:19). Only here is the seed of faith raised up and the saving power of the light realized.

Fox is not sanguine of the individual's resolve to stand in the reproof of the light, without the hearing of the gospel which scripture and preaching afford.[31] But he points, like Paul (Gal. 3; Rom. 4), to Abraham, who was saved not by a written law but by grace and faith. The gospel (the promise) was preached to Abraham by the Holy Ghost. By this Spirit, Christ, in fact, preached to spirits in prison as far back as the days of Noah (1 Pet. 3:19f), long before Moses and the beginnings of scripture.[32] Abraham's seed was blessed not because Abraham adhered to scripture, but because he "obeyed my voice" (Gen. 22:16). Christ's earthly ministry, the scriptures, and the preaching of the gospel play a vital role in Fox's message, as we shall see; nevertheless, it is clear that he does not consider a *propositional* knowledge of any of these to be essential to Christ's power to save those who love his light.

As we have already seen, much of the debate between Puritans and Quakers centered around the first two chapters of Paul's letter to the Romans. Owen and others construed a natural revelation from "that which may be known of God" in 1:19ff, and a natural law from the Gentiles' "law unto themselves" in 2:14f. This knowledge of the Creator and of good and evil, given to all, can keep them from sin and is the condemnation of those who rebel from this knowledge, so that they are without excuse, as Fox agrees. This is the wrath of God "revealed from heaven against all ungodliness and unrighteousness of men, who hold the truth in unrighteousness" (vs 18). But this apocalyptic revelation of judgment day breaking forth is *inseparable* from the revelation of the righteousness of God accomplished in Jesus Christ, which Paul proclaims in the preceding verse (vs 17). The revelation of wrath and the revelation of righteousness form a unity in Jesus Christ, according to Paul.

Therefore, in the final analysis, the Puritan conception of two lights, one a created light of condemnation and the other a saving light of the gospel, really amounts to the *Marcionite* error by which the one God is divided into a Creator God of wrath and a Redeemer God of love. Marcion believed that the Creator witnessed in the Old Testament was an inferior god to the Redeemer revealed in Christ. The Church long ago rejected this formulation in its Christology, yet here we see it cropping up again. But Fox invariably insists that there is one God and one light, known in the apocalyptic revelation of Jesus Christ, just as John's Prologue identifies Christ's light with the Word that created all things. Fox's insistence upon the universal light of Christ is fundamental to his understanding of the unity of the biblical faith.

When Fox counters his Puritan critics, he does so on a note of urgency toward those who, unlike the heathen, have long had the advantage of the scriptures and think they have salvation in them, yet are actually those who "stumble at the cornerstone":

> Therefore, while ye have time, prize it; seek the Lord while he may be found, and call upon him while he is near; lest he say, "time is past;" for the rich glutton's time was past [see Luke 12: 16-20]. Therefore, while time is not quite past, consider, search yourselves, and see if ye be not they that hate the light; and so are builders that stumble at the cornerstone; for they that hated the light, and did not believe in the light, did so in ages past [see Ps. 118:22; Isa. 28:16; Rom. 9:32f; 1 Pet. 2:6-8].[33]

Fox strikes here upon his key point. The scandal of the Quaker gospel is really no different from that of the early apostolic preaching of Christ. That the light came into the world in the person of Jesus Christ is a scandal well recorded in the gospels. Crowds hearing Jesus' preaching murmured among themselves, saying, "Is not this Jesus, son of Joseph, whose father and mother we know?" (John 6:42). The only thing apparent to the hearers of Jesus was that he was common (remember Luke's nativity story), if not outright inappropriate: "Shall Christ come out of Galilee?" (John 7:41). In other words, he seemed too "natural" to believe. Many were attracted to Jesus' message, but some fell away (John 6:66). It is asserted that Jesus knew from the beginning who would believe and who would not (John 6:64). Yet he believed himself fulfilling the prophecy that *all* would be taught by God, and all who heard and learned came to him (John 6:45; see Isa. 54:13). Even those who sat in patience under Jesus' teaching did not fully recognize him as the Christ. Real belief came only after he was raised up, fully revealing his identity.

Fox understands the light that enlightens every one according to the gospel of Jesus: "It is sown in dishonor; it is raised in glory: it is sown in weakness; it is raised in power" (1 Cor.

15:43). The light that came into the world in Jesus enters all men and women with the same commonness and impropriety. Thus, a grace which in its initial stages appears to be only of the basest sort, revealing and condemning sin, if waited upon, will reveal salvation. Thus, the second coming of Christ relives the drama of faith and disbelief witnessed by the gospels in the first coming. The difference is that the revelation of the risen Lord signals the end time. This is the last time to respond.

But with a universally bestowed light of Christ, what *is* the significance of the life, death, and resurrection of Jesus, and the writing of scripture? This recurring Puritan query must be answered; we may now turn our attention to this vital issue.

> *If Christ that is crucified be not within, and Christ that is risen be not within, I say you all are reprobates [2 Cor. 13:5]; and if the scripture be not within, which was spoken forth from within, you all want [i.e., lack] the spirit that gave it forth, and Christ the substance of it, and you have not eaten his flesh, neither are you of his bone [Eph. 5:30]; and this is not opposite to Jesus Christ without, that died at Jerusalem, but the same; for they who eat his flesh have it within them, and this is not a new gospel.* [1]

5. THE RELATIONSHIP OF EXPERIENCE TO HISTORY

George Fox's preaching of a universal enlightening presence of Christ has been viewed with both praise and scorn; both reactions have usually been due to misapprehension of his meaning. Modern liberal Quakerism has often portrayed Fox as a witness to an unnameable mystical experience, assuming that he applied Christian language to this experience simply as a matter of preference or cultural conditioning. He has, by this reasoning, been hailed as the prophet of a new age of universal mysticism.

Fox's contemporaries, however, condemned him as an antichristian seducer for much the same reasons. In his emphasis upon the work of the light of Christ that does not even require a knowledge of scripture to save, they thought they heard a denial of the importance and identity of the historical Jesus. They accused Fox and his Quaker followers of denying "that Jesus Christ is come in the flesh" (1 John 4:2f). [2]

Indeed, there are surprisingly few references in Fox's writings to the life of Jesus as recorded in the gospels of the New Testament It must be recognized, however, that in the society to which Fox preached, hearers were already familiar with at least the outlines of the life of Jesus; recounting his life was not of absolute necessity. This fact makes it significant, then, where Fox *does* emphasize the historical Jesus. In evangelical tracts written to Jews,[3] he goes to great lengths to show how Jesus fulfilled the promises and prophecies of the Old Testament. In answering Ranters,[4] he insists upon the importance of this historical Jesus in Christian faith. When Friends are suspected by civil authorities of being antichristian, Fox is very explicit about the Quaker belief in the Jesus born of Mary, who suffered outside the gates of Jerusalem. And when Fox establishes a meeting among Indians in America, he arranges for a local Friend to read the scriptures to them on a regular basis.[5] Thus, when the life of Jesus is unknown, or its significance questioned, Fox witnesses to it with conviction.

But Fox is not interested in drawing people into an assent to a set of propositions about the life of Jesus sixteen hundred years before. *That* was the cultural norm of seventeenth century England. His mission is to bring people into a *possession* of what they profess — to help them *incarnate* the life of Jesus Christ as well as to speak of it. That was far from the cultural norm.

In view of this, it is also revealing to look at Fox's *Journal*, the story of his own life, as a whole. Geoffrey Nuttall[6] observes that the *Journal* shows us a life thoroughly infused with the example of Jesus. It is a life of fearless preaching, healings, and even some acts considered miraculous by witnesses. In fact, the *Journal* is a remarkable document whose very construction is provocatively similar to the way in which modern scholarship believes the gospels themselves to have been written. Fox's classic of English and Christian literature is nothing less than a summary of his total message given in anecdotal form. He clearly sees his life as a series of events that declare and incarnate the Good News of Christ's victory over Satan in the cross. Both savage beatings and glorious in-gatherings are occasions with which Fox can summarize, "the Lord's power was over all." And, though the seemingly endless stream of conversations, disputes, and sermons recorded in the *Journal* can seem tiringly repetitive in a cursory reading, closer examination discovers that each incident relates some new facet of Fox's total message. Though the religious journal was a popular *genre* among Puritans and Quakers alike, Fox's contribution is clearly the masterpiece in that it shows the most profoundly organic grasp of the gospel, in terms of both content and form.

Thus, Fox's *Journal* relates a life whose experience and obedience *partake* of the life of Jesus Christ; this sense of internalization is the only kind of communion with the flesh and blood of Jesus that Fox considers important, as suggested in the opening quote of this chapter. But in partaking of the life of Jesus, one incarnates a life which in turn has fulfilled all the life of Israel which preceded it. Fox understands his experience of Christ's revelation as one that summarizes the salvation history of the Bible; this can be seen from the opening thirty pages of the *Journal*, which record his spiritual transformation. As we detailed that transformation in our last chapter, we saw how Fox's experience of Christ's light moved him from his alienated state in Adam, through an inward experience of the law, revealing his sins, and eventually to the power of the risen Christ, the seed within. Fox concludes this description of his spiritual development with this insight:

> I saw also how people read the scriptures without a right sense of them, and without duly applying them to their own states. For, when they read that death reigned from Adam to Moses, that the law and the prophets were until John, they read these things without them and applied them to others without them, but they did not *turn in* to find the truth of these things in themselves. But as these things came to be opened in me, I *saw* death reigned over them from Adam to Moses, from the entrance into transgression till they came to the ministration of condemnation, which restrains people from sin that brings death. Then, when the ministration of Moses is passed through, the ministry of the prophets comes to be read and *understood*, which reaches through the figures, types, and shadows unto John, the greatest prophet born of woman; whose ministration prepares the way of the Lord by bringing down the exalted mountains and making straight paths. And as this ministration is passed through, an entrance comes to be *known* into the everlasting kingdom.
>
> . . . Thus I saw . . . none could *know* death reigned from Adam to Moses, etc., but by the same Holy Spirit which Moses and the prophets, and John were in. They could not *know* the spiritual meaning of Moses', the prophets', and John's words, nor *see* their path and travels, *much less see through* them and to the end of them into the kingdom, unless they had the Spirit and

light of Jesus; nor could they *know* the words of Christ and his apostles without his Spirit. But as man *comes through* by the Spirit and power of God to Christ who fulfills the types, figures, shadows, promises, and prophecies that were of him, and is led by the Holy Ghost to the truth and substance of the scriptures, sitting down in him who is the author and end of them, then they are read and *understood* with profit and great delight [emphases mine].[7]

The statement bears careful reading to appreciate its immense implications. To summarize, Fox is saying that in Christ's light he has come to know the experience of Adam, Moses, the prophets, John, and the apostles *apart* from his reading of scripture — and *beyond* it as well. He can witness to the history recorded in the Bible because he has known it in his own life. He insists of his own experience: "This I saw in the pure openings of the Light without the help of any man, neither did I know where to find it in the scriptures; though afterwards, searching the scriptures, I found it."[8]

Fox follows the radical Christology of the Gospel of John in believing Christ to be the Word of God who, in his incarnation, life, death, and resurrection, has fulfilled the history and scriptures of Israel. Then, in his revelation within the individual, this same Word recapitulates *history* in personal *experience*. So the individual understands the history recorded in the Bible only by personal experience. Yet this key given by Christ's direct teaching works, it might be said, from either side of the door: the believer also understands scripture "with profit and great delight." This implies that with the Spirit of Christ, the scriptures may in turn aid the individual in better understanding his or her own experience. Experience and scripture interpret *each other*.

Here we begin to discover the significance of the historical Jesus in Fox's thought. But we must not jump to premature conclusions. Fox is not saying that the life of Jesus and the history of Israel function simply as an allegory by which a universal mystical experience is described. If that were the case, we could expect Fox's message to contain no significant historical or corporate dimension; the Bible would represent for Fox simply a set of universal archetypes upon which individuals might project their own experience, if they found it helpful to do so; Jesus would symbolize an escape from an essentially illusory world of history. But in fact we find that while Fox does insist upon the primacy of individual experience, he falls neither into a

96

negation of history nor into narcissism. Experience serves as a starting point toward Fox's overarching concern for the community of the Church and a strong engagement with history. In other words, personal revelation and historical apocalypse meet in Christ.

HISTORY, COMMUNITY, LANGUAGE

We can place Fox's teaching in its proper perspective by taking a moment to consider the inter-relationship between history, community, and language. These three elements combine powerfully in the faith of ancient Israel. The children of Abraham are galvanized into a nation by the revelation of God's power and love in history, the Exodus from Egypt and the conquest of the Promised Land. This community is defined and preserved by God's law for his people. Both the law and the mighty acts of God are recorded and preserved in scripture for all generations. Scripture becomes the center of the Israelite community and the interpreter of its history since only by some language system can a community exist, and since only through the linear quality of language can historical experience be made meaningful. The religion of Israel is a religion of the Word, and revelation comes to be understood *by* and *as* God's Word. The inter-relationship of language with history and community is well-attested in modern linguistic theory.[9] But apart from this twentieth century analytical approach, the same unity is more profoundly articulated in the Old Testament record of Israel's experience. This unity cannot be violated as long as one affirms that experience.

Fox affirms the historical experience of Israel because it resonates with his own personal experience and helps him to understand his own experience better. Therefore, he sees the same Word of God at work in both the historical revelation of Moses' law and his own personal experience of the light's revelation of sin, for example. The correspondence between the history of Israel on the one hand, and Fox's Christian experience on the other, is therefore not allegorical but *typological*. Israel's experience forms the historical antitype of the life of Jesus in the New Testament, and in turn for this same Jesus' work within George Fox. Typology is the dominant concept of correspondence in the Bible; it conveys a historical sense of comparison between a former event and a latter one. Typology is the chief way in which the New Testament writers understand the life, death, and resurrection of Jesus Christ as fulfilling the writings of Moses and the prophets; it is the way in which the New Testament conceives of the relationship of the first covenant, mediated by Moses, and the new covenant, mediated by Jesus.

Fox insists, however, that to the reader of the New Testament this can represent only a "notional" or propositional truth by itself. But as Christ re-enacts his fulfillment of the first covenant through the individual's personal experience, then he or she *knows* the truth of it and may *incarnate* that truth through obedience to it. Typology, then, must reach all the way into personal experience to become more than a literary device of the New Testament, appreciated by more than the intellect alone. The *Word* himself, not the *words* about him, brings it into embodiment in the believer.

Thus, as in the first covenant God *revealed* himself to his people *in history*, in saving acts, so in the second covenant God in the life of Jesus *reveals history*. George Fox, waiting in the light and power of the risen Lord, experiences history revealed, from the ministration of the law, all the way to the return to Eden. Therefore, he can state that those in Christ "comprehend the state and time before the law, the time of the law, the time of the Christians . . . ."[10] To his Puritan opponents who insisted upon the witness of scripture as the saving knowledge, Fox adamantly emphasizes the necessity of Christ's work within: "And thou sayest, thou art saved by Christ without thee, and so . . . are ignorant of the mystery of Christ within thee; for without that thou dost not know salvation."[11] "They that have the form of godliness [but deny the power — see 2 Tim. 3:5] can confess a Christ without them, and not within them."[12] "There is none knows Christ within, but he knows him without, the same yesterday, today, and forever [Heb. 13:8]; and there are none know him but they know him within . . . ."[13]

The Calvinism of the Puritans certainly attested that the work of the Holy Spirit in the heart is necessary for a saving understanding of scripture's witness. But this is still decidedly different from Fox's concept of history as directly revealed by Christ within the believer. To be sure, an explicit awareness that one is experiencing the history of Adam to Christ would naturally require a knowledge of scripture. This knowledge is important to a better understanding of the experience and may aid one in persevering in subjection to it. But this kind of knowledge is not fundamentally necessary. The difference between

Fox and his Puritan contemporaries, as we shall see repeatedly, is a difference in understanding of the Word of God. For Fox, Christ himself is the only Word, and in this role he himself mediates between history and experience. In his incarnation, life, death, and resurrection he has mediated between the historical religion of the Israelite community and the experience that he offers to all individuals. As we shall see later, the knowledge of scripture becomes particularly important for Fox not only for interpreting the individual experience, but also for gathering the Church — the new Israel — around that experience.

INWARD *VERSUS* OUTWARD

In order for us to explore Fox's thought further, we must first note what language he employs to describe Christ's mediation. We have already seen some of Fox's usage of "Christ without" and "Christ within" to describe the Christ of history and the Christ of experience. This usage is exemplary of a basic antinomy that runs throughout Fox's writings — namely, *outward* and *inward.*

Outward and inward represent in Fox's thought two different ways of knowing. Outward knowledge is rational or based in some way on sensory perception. As such, it is given to change and to fallibility. One may have an outward knowledge of salvation history through the reading or hearing of the outward letter of scripture; an outward knowledge of God's will is transmitted by the written laws of Moses and the recorded sayings of Jesus. Yet not only is this knowledge given to mis-apprehension through human frailty, but it cannot in fact become more than "notional" or intellectual — it cannot reach to the heart. This knowledge can lead only to the *form* of godliness at best.

Inward knowledge, on the other hand, is that which is revealed directly to the heart by the Spirit of Christ; it is a knowledge of certainty, never changing. It surpasses and judges the human mind. It gives a true knowledge of history and the *power* of God's will to live in true godliness.

There is no evil inherent in the outward knowledge nor in the outward world which it perceives; but if the outward mind is not kept in subjection to the inward Spirit of Christ, one will come to destruction. Satan constantly attempts to draw men and women out, into the outward mind, even as the serpent drew the first man and woman from obedience to the sure command of God, into a righteousness made by their own devising (see Gen. 3:1-7). The woman listens to the serpent's beguiling words, sees the fruit is good for food, and eats of the tree of knowledge. Fox summarizes this story, stating, "So man did eat: the eye out [i.e., went into the outward knowledge], the ear out, at last the mouth out too." The man and the woman "begot a wisdom by which in process of time they knew not God."[14] Forsaking inward knowledge for the outward, one forsakes the one living path for the many, all dead-ends in a wilderness of confusion; one worships not the one God but many gods, all of them changing and contradictory; one hears not the one Word, but many words, with no understanding.

Fox derives his usage of inward/outward, like all his theological vocabulary, from the Bible. The key reference here is Romans 2:28f, Paul's insistence that the true Jew is one inwardly, by the spiritual circumcision of the heart. A saying of Jesus makes a similar point: "Beware of false prophets, which come to you in sheep's clothing, but inwardly they are ravening wolves" (Matt. 7:15). Outward, formal religion may give the appearance, or form, of true faith, yet hide a different quality within. Other pairs of antinomies are frequently employed by Fox as parallels to inward/outward, like *spiritual/fleshly*, or *spiritual/carnal*. Like "outward," "fleshly" by no means implies something necessarily evil, but a realm vulnerable to the evil temptations of Satan. The flesh, whose perceptions are determined by the outward senses and human mind, must be overruled by the Spirit. The other antinomy in Fox's usage is *heavenly/earthly*, or *heavenly/worldly* (see John 3:12; Gal. 4:21-31; Heb. 12:22; Rev. 3:10-12).

The writings of Fox are thoroughly infused with these antinomies, always stressing the importance of the inward Jew, the circumcision of the Spirit, and the heavenly Jerusalem. Yet the outward Jew, the circumcision of the flesh, and the earthly Jerusalem are far from insignificant in his view of salvation. We must first focus on their role in his gospel message before we can fully appreciate the significance of the historical Jesus and the mediation that he makes between the outward and the inward.

THE FIRST COVENANT

The great redemptive work of God in history begins with Abraham. Fox follows Paul in viewing Abraham as a man initially without any unique relationship to God. He receives the promise in his uncircumcision and enters into an obedient relationship with God long before the time of Moses and the law. Hence, like any Gentile, he hears and responds to "the gospel" by inward spiritual experience, by Christ's preaching through the Holy Spirit (1 Pet. 3:18-20). The promise is reiterated and vouchsafed as a result of Abraham's faithful obedience to God's inward leadings — "because thou has obeyed my voice" (Gen. 22:18). This inward experience and its obedient response remain the vital core of Israel's faith, according to Fox.

Abraham's interaction with an unnamed God is not unique but a universal possibility. Yet God undertakes a unique historical plan with Abraham. This plan is suggested in the promise, "in thy seed shall all nations of the earth be blessed . . ." (Gen. 22:18). A redemptive plan is set in motion through the outward and fleshly means of Abraham's progeny. God's effort to reach men and women goes into this outward, historical mode because men and women are alienated and separated from God's inward teaching. They have been drawn into a barren and treacherous wilderness of outward knowledge by Satan's teaching, the serpent's temptation. Therefore, God's mission to redeem humanity must first invade this realm. The promise to Abraham's seed will ultimately be realized in Jesus Christ, the one seed, rather than the many (Gal. 3:16). Nevertheless, the entire line of Abraham, the nation of Israel, plays a vital role in this promise and fulfillment.

The historical role of Israel begins in earnest with God's mighty act of liberating the children of Israel from bondage in Egypt. This event is accomplished through the combination of God's outward lordship over creation (the plagues of Egypt, the deliverance through the Red Sea) and his inward guidance of his chosen leader, Moses. Through the ministry of Moses, this obscure ethnic group becomes a nation of God. Through Moses, this community comes into being (1) as the God of its ancestors reveals his name (Exod. 3:13f), (2) as Moses begins a language tradition that recounts God's mighty acts on behalf of his people (e.g., "The Song of Moses," Exod. 15), and (3) as the cultic and ethical boundaries of this community are defined by the laws given at Sinai. Thus, through the ministry of Moses, the *community* is established and maintained, and its *history* preserved through *language* (the communication of God's name, law, and mighty acts).

Fox characterizes the covenant mediated with Israel by Moses as an *outward covenant.*[15] It is made with outward Jews, the fleshly descendants of Abraham, whose membership is validated by circumcision of the flesh. This covenant sets forth an outward worship consisting of outward, earthly tabernacles, temples, and animal sacrifices, conducted by the outward priesthood of the line of Levi. It observes outward Sabbaths and festivals held at outwardly discerned times and seasons of the year. It establishes outward laws, written in outward words upon stone, the knowledge of which is to be preserved among the people by the teaching of the priests. And it grants the outward Jews an outward kingdom, established and maintained by the use of outward, carnal weapons. Thus, the outward Jews are to "hear Moses," that is, to follow the laws given through him, in all these things. In faithfulness to his covenant, Israel may know the righteous life which God demands, the forgiveness of sins that he offers, and the blessings that he bestows upon the land he has given.

The covenant mediated by Moses establishes a series of formal "signs" and "figures" — set behavioral patterns — by which the people may recognize God's grace offered to them. Fox affirms that the laws of Moses are "the pure and perfect law of God." [16] Yet Fox, following Paul, sees the dangers attendant in this outward formalism. Because they do not necessarily bring the mind inward from its outward confusion, the ethical demands of these laws serve ultimately as a curse (Gal. 3:10f), a ministration of death (2 Cor. 3:7) and of condemnation (2 Cor. 3:9). They serve only to expose *sins*, not to reveal the fundamental condition of *sin*, the alienation from God's inward voice. They cannot reveal the will of God. One may remain in confusion, without the inward clarity necessary for salvation; thus, the mind is blinded (2 Cor. 3:14), and the heart is hardened. Using this array of laws, men and women attempt to create their own righteousness (Rom. 10:3), not the righteousness of God.

Nevertheless, while the covenant and law of Moses are outward and given to these pitfalls, they do not necessarily lead to this outcome; Israel was by no means doomed to fail by this covenant. This law, being truly the law of God, may resonate with the inward revelation of God, the light:

> The pure and perfect law of God is over the flesh to keep it and
> its works, which are not perfect, under, by the perfect law; and

the law of God that is perfect answers the perfect principle in every one. And this law the Jews and the prophets were to perform and do.[17]

The inward *light of the law* (Ps. 6:23), or *spirit of the law*, Fox opposes to the outward letter of the law. Yet the two "answer" one another, just as a certain key "answers" a certain lock, according to an old English expression still in use today.[18] Hence, "the life of the law, the light, which is one with the light of God, in every man . . . with that they know that the judgments of God are upon them when they act unrighteously."[19] Thus, as we have already noted in this chapter, the outward, historical revelation and the inward, personal revelation confirm and interpret each other. But unless one loves the inward light of the law and comes to its inward condemnation, then one will never live in the life of the outward law, in the Spirit by which it was given. Instead, one becomes lost in the outward letter of confusion and alienation.

The tragedy of Israel's fall, recorded in the Old Testament, consists precisely in that outward path of alienation and oblivion. Fox asserts that the outward Jews became lost in the outward form of righteousness. They "were out of the life of the law, though they had the words, and . . . according as it is written, God hath given them a spirit of slumber, eyes that they should not see, ears that they should not hear [Isa. 29:10; Rom. 11:3] . . . having their minds reprobated . . . ."[20] The curse against Israel pronounced by Isaiah is essentially the same as that pronounced against Adam and Eve; it is less God's *imperative* against them than his *indicative* description of how their outward-mindedness has numbed them to his saving inward revelation.

The prophets of the Old Testament suggest that Israel failed to live in the life of the law; it failed to embrace the *Spirit* by which the law was given forth (e.g., Isa. 58:1-11), and it failed to meet the specific demands of the letter of the law (e.g., Isa. 10:1-11). Israel was warned by the prophets of the judgment that would come upon its waywardness. Not heeding these warnings, Israel was cast out of its Promised Land, just as Adam and Eve were cast out of Eden. Thus, Israel resisted the inward light of the law to which the outward law of Moses was to have turned them. Remaining in the outward knowledge and mind, Israel embodied, like all humanity, the curse of Adam.

Fox insists, however, that many Israelites *did* know and love the light of the law, living in obedience to it.

> For the promise was when God gave forth the law, the blessing, and they that were in the life saw to the end of it . . . the curse was to them that . . . came not to see the end of what they professed, and these went from the life of the law to men's precepts, and were such as called upon God with their lips, but their hearts were afar off [Isa. 29:13] . . . .[21]

The light brings both mind and heart to the will of God; ". . . this light *keeps* thee from adultery . . . *teacheth* thee not to commit adultery . . . ."[22]

Moses, mediator of the outward covenant and leader of Israel, had a profound inward relationship with God. In the light of the law, Moses saw to its end. Fox finds this confirmed in Deuteronomy 18:18f:

> I will raise them up a prophet from among their brethren, like unto thee, and will put my words in his mouth; and he shall speak unto them all that I command him. And it shall come to pass, that whosoever will not hearken unto my words which he shall speak in my name, I will require it of him.

Thus, Moses saw to Christ, the end of the law.[23] Moses' experience follows Fox's understanding of the light: the same light revealing your sin also reveals your savior.

The other Old Testament prophets also saw Christ and prophesied of his coming. Fox particularly points to Isaiah and his oracles of the Messiah as a light to the Gentiles (Isa. 42:6; 60:3) and ensign to the nations (Isa. 11:10). It is Jeremiah who speaks explicitly of a new covenant as an inward revelation: "I will put my law in their inward parts, and write it upon their hearts . . . for they shall all know me, from the least of them to the greatest . . ." (Jer. 31:31-34). This new covenant revealed to the prophets therefore confirms the covenant of Moses, yet its mode will be inward rather than outward. The "new thing" will gather Jews and Gentiles into a new community.

These prophets, and undoubtedly many other ancient Israelites, were "tender" to the light. Fox can allow this regarding individual Israelites, just as he can allow it regarding individual heathens or even individuals in the established Church of his own day, which he views as no holier than Israel at its worst. Israel as a community, however, was a scattered flock. Looking at this once again from our rubric of community, history, and language, the Israelite community in its corporate disobedience to the language, or terms of its outward covenant, received the terrible judgment of God in history. A broken outward covenant, then a broken outward people, and a broken history. Yet God is faithful to his outward covenant and will fulfill it as he establishes his new, inward one.

THE NEW COVENANT

The incarnation of the Word of Jesus Christ is to the fulfillment of the old covenant. As the Word made flesh, made outward, made earthly and historical Jesus states, "Think not that I am come to destroy the law, or the prophets: I am not come to destroy but to fulfill" (Matt. 5:17). The gospels are full of explicit and implicit references to this fulfillment in the birth, life, death, and resurrection of Jesus. He therefore *embodies* in one sinless life the law, history, promises, and prophecies — the *life* — of Israel, so that it can be said that the scriptures testify of *him*.

As the *Word* of God, he is the author of the outward words of scripture, through the inward inspiration of Moses and the prophets. Yet he is not recognized either as the author or fulfiller of scripture by the Jewish authorities, because their minds are gone into the outward words of the law: "and owning not the life of the law, they owned not Christ when he came . . . but were blind, and so Isaiah's words [Isa. 29:10] came to be fulfilled, which were spoken forth from' the life . . . ."[24] Jesus is thus rejected by the Jewish authorities and delivered to the Gentiles, the Roman authorities, who crucify him. In the cross, Jesus' fulfilling of the old covenant is completed; the incarnation of the Word, and the embodiment of Israel's glory in the outward life of Jesus terminates with his death. Both sin and the law of Moses, which defines sin, are nailed to the cross in the flesh of Jesus, and cancelled (Col. 2:13f). Thus, in effect, the outward religion and history of Israel end with the cross of Christ. Yet beyond this utter negation is revealed a still greater substantiation. With the appearance of the risen Lord, a spiritual body (1 Cor. 15:44), the weakness of the outward law is raised in the power of an inward light of Christ that teaches and empowers to do God's will. In the revelation of the risen Jesus, the apostles believe that they have encountered the end of history, the close of the world age and order that spans from creation, through Moses, the prophets, and John the Baptist, to the death of Jesus on the cross. They also believe that they have encountered the beginning of a new order and a new creation in him. This is a strongly *apocalyptic* sense of revelation, one that is nowhere more beautifully expressed than in the opening of the Epistle to the Hebrews: "God, who at sundry times and in diverse manners spake in times past unto the fathers by the prophets, hath in these last days spoken unto us by his Son . . ."(Heb. 1:1f).

The early Church's apocalyptic sense of destruction and new beginning in the crucifixion and resurrection of Jesus is rooted in a typological understanding of his life that is so powerful that it transforms the normal typological comparison of former and latter into an ultimate comparison of first and last, beginning and end. Paul, for example, shows Adam in his disobedience to be the antitype of Christ in his perfect obedience (1 Cor. 15:45). Paul finds many other aspects of the Old Testament witness to be figural of Christ's work (e.g., 1 Cor. 10:1-6). The typological interpretation of Jesus as the Prophet-like-Moses is found among what may be the earliest forms of apostolic preaching (Acts 3:22; 7:37) and is an important theme in the Gospel of John (John 1:21, 25; 6:14) and the Synoptic gospels as well (note the Transfiguration scenes of Matt. 17:3-5; Mark 9:4-7; Luke 9:32-35). The comparison of earthly and heavenly Jerusalems, already mentioned in this chapter, is a typological comparison in which the earthly reality forms the antitype of the heavenly one.

But the typological interpretation of Christ's significance is most elaborately set forth in the Epistle to the Hebrews. Because of its importance in Fox's preaching, we should briefly describe the typology of Hebrews here. The institutions of the old covenant are represented in Hebrews as *figures* or *types* (9:9, 24) and *shadows* (8:5; 10:1), as opposed to Christ the *body* (10:5, 10) or *substance* (11:1) of them. So the types, figures, and shadows of the first covenant have found their substance in the new covenant made in Jesus Christ. The language here is drawn from Platonic philosophy in which human perception in the material world is a mere *shadow*, compared to the heavenly reality of things as their *body* or *substance*. This concept is premised upon a static view of two different planes of reality, one consisting of pure, divine idea, and the other consisting of corrupt human perception. But Hebrews employs the terms to serve a more Hebraic, temporal comparison, by which the former is a "prefiguring" or a "foreshadowing" of the latter, the true embodiment or substantiation. In this case, full truth is revealed not by metaphysical transcendence of materiality to behold the divine idea, but by a temporal confrontation with the embodiment, the fulfilling *incarnation* of things hitherto known only figurally.

The typological focus of Hebrews centers upon the priestly institutions of the old covenant and their fulfillment in Christ. Jesus Christ is the great high priest whose priesthood is greater than that of the Levitical line of Aaron. In his new covenant, he abolishes the old: "Now that which decayeth and waxeth old is ready to vanish away" (Heb. 8:13). Thus we find a radical discontinuity between the old and the new. This is in line with the prophecy found in Isaiah, regarding God's new act of creation: "and the former shall not be remembered nor come into mind" (Isa. 65:17).

Yet there is also a continuity in that the institutions and commandments of the first covenant have provided the types and figures by which the new salvation in Christ may be understood. Thus, continuity and discontinuity[25] are held in tension in Jesus Christ, who substantiates the old covenant — he fulfills and ends it in the cross, and he embodies the power of it in the new covenant of his risen glory. This tension between the outward and the inward revelation of Christ is what makes the witness of the resurrection by those who had been his disciples so important. The testimony of these individuals, men and women, who recognized the risen Christ to be the same person that they had known in Jesus of Nazareth confirms that this new revelation is not simply some floating spirit, unconnected with history, unrelated to the revelation of the first covenant. It is a witness to an inward revelation of that person in whom the entire outward history of God's dealings with his people has culminated.

This conclusion has major implications for the meaning of scripture. The purpose of the apostles' writing the gospels is not that people might *know* Jesus but that they might *recognize* him. The Lord was revealing himself to people before there was a New Testament, just as Abraham was called before the law of Moses was given. The crucial role of remembering Jesus of Nazareth is therefore that the memory of him names and interprets the inward experience of him, discerning Jesus' Spirit from the other spirits (1 Thess. 5:19f; 1 John 4:1).

This is the radical understanding of scripture advanced by Fox. It places inward knowledge in first place over outward knowledge — experience over scripture — while maintaining a mutually-informing relation between the two. Fox criticizes the Puritans and "the generality of Christendom" for having placed the writings of the apostles, and the doctrinal formulations derived from them, above the experience of the risen Lord. When Christ within is denied or subordinated, the Church retreats from the radical Christology of the apostles themselves. Forsaking the oneness of inward knowledge, the Church wanders into the many paths of outward knowledge, breaking down into many "rudiments, inventions, handiworks, and traditions, and cannot sit long in them, therefore turn one against the other."[26] Turning from the one head, Christ, the Church has many heads, "then come the warrings with carnal weapons about earthly churches, and religions, and worships, and ministry, which have been set up since the days of the apostles, and since the fall."[27] We shall see how Fox connects the apostate Church with the many-headed beast of Revelation in our chapter on his salvation-historical teaching.

Fox accuses the Church of having stepped back from the apocalyptic turn of the ages that is known in Christ; they have forsaken the substance, the body of Christ experienced within, and instead chosen the types, figures, and shadows of him that were provided in the first covenant. Worse, they have also adapted religious customs of the pagan world, which God never commanded. They have rejected the *immediate* work of Christ's Spirit for the *mediated* religiosity of holy men, holy places, and holy days and seasons. They "are such as Christ said should come, inwardly ravening forth from the spirit of God, [yet] have got sheep's clothing" (Matt. 7:15).[28]

Fox's Puritan contemporaries sometimes accused early Friends of "denying Jesus Christ is come in the flesh" (1 John 4:2ff), because of their emphasis upon Christ known within. Fox hurls the same accusation back, asserting that they have cherished the Jesus of scripture without truly understanding his significance in history. Christ came to end the outward priesthood, its tithes, rituals, etc. Those who love the light witness Jesus Christ come in the flesh by denying priests, tithes, rites, and all figures; "and you that hold up the figures deny Christ come in the flesh."[29]

As the first covenant was ended by the outward incarnation of Jesus Christ, so the second covenant is entered through the inward incarnation of Christ in all who love his light. Again, we find both discontinuity and continuity between those two incarnations; the discontinuity consists in the death of Jesus on the cross; the continuity consists in this same Jesus being recognized inwardly as the risen Lord. "And Christ Jesus, who is born (of a virgin), crucified, and is ascended (and there is no other) all of you, that are turned to the light, wait to have him born in you . . . ."[30]

FOX'S PREACHING OF CHRIST

The aim of Fox's preaching, then, is "that all who profess themselves Christians may walk in the Spirit of Christ."[31] A great part of this task, therefore, is to bring men and women out of all their apostate "notions" of the gospel, to the power and order of it. This program is exemplified by Fox's description of his historic sermon at Firbank Fell. On that day, Fox began by disabusing his hearers of any assumption that the steeplehouse they stood by was a holy "house of the Lord." It was not commanded by God; neither were the Christian priesthood, tithes, and other rudiments of the world (Col. 2:8, 20), which had been developed since the apostles' days. Christ came to end these, saying "Learn of me" (Matt. 11:29); God said, "This is my beloved Son, hear ye him" (Mark 9:7). All are to know Christ himself as their teacher, counsellor, shepherd, bishop, and prophet. Their bodies were temples in which God and Christ might rightly dwell. "And so I opened the prophets and the figures and shadows and turned them to Christ the substance."[32]

In relation to the old covenant, Fox preaches Christ first and foremost as the Prophet-like-Moses (Deut. 18:18f; Acts 3:22; 7:37).[33] As such, he is to be heard in "all things" (see John 4:25, 29; 14:26; 15:15), even as Moses was to be heard through his outward laws in all aspects of life. "For as Moses said, 'Like unto me will God raise up a prophet, and Him shall ye hear in all things;' so, said I, this prophet, Christ, is come, and all the Jews in spirit, the true believing Christians in the light . . . are to hear Christ . . . ."[34]

Christ also stands as fulfiller of the type of Moses as *mediator* between God and his people. He has mediated between God and sinful humanity by a covenant made with his own blood. While this sacrifice fulfills the old covenant's practice of sealing a covenant (Gen. 22:13) and of atonement for sin (Lev. 4-9) by the blood of animal sacrifice, it also serves a revelatory function. In the cross, Jesus fulfills and ends the law, thereby taking the sin exposed by the law upon himself and cancelling it. In his resurrection, he substantiates the law through the inward revealing power of his light, giving to all a more intimate sense of sin and the law's condemnation of it.[35] Following this same universal theme in Isaiah 42:6, Fox calls Christ the *covenant of light*. Thus, Christ who died for all also enlightens all. In the intimacy of this covenant, "nothing may get between you and the Lord God."[36] The mediation of Christ is one of immediacy.

As we have already seen, Fox also emphasizes Christ as the *seed*, the will of God risen up within. He summarizes thus:

> The substance is the seed, the top stone, on top of the law, on top of the prophets, on top of the types, figures, shadows, parables, and ends them all, and on top of all heathens' inventions, though it hath been a mystery hid from the ages [Col. 1:26; Eph. 3:4, 5, 9] . . . .[37]

That mystery, as the writer to the Colossians goes on to state in 1:27, "is Christ in you, the hope of glory." It is the inward mystery unknown to history, to the outward knowledge of the world. But this incarnation "is made manifest to [or in] his saints" (vs 26).

THE CHURCH

The inward experience of the risen Christ does not swallow history into a privatized phenomenon. It engages with history, with the outward world, as it gathers a community around the preaching of the gospel.

Fox is a revolutionary thinker in Christian history for his claim that one need not know the gospel outwardly in order to respond to its inward revelation. Yet this experience and obedience cannot alone form the community of faith foreshadowed in Israel, nor enter the realm of history. The Christian community of faith, which truly becomes the agent of God's work in the history of the world, must be gathered by the outward hearing of the gospel, the language that interprets the inward experience of Christ and gives a solidarity of understanding and action. In the Church, the inward incarnation of Christ reaches its full stature, bringing inward experience and personal obedience to grips with the social dimensions of the world and its history.

Perhaps because Fox lived in a religious culture dominated by the language of the gospel, he is never very explicit on this important point. Nevertheless, he does demonstrate his thinking on the subject with his one occasion for contact with those completely unfamiliar with the Bible; namely, his visits with Native Americans. He records about a dozen such meetings, some of them personal conversations, others large gatherings. While all these contacts appear to be friendly and affirmative, only two result in Indians joining with or starting Friends meetings. In Maryland, Fox preached twice to a group of Indian leaders:

> . . . and they heard the word of the Lord and did confess to it. And what I said to the kings and emperor . . . I desired them to speak to their people, that God is setting up his tabernacle of witness in their wilderness countries and setting up his glorious ensign and standard of righteousness. And they asked when we had meetings and they said they would come to them and were very loving.[38]

The other occasion was on Shelter Island, Long Island, in which Fox addressed about one hundred Indians in a two-hour meeting:

> . . . they said all was truth and did make a confession of it after the meeting. So I have set up a meeting among them once a fortnight, and Friend Joseph Silvester is to read the Scriptures to them, negroes and Indians . . . . A great desire there is and a great love and satisfaction were among the people, blessed be the Lord. His name spreads and will be great among the nations and dreadful among the heathen [Mal. 1:14].[39]

So the occasion for the gathering into meeting, the corporate life of the Church, is the *confession* of the gospel, though Fox maintained a respectful and brotherly disposition toward other Indians who could testify to a similar inward experience and appear to live in the life of it.

The *Church* is the ultimate concern of Fox; it is the goal of all his preaching and writing about the intimacy of Christ's work within the individual. Though it begins on the personal level, the Church fulfills God's great historical work with Israel in the first place. It is raised up in the outward world of history in order to wrestle against Satan and his sway over the world, and against the temptation with which he draws men and women into ruin. It puts on the spiritual armor of God and takes up the spiritual weapons of apocalyptic holy war, to "wrestle not against flesh and blood, but against the rulers of the darkness of the world, against wickedness in high places" (Eph. 6:12).

The Church engages in this battle among the kingdoms of this world, seeking to bring their subjects to the kingdom, or rule, of Christ. But this does not mean the establishment of an outward kingdom, like the "typical kingdom" of Israel, or the state-church power structures of official Christendom. The Church must not join with the principalities and powers, but make known to them the manifold wisdom of God (Eph. 3:10).

> And those are Christ's ministers of the spirit, and believers, and true Christians, that stand in this armour, and have these weapons, and follow Christ, and fight under his banner of love . . . and follow not the Jews in their carnal armour and weapons, and signs, and shadows; for the substance has come.[40] So the King of kings was far off from giving them commissions or licenses, to beat people into his religion, way, and worship, church, or belief, with carnal weapons . . . .[41]

The only legitimate power of the Church is the power of the cross of Christ, its head; the only legitimate force of the Church is the force of its witness to his work in its members, in their words and deeds of love. This is no ordinary battle.

The struggle for personal and social transformation is the Church's mission in following its commander in *ending the world, ending history* in human experience. This mission begins with the act of corporate worship, unencumbered by the vestigial remains of the old covenant — priesthood, ritual sacrifice (the eucharist), liturgy, outward vestments, etc. — or the "beggarly rudiments" of Church tradition that have sprung up since the apostles' days. Thus, it begins with *the end of worldly religion*, so that Christ may be experienced in all his offices of mediation.[42] Fox describes the apocalyptic power of this experience:

> In this gathering by the power into the name of Christ (which is the power), with the power he is felt in the midst, who is King of kings, and Lord of lords, and prince of life and peace, and

prophet to open by his power and light in you all, ye will have
every one of you, in your own particular, joy, peace, comfort . . .
when all gatherings, meetings, heaven and earth, types, and
figures, and shadows, and prophets, and prophecies are ended
. . . . So all ye that have felt the light, and have been turned to it,
in that light ye feel the covenant with God, who is light . . . .[43]

So this is a total experience in which Christ is everything to the
believer, mediating at all points, so that not only mediated
worships, but even heaven and earth pass away in this experience.

Worshiping in the immediacy of Christ's Spirit, the Church
finds itself "sitting in heavenly places" [Eph. 2:6] in Christ Jesus
the first and last, the beginning and ending," and views all things
from the end of the world. Christians come to see where Adam
and Eve "sat in paradise," and where they sat after the Fall:

They see where the Jews sat, in types, figures, and shadows,
and temples, and oaths, in offerings and sacrifices, and there
were to sit till Christ the substance came to end them all; which
Christ the substance was before they were . . . . They see where
the Gentiles sit, in the traditions, inventions, idols' temple,
which God never commanded. They see where all the apostate
Christians have sat since the apostles' days, in the rudiments,
inventions, handiworks, and traditions . . . .[44]

In true Christian worship, then, the Church gains "insight by
which false, outward worships are recognized and cast out. The
new creation begins here:

. . . now once Christ in the end of the world hath appeared to
put away sin, by the sacrifice of himself [Heb. 9:26]; so in the
end of the world, of all worldly things, worldly sanctuaries,
tabernacle and carnal ordinances . . . he is the beginning of a
new world with his heavenly things, who makes all things new
[Rev. 21:5].[45]

This is the astonishing claim of Christian worship in Fox's
message: in the apocalyptic revelation of Christ, the old world
begins to end, and a new world is in the making. But this is only
the beginning. In our next chapter, we shall go on to see how
Christ's revelation maps out the new world to the eyes of faith,
leading us to the apocalypse of the Word itself.

*The hour is coming and now is, when the dead shall hear the
voice of the Son of God: and they that hear shall live . . . . And
the Father himself, which hath sent me, hath borne witness of
me. Ye have neither heard his voice at any time, nor seen his
shape. And ye have not his word abiding in you: for whom he
hath sent, him ye believe not. Search the scriptures; for in them
ye think ye have eternal life: and they are they which testify of
me. And ye will not come to me, that ye might have life [John
5:25, 37-40].*

6. THE APOCALYPSE OF THE WORD

In the preceding chapter we saw that the light's inward revelation of God moved into an outward manifestation in God's
historical work with Israel. This outward, historical work culminated in Jesus Christ, who in his very person became God's
new covenant with all humanity. We saw how each of the
provisions of the first covenant is fulfilled inwardly in the
experience of the risen Lord's power to mediate between
humanity and God.

The new covenant is entered as the provisions of the old
covenant are left behind in pure, inward worship. Yet this
experience not only transfigures the old cult; it extends to
transform the old created order in the vision and action of the
Church, the body of Christ, the beginning of the new creation.

Here we come to one of the boldest expressions of Fox's
apocalyptic spirituality. In one remarkable tract,[1] he deals extensively with this dimension of his message. He begins by describ-
ing the human condition as "Man being drove into the earth out
of Paradise." There, "the god of this world cometh in and takes

the dominion, and so your minds are blinded, and your understandings darkened . . . ."[2] But even as humanity dwells in this confused state, God provides with scripture a kind of "travel guide" out of this outward wilderness, to the safety and certainty of inward knowledge. In scripture God has pointed to outward things as figures and parables of an inward world, "so figures are spoken to the carnal part in man."

These figures are interpreted and their inward counterparts revealed by the inward light of Christ: "And as the light opens and exerciseth thy conscience, it will open to thee parables and figures, and it will let thee see invisible things, which are clearly seen by that which is invisible in thee . . . ." In this light, "thou canst go no way but thou mayest read thy figure." The most obvious example of this parabolic speech would be the parables of Jesus, in which everyday life situations are employed to describe the inward working of God's grace, the discovery of the kingdom of heaven, etc. But Fox appears to view *all* the descriptive language of scripture as functioning potentially in this figural, parabolic manner of pointing toward inward, spiritual realities. Indeed, modern Old Testament interpreter Gerhard von Rad[3] similarly asserts that the possibilities of typological interpretation are limitless. Fox explores these possibilities extensively in his outward/inward typology, finding the realities of the outward world described in scripture to be types of the inwardly revealed new world.

So, as there are harvests, earthquakes, wolves, and mountains without, they are seen within as well by the "invisible eye." As there are serpents without, there is the nature of the serpent within. Fox lists dozens of examples like these. Therefore, the

> light of God which gave forth the scripture, this light of God
> according to its measure will open the scripture to thee . . .
> the Lord speaking low things, comparisons like to that nature
> in many; that man may look upon the creation with that
> which is invisible, and there read himself; there thou mayest
> see wherever thou goest.[4]

As this "inner landscape" opens up, a new life is begun and a new world is revealed:

> . . . as [there are] sons and daughters without, born by the will
> of man, so there are sons and daughters of God, born by the
> will of God, heirs to another world; as these are born in this

world, and as there is a world without you, so there is a world
in the heart . . . .[5]

This is a radical understanding of typology, to be sure. It must be
termed an apocalyptic typology for two reasons: first, it places a
total emphasis upon the apocalypse, or revelation, of Christ by
his light; and second, the scope of this revelation embraces "all
things" — a typology that includes not only Moses/Christ, Israel/
the Church, but even old creation/new creation. As we noted
earlier, Fox's typology should not be confused with allegoriza-
tion. The Hellenistic Jewish philosopher Philo (born ca. 20 B.C.E.)
freely allegorized the Old Testament, reducing Sarah, for
instance, to the attribute of *sophia*, wisdom. Fox's approach is
not one that makes such abstractions; it seeks instead to find the
inward and new revealed in counterpart to the outward and old.

Nor is this a retreat from the world without to a secret "world
of the heart." The revelation within does not abandon the world
without to Satan's dominion. This is beautifully articulated by
Fox in a later tract, touching upon Mount Zion and Jerusalem.
Citing Hebrews 12:22, that the faithful are come to the heavenly
Zion and Jerusalem, Fox concludes:

> . . . outward Jerusalem and the outward Mount Sion, was a type
> of the heavenly Jerusalem and the heavenly hill Mount Sion.
> And upon that outward hill Mount Sion, a man might see a great
> way in the land of Canaan, but upon heavenly Mount Sion in
> heavenly Jerusalem, the spiritual man may see over the whole
> world or earth; for it is the joy of the whole earth.[6]

The old world passes away as the faithful "see over" all the
earth. If this were to remain only an inward revelation, it would
amount to nothing more than a gnostic negation of the outward,
material world. But the Church is given an active role in establishing a new world order above the old. Even as Fox writes of a
world revealed in the heart, he also insists that "this light will
bring you to walk in the commands of Christ."[7]

The Church stands between the old world order and a vision
of the new. The apocalyptic battle is joined at this interface
between the new and the old, experience and history, spirit and
flesh, heaven and earth — between command and obedience. In
other words, it stands always at the *cross of Christ*. This is
where Jesus has decisively achieved the victory over Satan and
has begun the end of the world, the turn of the ages. This is

where the Church must struggle until the restitution of all things (Acts 3:21) — that is, the final resolution of all history, the resurrection of the dead, and the full assembling of the Church.

The Church incarnates Christ's ending of history in the same way that he accomplished it in his earthly ministry; it *reveals history* to the world in the preaching of his gospel. It does so by showing Jesus Christ to be the culmination of God's historical dealings with the Hebrew people in the first covenant. But for Gentile hearers, who have never been involved in the first covenant, the gospel reveals — interprets and answers — the *experience* of salvation history that they may know through the universal light of Christ.

The individual's response to the light's revelation and to the preaching of the Church is not simply a matter of personal preference, or taste. Fox warns those who resist Christ's inward power and remain in the outward:

> The Lord is coming in flames of fire [2 Thess. 1:8], flames of fire without you, [therefore,] as you see with a natural eye, see flames of fire within, who have the light come upon you . . . .[8]

The inward experience of the risen Christ is an advance view of the consummation of the outward in history. The loving and obedient response to this experience now is the means by which the saints shall stand in that terrible day.

THE END OF TIME

Time (Fox's use of the term "time" includes what we today would call "history") is seen from a different perspective in the light. Fox can testify to this from his own experience: "For sometimes when I would set myself to sleep, my mind went over all to the beginning, in that which is from everlasting to everlasting."[9] He is more explicit about the content of this experience in an epistle to Friends:

> So [you] who are in this royal seed comprehend the state and time before the law, the time of the law, the time of Christians, and the time of the apostasy: for the seed Christ is the first and last, the beginning and ending . . . .[10]

Fox's language here of "comprehension," like "seeing over," describes the understanding, as well as overcoming, of things that are ended in Christ. Standing in this seed, in the beginning and end of all things, the Christian sees that "all figures and shadows were and are comprehended in time."[11] This seed, as we saw in the previous chapter, is raised up in the revelation of the light of Christ. In Fox's words, this is the revelation by which "the unknown truth, unknown to the world [is] made manifest, which draws up that which lies in prison, and refresheth it in time, up to God, out of time, through time."[12]

With these three directional prepositions relating to the word "time," Fox describes the life of faith — *out* of time (or history) as a primary reference, yet still *in* time and *through* time. As we have already stated in a slightly different way, this interface between time (the old, present age) and the everlasting (the new, coming age) is the place of the cross. Fox's description of this entry into the new age, even while one is still engaged with the old age, suggests a relationship between the two in which they do not simply join end to end (as one year succeeds another), but in which the new age diverges from the old into a new dimension of experience.

Until one responds to the light, the seed is "in prison in time."[13] Like the outward world and its knowledge, time is not evil as such, but is used by Satan to "captivate,"[14] to draw people into confusion over the many things, many times. The apostate Church has been led into this captivity. The apostate "spirit's work . . . is to bring into such forms in time, which are out of the spirit, and truth, and power of God . . . [which] was before time."[15] But "there will be an end of old Adam's and the devil's [government], which began in time and will end in time, but there will be no end of [Christ's] [Isa. 9:7], that was set up from everlasting to everlasting."[16]

Fox wrote these words while he himself was in prison, in 1673. The seed raised up in the Quaker movement prompted Adam's government to attempt its recapture, as thousands of Quakers were sentenced to "serve time" in prison for their witness. Always encouraging other Friends in persecution, Fox exhorts them to keep the everlasting perspective of faith, and "think not the time long."[17] All this suffering was the result of Friends' refusal to "serve time" by conforming to restored Church's Common Prayer book with its liturgical calendar of appointed worships, feast days, and fasts. These were important in the first covenant, as the "shadow of things to come; but the body is Christ" (Col. 2:17).

Fox constantly attempts in his preaching to raise people's consciousness from this calendrical *time* to see the timely *day* of visitation, the day of the Lord, in which the light of Christ is seen and followed in experience and obedience. He urges them to "receive this day in your time."[18] While imprisoned at Derby in 1650, Fox wrote with delicious irony a word of warning to the bell ringers ("time keepers") of the local steeplehouse:

> . . .prize your time now while you have it . . . . The time will come that you will say you had time, when it is past. Oh, look at the love of God now while you have time . . . . Oh, consider, time is precious![19]

FOX'S UNDERSTANDING OF THE WORD

In 1653, George Fox was arrested for his preaching at Carlisle. At his trial, he was asked a series of questions about his faith. One question demanded that Fox state whether he affirmed scripture to be the Word of God:

> I said, God was the Word and the scriptures were writings; and the Word was before the writings were, which Word did fulfill them. And after a long examination they sent me to prison, as a blasphemer, a heretic, and a seducer . . . .[20]

This was not the only time Fox ran into trouble for his preaching on the Word. In fact, as we saw in our historical chapter on Fox's life, his first arrest occurred when he could not resist interrupting a sermon to contradict the assertion that the scriptures are the "more sure word of prophecy" (2 Pet. 1:19). Even with Baptists, whom Geoffrey Nuttall and Hugh Barbour closely identify with Quakers as radical, spiritual Puritans, Fox had vigorous disputes over the Word of God.[21]

That Fox found the question of the Word so central to his message that he was willing to go to prison because of this belief and that he had strong disagreements over it even with close religious contemporaries is more significant than most modern interpreters have recognized. This has been the problem particularly with the Protestant interpretation of Quakerism as a form of radical Puritanism.

Geoffrey Nuttall devotes an entire chapter to "the Spirit and the Word." Perhaps due to his own viewpoint as a Congregationalist, he assumes the Puritan identification of the Word with scripture. He shows the basic Puritan understanding to be that the Word (scripture) must be interpreted with the help of the Spirit in order to save.[22] He portrays Quakers as normally holding to this outlook and thereby to be classified as Puritans. But he admits that Quakers sometimes gave the Spirit in themselves primacy over the Spirit in the Word (scripture). He calls this "opposing" the Spirit and the Word,[23] leaving the reader to conclude that such a position is indefensible as a Christian theology — which is true.

But Nuttall never countenances the fact that Fox and the other early Friends *did not accept* scripture as the Word of God. This is a prominent theme in Fox's writings. Far from opposing the Word and Spirit, Fox *fuses* them, finding Christ the Word to be present and active within the believer by his Spirit.

Hugh Barbour similarly misses the Quaker understanding of the Word. He rightly points to the issue of Christ's light as an area where better Puritan-Quaker understanding was needed; but he goes on to say that "this issue was sometimes wrongly narrowed down to a clash between the authority of the Bible and the authority of the Light of men . . . ."[24] The question of primary authority was *precisely* the point of the issue. Like Nuttall, Barbour points to the Puritan belief in the importance of the Spirit's work with scripture for conversion as suggesting an essential unity between Puritans and Quakers.[25] He summarizes the Quaker position thus:

> Friends conceded that the Bible was authoritative and then talked about the Spirit. The key difference between puritan and Quaker was in their ideas about the relationship of the inward Spirit and the outward Word in the life of Christians. Where Quakers made these independent, the puritans saw them as working together . . . .[26]

Following Nuttall, Barbour misses the weight the Quakers placed on the inward Word as the only true Word to be known and followed.

What both writers, like Fox's contemporary Puritan critics, have failed to appreciate is that ultimately the Word must be viewed as part of the inward/outward typological interpretation of Christ's salvation. Indeed, because the Word of God is Christ's most important title (at least in relation to the biblical concept of revelation) the Word constitutes the most important aspect of Christian typological interpretation.

To see this more clearly, we return to the Epistle to the Hebrews. As Graham Hughes[27] notes, the opening verses of Hebrews make an impressive opening statement on the revelation of God's speaking in Jesus — almost a *logos* Christology like that of John's Prologue. Yet it would seem that this grand theme is suddenly dropped, as the writer goes into a long development on Jesus Christ as the great high priest whose sacrifice has conferred salvation upon all who believe. One might conclude, as some have, that these opening verses of Hebrews have no real connection with the rest of the epistle. Yet, as Hughes shows, the rest of Hebrews is in fact a substantiation of this initial assertion. Jesus' high-priestly self-offering not only ends the worship patterns of the old covenant, showing them to be figural, but its greatest effect is to gain for his followers entrance into the heavenly sanctuary of God (10:9ff), so that they may miraculously stand in his presence (4:16; 12:22ff).[28] His sacrifice thereby achieves not only atonement for past sins, but a new possibility of radical obedience to the will of God through the direct hearing of his voice. Therefore, the author warns his brethren, "See that ye refuse not him that speaketh" (12:25).

The thrust of Fox's message proceeds along the same lines. But while he occasionally follows explicitly the high-priestly understanding of Christ's revelation set forth in Hebrews,[29] he more typically develops it according to the Prophet-like-Moses Christology. A good example of the way Fox can interconnect these themes is seen below:

> The Lord saith, "this is my beloved Son, hear ye him [Mark 9:7]; this is the prophet which Moses saith, like unto him that God would raise up, whom the people should hear, whom we do hear, that speaks from heaven [Heb. 12:25]; at sundry times, and in diverse manners, God spake to the fathers by the prophets, but now in these last days hath spoken to us by his Son [Heb. 1:1f] . . . who fulfills the prophets and ends the . . . first covenant . . . .[30]

The implications of this prophetic Christology, combined with Fox's emphasis upon experience, are profound. He is not unusual for his time to chide Judaism for having failed to recognize its Messiah when he came 1600 years before;[31] but he makes a bold leap in making the same charges against his Christian contemporaries:

> As the Pharisees got the words of the true prophets and Moses, out of the life, so the Papists and you have got the words of Christ and the apostles, and are out of the life, and persecuting them that are in the life, as the Pharisees did . . . . And you, with your dark eyes, have looked upon the scriptures ever since the apostasy, and ravened from the spirit of God and the pure eye . . . you are apostatized from the apostles in life, and power, and doctrine, and so are in heaps about their words, out from that which is the ground of communion, the bond of peace.[32]

It is important for us to take a moment to consider the period in Church history to which Fox spoke. He addressed a newly-formed Protestant Church establishment which owed much of its character to the Guttenberg watershed. The printing of English Bibles, first the Geneva Bible, then James I's Authorized Version, had brought the scriptures to the English people with much the same explosive effect that the translations of Luther and others had created on the Continent. The printed word expanded the arena of theological inquiry and debate; it also had a profound effect upon devotional life and worship. The Bible became the center of Puritan life, from daily personal and family readings, to the avidly followed preaching and debating of scriptural texts by pastors. Sermons, lectures, meetings for prophesying — all centered around the exegesis of these inspired texts now available for all to study.

The radical Puritan movement of the mid-seventeenth century began to articulate the limitations of this intense scripturalism. The spontaneous direction of the Spirit received increasing emphasis as an important supplement to scripture's authority. Not only could it give a true understanding of the Word in scripture, but it could lead Christians in the proper worship of God and aid scripture in shaping one's daily actions as well. But the *Word* continued to be invested in this technological break-through with ink and paper (and/or the preaching from it) which had catalyzed a religious and social revolution in England.

Puritans read the New Testament polemic against legal preoccupation among the Pharisees; yet they failed to recognize their own tendency in the same direction — namely toward bibliolatry. The radical Puritan emphasis upon the Spirit along-side scripture appears to have been an effort at correction. Yet, contrary to the suggestions of Nuttall and Barbour, this emphasis really has the effect of *opposing* the Word and the Spirit. Even if it is asserted that the Spirit is essential in the writing and understanding of scripture, one still is left with a mechanistic conception of the Spirit's relation to the Word.

It is perhaps Fox's most valuable contribution that he rejoins the Spirit and the Word in the prophetic experience of the risen Christ. While he presents Jesus Christ as the one Word of God, present and teaching by his Spirit, he places scripture, the historical record of the Word's work, as the *words* of God. The true Word is the Christ who is speaking now.

While Fox makes this witness with searing polemics against his Puritan opponents, we should not gather that he belittles scripture.[33] He records in his *Journal* that "I had no slight esteem of the holy scriptures, but they were very precious to me, for I was in that spirit by which they were given forth, and what the Lord opened in me I later found was agreeable to them."[34] His knowledge of scripture was legendary; when he preached, hearers said, ". . . they had never heard the scriptures so clearly opened before, for said they, 'He hath them at his fingers' ends [as if] a man should read them in a book and hold it open before him.' "[35]

As may be seen in quotations throughout this study, Fox's theological vocabulary keeps carefully to the language of scripture. A good example of his persistence in this practice is found in his accounting of his trial at Lancaster in 1652. Asked if he did affirm that he had the divinity "essentially" in him, Fox replied, "For the word essentially, it is an expression of their own, but that the saints are the temples of God and God doth dwell in them, that I witness and the scripture doth witness . . . ."[36] We also note that in his above-mentioned tract on the mirroring of outward realities within, though Fox seems to imply that all the outward creation may be figural of inward realities, the only examples he uses happen to appear in scripture.

Fox sees scripture as vital for the propositional knowledge of salvation history and the revealed truths of God that it records. Yet it is without any power to *reveal* God's truth and to *incarnate* the substance of the scriptures in men and women. These are requisite for salvation, and must be given by the living Word himself:

> The holy scriptures . . . are to be read, and believed, and ful-
> filled, and he that fulfills them is Christ; and they are "profit-
> able for doctrine, for reproof, for correction, for instruction,
> in righteousness, that the man of God may be perfect, thorough-
> ly unto all good works [2 Tim. 3:16f] . . . . And we do believe
> that the scriptures are the word of God . . . .[37]

> The scriptures of truth are the words of God and not the word;
> and Christ who was before the scriptures were given forth, by
> whom the world was made, is the word of God, who fulfilled
> the words; the scriptures end in him, who was before they
> were spoken forth.[38]

Thus, Christ is the *substance* of the scriptures;[39] present by his
revealing light and Spirit, he is "scripture within thee."[40] Only
by heeding this light, which is "life in the Word,"[41] does one
come to the life of the prophets and the apostles. Here Fox's
incarnational emphasis comes through with full force:

> . . . for feeling God's word in the heart to obey it, you come to
> know that which the prophets and apostles witnessed, the
> word of life which became flesh [John 1:4], which is Christ in
> us . . . .[42]

This incarnation receives its highest realization, as we have
previously noted, in the Church: "[the] word became flesh, and
dwelt among us; so he (Christ) is the head of the church . . . ."[43]

It is the power of this Word, not the letter of scripture, that
gathers the Church. It is true that the New Testament witnesses
to the life, death, and resurrection of Jesus in history and provides the language by which the community of faith understands
its experience and its purpose in history. But even with the most
careful exegesis, the example of Jesus and the early Church
cannot be used to re-constitute the Church today. It must be
organically gathered by Christ's Spirit, rather than mechanically
fabricated from New Testament precedents. Fox calls the latter
an "imitation" of the Church. As outward example and inward
revealer, Jesus is both the author and finisher of the Church's
faith and life together (see Heb. 12:2).

Fox repeatedly assails bibliotary, preoccupation with the
words of the scriptures. The children of God are "sanctified by
the word," while the children of the world are "painted with the
words;"[44] like whitewashed sepulchres, they are beautifully

adorned with outward knowledge of the Bible, but utterly dead within (Matt. 23:27).

Fox relates that from an early age, God taught him that he must order his words, like the other creatures around him, to God's glory. This understanding of words, even the inspired words of scripture, as creatures, may constitute the heart of his critique of bibliolatry; it is simply a more subtle form of idolatry (abstract, printed images, rather than the representational, graven ones denounced by the prophets). To paraphrase Romans 1:19-25, we might say that bibliolatry exchanges the glory of God's incorruptible Word for the image of corruptible words and the truth of God for a lie, by worshiping and serving the creature more than the Creator of all things. Professing to be wise, the bibliolater becomes foolish. Against the vast weight of English Protestantism, Fox demands that that which may be known of God, his Word, is manifest within all men and women; the words of scripture spring from this inward Word, as must the words and acts of all Christians. Those who shun or deny this inward revelation are "without excuse."

Fox questions the Protestant exegetical establishments of Oxford and Cambridge, particularly in their training of ministers in the biblical languages for a better understanding of God's Word:

> For the many languages began at Babel [Gen. 11], and to the Greeks that spoke the natural Greek, the preaching of the cross of Christ was foolishness to them; and to the Jews that spoke natural Hebrew, Christ was a stumbling block to them, and as for the Romans that had Italian and Latin, they persecuted the Christians; and Pilate, one of the Roman magistrates, could set Hebrew, Greek, and Latin a-top Christ the Word when he crucified him. So . . . they set [languages] a-top Christ the Word when they crucified him [John 19:19f].[45]

Thus Fox accuses his contemporaries of following in Pilate's footsteps when they delve so deeply into the study of "original" languages of the Bible, even as they deny the inward revelation of the true, original Word. Over against Babel's confusion of outward language, the inward revelation of the Word is "the power where all men shall agree."[46] This perspective, however, did not stop Fox from doing some study of Hebrew and Greek on his own over the years.

The scriptures, like all the other outward provisions of the first covenant, served according to God's command until Christ came. And as those who search Moses' law for salvation have a veil over their heart (2 Cor. 3:15), so those Christians who look to the scriptures for salvation shall suffer the same darkness. "Nevertheless, when a man shall turn to the Lord, the veil shall be taken away" (2 Cor. 3:16).[47] Fox describes this experience forcefully in his own words:

> And I saw the state of those, both priests and people, who in reading the scriptures, cry out much against Cain, Esau, and Judas, and other wicked men of former times, mentioned in the holy scriptures; but do not see the nature of Cain, of Esau, of Judas, and those others, in themselves. And these said it was they, they, they that were the bad people; putting it off from themselves: but when some of these came, with the light and spirit of Truth, to see into themselves, then they came to say "I, I, I, it is I myself that have been the Ishmael, and the Esau."[48]

Here we return to our preceding chapter's observation: Fox sees experience giving true knowledge and interpretation to the history recorded in scripture, even as scripture helps one understand his or her own experience. The Word's action in history, as recorded in scripture, cannot truly open one's self-understanding — it cannot speak to one's condition — unless the same Word takes away the inward veil in experience. This apocalyptic "uncovering" is the event to which the gospel and the entire history of the Bible point. God has written it across the face of history, etched it upon stones, and written it upon paper — not that we should search these for final proof and assurance, but that it should "answer" something known deep within the hearer.

In this "uncovering" one must first stand terribly naked before God, silently bereft of the "fig-leaves" of scripture, of liturgy, of all one's nervous babel. Yet, loving this Word, this revealing light, and waiting in it, one comes "in time, through time, and out of time" to live in a power that the world does not know. Here we look forward to the subject of our next chapters, the understanding of preaching and worship held by Fox and the early Quakers.

I asked them whether any of them could say they ever had a word from the Lord to go and speak to such or such a people and none of them durst say so. But one of them burst into a passion and said he could speak his experiences as well as I; but I told him experience was one thing but to go with a message and a word from the Lord as the prophets and the apostles had and did, and as I had done to them, this was another thing . . . . I told them the false prophets and false apostles and antichrists could use the words and speak of other men's experiences that never knew or heard the voice of God and Christ and such as they might get the good words and experiences of others. [1]

7. THE ROLE OF CHRISTIAN PROCLAMATION

The exchange related above took place in 1652 during a meeting with a group of local clergymen while Fox was staying at Swarthmoor Hall with his new-found allies Judge Thomas and Margaret Fell. The outburst of the minister in this account suggests that he took Fox's message to be concerned solely with individual experience. If this impression were correct, his objection would have been justified; everybody has his or her experiences to tell, but what is to keep this from digressing into a spiritual relativism?

But, as Fox shows, his concern by no means ends with the inward experience of Christ. Not only does he understand his Christian experience to be no different from that of the prophets and apostles, but he also sees this experience leading to the same quality and manner of preaching and worship that they established.

In Fox's thought, prophetic and apostolic preaching are the only way in which the true Israel, the true Church, can be gathered and maintained. He contends that this preaching has generally been in eclipse from the end of the apostolic age all the way down to his own time; he finds this confirmed not only in the posture of the Church through history, but particularly in the attitudes and practices of ministers like those that visited him that day at Swarthmoor. They are unwilling even to *claim* the preaching power of the apostles, let alone *practice* it in truth.

The preaching of the early Quaker movement is thus seen to be a new beginning for the Church:

> This work of the Lord is beginning again, as it was in the apostles' days. People shall come to receive an unction in them again from the Holy One, by which they shall know all things [1 John 2:20], and shall not need any man to teach them [1 John 2:27], but as the anointing doth teach them; and also to know what the righteousness of faith speaks, the Word nigh in the heart and mouth [Rom. 10:8], to obey and do it. This is the Word of faith the apostles preached; which is now received and preached again, and which it is the duty of all true Christians to receive. Now people are coming out of the apostasy to the light of Christ and his Spirit, and to receive faith from him, and not from men; to receive the gospel from him, their unction from him, the Word; and as they receive him, they declare freely, as his command was to his disciples [Matt. 10:8], and is still to the learners and receivers of him. For the Lord God and his Son Jesus Christ is come to teach his people . . . .[2]

Fox claims to preach a gospel which will not require a new installment from him the next Sunday, but which leads people to Christ, who will teach them all things needful for righteousness. And as Christ proclaims freely by his inward grace, so all preachers who bring men and women to him must also preach freely.

This understanding of gospel preaching led Fox to a strategy and stature of ministry markedly different from comparable Protestant leaders. He did not have the university as a haven in which to write and teach disciples, as Luther had at Wittenberg, or as John Owen had at Oxford. Nor did he establish himself as pastor to a congregation of followers, as Richard Baxter did, or become a powerful state theocrat, like Calvin. The ministry of Fox and the early Quaker "Publishers of Truth" was more like that of the prophets and apostles themselves. It was strictly itinerant, a preacher staying with a group of newly convinced

Friends only long enough to settle them solidly under Christ's teaching, then moving on.

Fox and his associates preached in a variety of places and situations: in taverns and inns, in homes and in prisons, in open fields and on hilltops. They often preached in market places, like the apostles sometimes did (Acts 17:17). In the tradition of the Old Testament prophets (e.g., Isa. 58:6; Amos 8:4-6), they condemned deceitful merchandising and oppressive employment. They walked through towns, preaching repentance and the day of the Lord.

But perhaps the most strikingly apostolic aspect of their preaching was their practice of going into steeplehouses in order to draw people out. This is the approach that the Lord had revealed to Fox while he was imprisoned at Derby, and which became the systematic practice of the Quaker movement in parishes throughout England. Fox saw this practice in the tradition of the apostles entering the synagogues to bring their former co-religionists from the Torah to Christ. This confrontation epitomizes the foundational difference between Quaker and Puritan preaching. Both claimed to preach the Word; Puritans preached and lectured by expounding the texts of scripture, while Quakers preached Christ, the living Word within them, speaking through them (see 1 Cor. 13:3). They saw their own calling as no less than Paul's: "The God of our fathers hath chosen thee, that thou shouldst know his will, and see that Just One, and shouldst hear the voice of his mouth. For thou shalt be his witness unto all men of what thou has seen and heard" (Acts 22:14).

Puritan preaching of scripture harkened back to the power and authority of the apostolic generation as the golden age of the Christian revelation. While a coming age of glory was also expected, the main reference point was the glory of the past, recorded in scripture. Puritan ministers simply did not expect to preach by the same revelation and with the same power that the apostles had.

Quaker preaching of Christ's coming to teach his people shifted the frame of reference dramatically. The future event expected by Puritans was vividly known in the present experience and preaching of Quakers. This by no means made the apostolic experience and record irrelevant; it *confirmed* the apostolic teachings with a new experience, as the new age was seen unfolding.

Early Quaker preaching follows that of the prophets and apostles not only in *style*; it also renews the basic *message* of their preaching. It does this by making the *content* of preaching the justice of God and the *context* of that justice the awe-ful day of God's judgment. It is important that we briefly review the content and context of the biblical preaching tradition before we proceed further in our examination of Fox's own message.

When the prophets of the Old Testament declared their oracles, the issue at hand was always God's justice. This begins with the ministry of Moses, declaring God's liberation to the children of Israel in bondage. When the prophets state, "thus saith the Lord," they spoke for the divine judge who had seen the actions of his people and now declared his judgment in a coming day of reckoning. A succinct example of this preaching may be found in the great prophet to the northern kingdom, Amos. Reading Amos, we see that prophecy is not a matter of speculative prediction, but God's revelation of future implications for the concrete moral situation of the present.

The great prophets of Judah — Isaiah, Jeremiah, and Ezekiel — evoke the same sense of a sudden, unexpected "day in court;" they proclaim God's juris-diction, his Word of judgment, his divine authority, over the affairs of men and women. This same God can also pronounce, through the same prophets, the offer of forgiveness (Jer. 18:8), or the promise of renewal for a broken nation (Isa. 40ff); but always the plumb line of God's justice is set in the midst of his people (Amos 7:7).

The prophetic preaching of the Old Testament declares the reality of a coming day that will reveal God's justice and/or mercy in history. In the latter prophetic texts of the Old Testament, this theme of hope intensifies, broadening the scope of God's coming action to include not only Israel's future, but also that of all humanity and the entire created order (see Isa. 60-66; Dan. 7, 10-12; Zech.). This trend culminates in the Jewish apocalyptic literature of the intertestamental period, where God is seen bringing all history and order, as they are presently known, to a cataclysmic end and new beginning (see IV Esdras 3-14; 1 Enoch 90; Jubilees 23:18-32). But at the same time, this later literature loses much of the specific and concrete bearing upon present moral conditions in history which characterizes prophetic preaching. The "trial scene" which calls men and women into question now gives way to more distanced speculation about the future. Confrontational public preaching becomes esoteric knowledge given to a select few.

Nevertheless, it is within this expanded horizon of apocalyptic thought that the apostolic preaching of Christ's salvation revives the prophetic tradition. This revival begins with John the Baptist's fiery preaching of repentance, but unfolds more fully with Jesus' preaching of repentance *and* the kingdom of God: "The time is fulfilled, and the kingdom of God is at hand: repent ye, and believe the gospel" (Mark 1:15). Again, the content is moral — God's justice for people's lives — and this justice is revealed in the context of an apocalyptic judgment day.

The apostolic preaching following Jesus' resurrection continues this prophetic renewal. Paul, for example, understands his calling to be an apostle of Christ in the same terms that Isaiah and Jeremiah had understood their own prophetic callings (Isa. 49:2; Jer. 1:5; Gal. 1:15). He evokes the apocalyptic "courtroom drama" best in his letter to the Church of Rome, his most complete extant statement of the gospel.

Romans 1-8 forms a particularly strong unit. In the first two chapters, Paul witnesses for the prosecution. Gentiles and Jews alike are under God's condemnation for sin; Jews have the laws of Moses, while Gentiles have a sense of the "law written upon their hearts;" both are "without excuse."

In Chapters 3-8 Paul brings in a new witness (not for the defense, for there is no defense), the revelation of God's righteousness, or justice, in Jesus Christ. Humanity may be justified before the throne of God by faith in Jesus Christ. who has accepted retribution for the sins of the ungodly: "being justified by his blood, we shall be saved from wrath through him" (5:9). By the Spirit of the risen Christ within (8:10), men and women come into God's righteous life, to be adopted as children of God along with him (8:15). Concluding with 8:18ff, the full apocalyptic horizon of this drama comes into view; the entire created order waits expectantly for the manifestation of God's children (8:20). Paul ends with this triumphant verdict: "If God be for us, who can be against us? . . . Who shall lay any charge against God's elect? It is God that justifieth. Who is he that condemneth?" (8:31, 33f).

In Romans 1-8 we see Paul's explicit statement of the apocalyptic judgment day that forms the context of the gospel, as well as the justice of God revealed as its content. But he is more explicit elsewhere in stating what he believes to happen in the experience of the hearer when the gospel is preached. His most extensive writing on this subject is found in his second letter to the Corinthians, particularly in Chapters 3-4. His portrayal of his own ministry suggests that it involves not only his words but also his actions, even his very demeanor in the world. All these aspects together are the way in which Paul and his fellow ministers become a "manifestation of the truth commending ourselves to every man's conscience in the sight of God" (4:2). Indeed, Paul's own hardship and suffering in the ministry, his participation in Christ's cross, are stressed in 2 Corinthians 4:8-18 as well. This concept of preaching with the totality of one's words and actions is echoed in other letters of Paul (Phil. 3:17; 4:9; Gal. 3:1).

The same personification of the gospel is seen in those who receive Paul's preaching:

> Ye are our epistle written in our hearts, known and read of all men; forasmuch as ye are manifestly declared to be the epistle of Christ ministered by us, written not with ink, but with the Spirit of the living God; not in tables of stone, but in the fleshly tables of the heart [2 Cor. 3:2f].

This strong statement on the incarnation of the Word in the heart and actions of the believer is followed by Paul's strongest diatribe against the efficacy of scripture for salvation. The law of Moses is a ministry of death and condemnation (3:8f), and his writings are read with a veil upon the heart (3:15) until one turns directly to the Lord. Only then is the veil taken away.

This transformation is the ultimate goal of gospel preaching. Paul describes the gospel as a light that shines upon the hearer. When a hearer responds, Paul describes the birth of faith thus: "For God, who commanded the light to shine out of darkness [Gen. 1:3], hath shined in our hearts, to give the light of the knowledge of the glory of God in the face of Jesus Christ" (4:6). The hearing of faith is so powerful, so elemental, that Paul can compare it only to God's act of the creation of the world in the beginning. In the next chapter, Paul makes this apocalyptic theme of new creation explicit: "Therefore, if any man be in Christ, he is a new creature: old things are passed away; behold all things are become new" (5:15 cf. Isa. 65:17).

For Paul, the receiving of the gospel is an inward experience of the light shining in the darkness. As this occurs in response to the light of the gospel, this new revelation comes to be understood in the "face," or person, of Jesus Christ. This inward knowledge is a divine gift, not a human capacity (4:7).

Paul wrote his epistles in order to respond to specific situations in individual churches; hence, the overall corpus of his extant writings does not provide us with a ready-made, interlocking system of his thought. Yet, if we compare his description of the preaching event in 2 Corinthians 3-4 with his assertions in Romans 1-2, we find a basic harmony of themes. In the latter passage, we saw that the heathen know inwardly the wrath of God "revealed from heaven against all ungodliness and unrighteousness of men, who hold the truth in unrighteousness" (Rom. 1:18). Thus, even without a knowledge of the law or the gospel, all know at least the judgment of God (Rom. 1:32).

Therefore, when Paul, a minister of the gospel, manifests its truth in his words and deeds, this gospel communication speaks powerfully to "every man's conscience in the sight of God" (2 Cor. 4:2). The receiving of the gospel is that moment when the inchoate yet insistent experience of God's judgment within, informing the human conscience, becomes the revelation of this same God's glory in the face of Jesus Christ, who has come to save, as well as to judge, the ungodly.

We also find the prophetic content and context of preaching continued in the Johannine literature. Here the key word is not Paul's *euangelizo*, "to preach," but *martureo*, "to witness." In John 5, a "courtroom" scene is strongly evoked, as Jesus defends his claim to Sonship against the attack of the religious leaders. The key confirmation of his witness to himself comes from the witness of the Father, whose Word abides in those who heed it (John 5:37f). Jesus then turns the prosecution back upon his opponents, stating that in their obsession with the scriptures they have repressed the inward witness of the Father and failed to recognize the Son, to whom the scriptures point.

This theme is extended in the First Epistle of John, where it is stated that those who believe in the Son do so because they have the witness of God within (1 John 5:9f). Moreover, the hope of overcoming sin is tied to this abiding Word within (1 John 2:14).

Therefore, we find strong affinities between the proclamational theologies of John and Paul; the preaching of the gospel must "answer," or corroborate, some witness of God known within the believer. When it does, the light revealed in the believer is recognized in the gospel of Jesus. Both John and Paul, then, see preaching as the effort to help men and women recognize in Jesus a person they have already known in glimmering ways in their own experience.

FOX'S UNDERSTANDING OF PREACHING

Some sixteen centuries later, George Fox found the content and context of prophetic and apostolic preaching to be seriously eroded in the preaching of the established churches. God's justice had been greatly compromised by both Catholicism and Protestantism. The Roman Church prescribed indulgences for Christian sin, gradually sublimating the urgent call to repentance into a measured system of penance. The Protestant Reformation rejected that system. Yet the reformers substituted for it a doctrine of *imputed righteousness*, a truncated gospel: Christ dies for the continuing sins of his believers, but he does not give them a direct revelation of God's will for their lives, nor the power to obey.

Fox rejects such a gospel of Jesus as a Pyrrhic victory. If God's justice is not served, men and women can never serve God in righteousness. He is certain from his own experience that there is more power to the gospel than that. Therefore, in his preaching he revives the prophets' and apostles' unsparing prosecution, summoning all to God's day of trial. Going from town to town, preaching the day of the Lord, he pronounces God's condemnation upon all humanity, both pagans and "those that have long had the scriptures," yet who fail to fulfill them. At the same time, he holds up Christ, who has died for all *and* who enlightens all, revealing not only personal sinfulness, but also a positive sense of God's will in one's circumstances. The believer is by no means vindicated, but *saved* through subjection to the will of the seed Christ, raised up within.

The juridical context of early Quaker preaching is seen explicitly in the term which is used to describe its immediate goal — *convincement*. As we have noted earlier, the term in seventeenth century usage connotes not only an intellectual assent but also what we would today call *conviction*, being found guilty. Quaker preaching seeks first of all to bring men and women into a decisive sense of their own sin and inability to be saved from sin by their own powers. But this does not mean that a "catalogue of sins" must be unleashed upon the hearer as a "scatter-shot" effort to find some hidden vice. Such a listing would, in fact, suggest in itself a moral code or system, the outward understanding and legalism that the gospel must overcome. The paths of sinfulness may be endlessly enumerated. But the path of God's righteousness is singular; this path is known only as one knows God. Quaker preaching, therefore, points essentially to one sin: alienation from God, from the light of Christ. Men and women are alienated from this inward revelation because its discovery of sin is painful (see John 3:19ff). Quaker preaching, then, is less explicit about the various *kinds* of sins than in pointing to the *experience* of sinfulness and the recognition of him who can save.

Of course, not all are reached by the preaching of the gospel. Some remain "convinced in their judgments, coming not into obedience;"³ that is, resisting the revelation of God's righteousness in favor of their own righteousness (see Rom. 10:3). But all those who do respond to this gospel are convinced because it has answered some hidden experience of God within:

> There is no people convinced of sin, but they are convinced within themselves, and with the light within them; and it is the light that makes manifest to a man when he is convinced: it answers to something, and reaches to something in their particulars though the words be spoken without them from the light.⁴

The gospel, preached from the preacher's own inward leadings of Christ's light, reaches through outward words to the hearer's inward light.

Fox reserves his most heated prosecution for the Church establishment itself; in apostasy from the Spirit of Christ, it has *kept people in alienation* from the power of God, causing them to follow outward teachers. Church leaders have disallowed the testimony of the light, stressing the mercy of God at the expense of his justice. Christ has come, not to impute righteousness, but to teach it; he has come to forgive *and* to reign.

In "The Lamb's Officer,"⁵ the apocalyptic scene of the judgment day trial is most vivid. The subtitle of the tract states "[The Lamb's Officer] is the witness of God in all consciences, to call them up to the bar, the judgment of the Lamb, in this his day which is come." Fox's opening statement calls a startling court into session: "The Lord Jesus Christ is come to reign, and his everlasting kingdom and sceptre is set up, and the bar of judgment, and all are called to it . . . ." What follows is a blazing indictment of the established Church, delivered in driving cadences, charging the Church with count after count of obstructing Christ in his divine offices of grace, which he must minister to people himself. From preaching by the hour glass to imprisoning, torturing, and murdering those who dissent, he lays the charges, punctuated frequently by refrains like "Come now, priests, guilty or not guilty?" Just as the new world is discovered and begun with authentic Christian worship (see our preceding chapter), so also inauthentic worship and Church order are the foremost objects of judgment, according to Fox's preaching. From the misdirected worship of God the Church has fallen into a multitude of sins, just as the first man and woman, the primordial Church, began their fall from grace with their disregard of God's immediate teaching. And just as they in their alienation lost the inward knowledge of God's voice, the goal of Quaker preaching is to bring men and women again into the hearing of God. As it calls the court into session, this preaching seeks to convince by calling the key witness for the prosecution and salvation; Fox calls this "reaching to the witness of God in everyone."

We have in this chapter portrayed the prophetic and apostolic tradition of preaching and the way Fox employs this tradition as the framework for early Quaker proclamation. We may now move on in the next chapter to examine the program of Christian witness that Fox finds implied in "reaching to the witness of God in everyone." We will also look at some of the unique characteristics of early Quaker preaching as it sought to revive the tradition of the prophets and apostles.

For the Lord had said unto me that if I did set up one in the same spirit that the prophets and apostles were in that gave forth the Scriptures, he or she should shake all the country in their profession ten miles about them . . . .[1]

8.   FOX'S PROGRAM FOR CHRISTIAN WITNESS

We have seen thus far a number of crucial insights in Fox's understanding of Christ's power, as well as some key critical insights into the problem of the Church. What is equally impressive, however, is the way in which Fox finds in these basic insights a radical program for Christian proclamation, worship, and Church order. In this chapter, we begin to focus on this program, examining his agenda for Christian witness.

Lewis Benson points out that Fox's use of the term "that of God in every one" is found most repeatedly in his epistles, where he is writing pastorally to Friends about the life in Christ or exhorting Quaker ministers in their work. The incessant refrain to his exhortations is that all their endeavors are to "sound deep to the witness of God in every man" (see 1 Thess. 1:8).

Fox's program of preaching is radical, extending beyond even the renewed emphasis that the Reformation had placed upon proclamation. It includes the preaching that takes place in the context of Christian worship and evangelism, but it also extends into the ethical life of Friends and the order and posture of the Church in the world. For Fox, the entire Christian existence can be seen in the prophetic terms of receiving and preaching the Word of the Lord. Lewis Benson[2] helpfully divides this program into basic categories. We will adopt these categories in our presentation below.

VOCAL PREACHING

Preaching the gospel in words is, of course, a primary way of answering that of God in every one. While this includes written communication, it was mainly carried out orally among early Friends. In 1656, as the Quaker preaching offensive was at its peak, Fox wrote to his fellow ministers of the Word:

> Let all nations hear the word by sound or writing. Spare no place, spare not tongue or pen; but be obedient to the Lord God and go through the work and be valiant for the Truth on earth . . . .[3]

Fox's exhortations to Quaker preachers often raise the theme of holy war, in which God's conquest is total, sparing no one (see 1 Sam. 15:3) from the sword of the Spirit, the Word of God (Eph. 6:17).

Indeed, a battle has been joined in the Quaker movement. Bringing men and women into this knowledge of God within themselves, the gospel is a word against all worships that do not serve this inward knowledge. "Let them know the living God; for teachings, churches, worships, set up by man's earthly knowledge, and will, must be thrown down by the power of the Lord God."[4] As this inward knowledge is found, men and women become new creatures and are like Adam and Eve in Eden before the Fall: "The Word of the Lord is that which was in the beginning, and brings to the beginning."[5]

Fox's preaching unfolds around his declaration that "Christ is come to teach his people himself." Jesus Christ is present in this "mighty day of the Lord" to lead by his Spirit into righteousness:

> And John told the saints that the anointing which abides in them would teach them all things [1 John 2:27] . . . and this was the ministers' work . . . to direct the hearing of faith, which Christ is the author of, whereby they receive the spirit. And the apostle brought the people to their teacher within them, which

is the light, and turned people from darkness to light, and from the power of Satan unto God [Acts 26:18]; which light shining in their hearts, gives them the light of the knowledge of the glory of God [2 Cor. 4:6].[6]

Fox accepts Paul's explanation that those who do not receive the gospel have been blinded to its light by Satan (2 Cor. 4:4). But for those who do receive the gospel, it

> brings life and immortality to light [2 Tim. 1:10], in every one of your hearts, and lets you see over him that darkened you. Now every man and woman here will have the testimony in your own hearts [1 John 5:20], of [Christ's] order and fellowship, being heirs and inheritors of it; by which you see over all the false orders and fellowships, that are or may be set up or made.[7]

Thus, false orders and worships are among the ways Satan blinds people to the light of the gospel. But as the gospel is received and Christ's free teaching set up, it gathers into the true Church, the fellowship of Christ, above all human fellowships, orders, and teachings.

The Christ who was crucified at Jerusalem is the same Christ who has been crucified within by alienation from his guidance. The liberation of this witness is the salvation of the believer. Writing to Friends in the ministry, Fox instructs:

> And him, who was promised to be the covenant of God to the Gentiles, and the new covenant to the Jews, hold forth to them both; that all may know him their leader to God, and the prisoner to come forth unto him.[8]

So we see that the Jesus Christ of history, preached in the gospel, answers and calls forth the Jesus Christ of experience in the hearer. The one who unjustly died for the ungodly, and is imprisoned within, is freed so that the ungodly may be justified.

In this day of trial, Fox offers a gospel which is unsparing in its condemnation, yet unlimited in its liberating power. Though its judgment is unrelenting, its salvation is overwhelmingly glorious. But to those Puritan critics who continue to resist this gospel, Fox issues a stern warning:

> The witnesses in all your consciences shall answer for me, and let you see that your own words are your burden; and a heavy

cry will come upon you when you feel it . . . come to the witness, else eternally you will be condemned.[9]

The gospel brings the great day of reckoning into the present,
that hearers may turn now, while there is time.

PREACHING BY EXAMPLE

While the witness to the gospel in words is essential to
Christian preaching, that men and women "be valiant for the
name of Jesus" in their speaking to the world, Fox also lays great
stress, like Paul, upon the posture and activity that preach Christ.
This is the work not only of those who are recognized as
ministers and who travel in the gospel ministry, but of all
Friends, for the world will keenly scrutinize a people that claims
so much for Christ's power.

> Dwell in the life of God, that to all the spirits in prison [1 Pet.
> 3:19] ye may be made manifest, that ye are no deceivers, but
> saviours, and such as are sent to lead from all deceivers, and to
> testify against them.[10]

The Church as a body which does the will of its head, Christ,
witnesses his lordship to the world.

> For now Friends are become a people gathered in the holy name
> of Jesus. Therefore all are to walk worthy of the gospel, which is
> the power of God . . . that in that your life may shine before men
> to answer that of God in all, that they may behold your good
> works, and glorify your Father which is in heaven. And so, walk
> in the light as children of the light and of the day.[11]

Here we may see a glimpse of Fox's appropriation of the concept
of Christian witness in John 5. Walking in the light, Friends
perform that work given them by the light to do (John 5:36; also
John 14:12 — "He that believeth in me, the works that I do shall
he do also; and greater works than these shall he do also . . . .").
Their deeds act out a second witness, confirming their words,
and more convincingly reach to the all-decisive witness of God,
the Word abiding in people. Fox goes on to say:

> And now that Friends are become a great people, shall not
> judgment, and justice, and righteousness run down our streets

> as a stream and a flood [Amos 5:24], to drive away all the filth
> from amongst us. And now Friends are become a good savour
> [2 Cor. 2:15] in the hearts of all people, they have a friend in
> their house that will plead for them; by which Friends have
> been kept and preserved in the life, to answer the friend in
> their house.[12]

In other words, this "friend in their house" is that witness within
that will respond to the testimony of Friends in words and deeds.

Fox repeatedly denounces those who do not walk in the light
they claim in words to know; these are the greatest deceivers,
leading the world astray. He is confident that by being living
examples, living epistles, of God's righteousness, "your lives and
conversations may preach."

If this gospel must bring each person low before the judgment
seat of God, then the demeanor of Friends must not humor men
and women in their false sense of dignity and honor. When Fox
describes his commission from the Lord to preach, he includes
God's demand that he say "thee and thou" to all, high or low,
that he not bow or take off his hat to anyone, etc. This behavior
was a refusal to humor the wealthy and powerful in their false
glory. It often inspired hatred and abuse from clergy and
magistrates:

> But the Lord's power carried me over all in his glory, and many
> came to be turned to God in a little time, for the heavenly day
> of the Lord sprang from on high, and broke forth apace, by the
> light of which many came to see where they were. But oh, the
> rage that then was in the priests, magistrates, and professors . . . .[13]

Fox and the early Friends presented a stern and solid front
against the "graces" of the social, ecclesiastical, and legal
establishments of their day. Their plain-speaking, non-deferring
demeanor had a disorienting effect upon those they confronted,
whether the local priest or Oliver Cromwell, revealing decorum-
as-usual to be like the emperor's new clothes before God. Even
the customary platitude, "good day," was withdrawn in order to
bring people to a consciousness of the Lord's mighty day of judgment.[14] The point of their conversation was to be Jesus Christ
(see Heb. 13:7f). Again, the trial scene of John 5 looms, as Fox
suggests that it is God's honor, not men's, that must be fervently
sought (John 5:44). So even as Friends were brought to trial
before the world's magistrates, they sought to bring worldly

authority at that very moment to the ultimate trial before the divine judge.

Fox kept his own stature low, condescending to all conditions (Rom. 12:16), despite his testimony to the Lord's great work in him. Fox's stubbornly apostolic style of ministry throughout his life, his willingness to labor with even the humblest seeker of truth, and his refusal either to join with the religious and academic establishments of his day, or to create his own, probably go far to account for the obscure corner he has occupied in Church histories down to this day. His vision, however, dictated a simplicity in life and words which was remarkable in its ability to reach those whom he addressed.

We begin to discover in this examination that the famous social testimonies of the early Friends arose not out of a political or sociological analysis, presented with a few biblical proof-texts as garnish. These early testimonies instead began simply as those things which Friends could no longer do without diminishing or even belying the message of Christ's salvation that they preached. Thus, they could no longer honor men and women while trying to bring them to the judgment bar; they could no longer glorify themselves with the possessions of the world, but lived in a simplicity that allowed their best energies to glorify God; they could no longer join in wars to defend the kingdoms of this world, when they were already joined in the spiritual struggle of the gospel to build the kingdom of God; they could no longer stifle the ministry and leadership of women when God's Spirit was so gloriously upon them to preach and lead.

> So speak the truth, whether merchants or tradesmen, and all sorts of people whatsoever, in all your occasions, and in all your tradings, dealings, and doings, speak the truth, act in the truth, and walk in the truth, and this brings righteousness forth. For it answereth the witness of God in every one; which lets every one see all the deeds and actions they have done amiss, and words which they have spoken amiss. So the witness of God within them ariseth a swift witness against them . . . and brings them to the judgment bar, and to condemnation. Here righteousness goes forth, and here the sweet savour to the Lord God begins to ascend; and truth and equity arise both to be acted and spoken.[15]

The preaching vocation is seen to call men and women in whatever their livelihood might be. Friends are urged to keep to their plain clothing and simplicity of life, that these things "may preach to all that you have to deal with . . . answering the equal principle in all, that God in all things may be glorified."[16] In Fox's writings, ethical matters arise not only for the individual's sake, but for the sake of those who witness his or her actions.

Walking in the light, dwelling in the seed that was promised to Abraham, Friends are to walk upon the earth, fulfilling God's most ancient promise to his people: "Then you will come to walk cheerfully over the world, answering that of God in every one; whereby in them ye may be a blessing, and make the witness of God in them to bless you" (Gen. 12:2f).[17]

LOVE AND UNITY

Two closely related ways that the community of faith as a whole answers the light in men and women are the love and unity of Friends with one another. Fox in his own life had a profound sense of God's love, so much so that he speaks of being "ravished" by the love of God.[18] And his life in this relationship with God bespeaks a dynamic in which his love for God is not one of pious gratitude, as Calvin describes the Christian life,[19] but of passionate desire.[20] In the community that his message gathered, this love spreads in all directions, as the Friends of Christ (John 15:14) are bonded in love, joined in the one seed.

This love and unity are a powerful witness to the world, one which convinced many who saw Quakers together. It is not a coalition of shared self-interests, but a self-giving faithfulness in which the seed in one person nourishes the seed in the other.

> Therefore I desire, that ye may all feel his love shed in your hearts, and in it live (above the love of the world, which is enmity) . . . . For love edifies the body of Christ . . . and brings and keeps all in true humanity and in the true divinity . . . . There is the hill or mountain, where the light shines to the answering of the witness of God in all . . . .[21]

Where people are gathered in the seed of Abraham, love unites and enmity is cast out. People will abandon their habitations in Babylon to migrate to this city.

Writing to Friends in America, Fox is certain that this is a sure way to reach to those who are not familiar with the gospel, as well as to those who are.

> Stir up the gift of God in you [2 Tim. 1:6], and the pure mind, and improve your talents [Matt. 25:14-30], that ye may be the light of the world, a city set upon a hill [Matt. 5:13f]. Let your light shine among the Indians, the Blacks, and the Whites, that ye may answer the truth in them, and bring them to the standard and ensign, that God hath set up, Jesus Christ.[22]

To non-Christians who may already be tender and responsive to Christ's light as individuals, the solidarity of the Christian community confirms that community's witness to Jesus in the language of the gospel, to answer that light in them and to draw them into faith and community in the name of Jesus.

All the outward works and words of the Christian community in the world must flow from the truth within its members. Fox writes beautifully of this divine flow of grace into the outward:

> And from the truth floweth justice, equity, righteousness, and godliness, mercy, and tenderness, that brings a man's heart mind, soul, and spirit to the infinite and incomprehensible God, and from [the truth] love flows to all the universal creation, and would have all come to the knowledge of the truth; and it bends every one to their utmost ability to serve God and his truth, and to spread it abroad . . . . As to unity, [truth] makes all like itself, that do obey it. Universal, to live out of narrowness and self, and to deny it.[23]

This truth is the love of God definitively revealed in history by the self-emptying life of Jesus.

This love of Christ that flowed in the Quaker community shook the world in its judgment as Friends volunteered to lie in prison for one another when family hardship or ill health threatened life. As early as 1655, Fox urged Friends in persecution to "lay down and offer up your lives for one another. Here is the love of, and unto the brethren manifest, to lay down their lives for one another [see John 15:13] . . . . So dwell low in the life, that ye may answer that of God in every one."[24] Fox's emphasis upon love follows Johannine lines, in that the love within the community is stressed more explicitly than love to the world in general; nevertheless, this love is the beacon of a city whose gates are open both night and day (see

Rev. 21:25). In a world "order" continually rent by enmity and strife, the love and unity of the true Christian community stands as witness to a new order, one in which outward divisions are judged and forged into a new creation (see 2 Cor. 5:16-18; Gal. 6:15) by the fiery apocalypse of Christ's love.

CONFOUNDING DECEIT

The final category in answering the witness of God is what Fox calls "confounding deceit." This effort was a major focus of the energies of Fox and other early Friends as they constantly strove to reveal the false teachings of the established churches and to answer the attacks of Puritan critics. His largest single work, *The Great Mystery*, published in 1659, is devoted entirely to the point-by-point answering and counterattacking of over one hundred published criticisms of Quakerism.

As the *Journal* amply illustrates, Fox was ever ready to engage a local clergyman in dispute. His public debates often did reach to the witness in people, sometimes gathering entire communities into the Quaker movement. Confounding deceit, in fact, was a major aspect of Fox's synagogue strategy — to counter the minister's teaching after the sermon was finished and draw sympathizers out. It is a small wonder, given the skill of Fox in debate on the scriptures, that sometimes the local minister simply fled upon Fox's approach.

Again, the holy war theme is clear, as Fox urges Friends to answer every public criticism and every false teaching, published or spoken, much the same as Deuteronomy's unsparing commands against the worshipers of false gods (Deut. 13:8). Fox counsels Friends in the ministry to

> be a terror to all the adversaries of God, and a dread, answering that of God in them all, spreading the Truth abroad, awakening the witness, confounding deceit, gathering up out of the transgression . . . tread and trample all that is contrary under [Gen. 3:15; Ps. 91:13; Isa. 63:3-6] . . . . Spare no deceit. Lay the sword upon it; go over it . . . .[25]

If the preaching of early Friends is in the type of Israel's conquest of Canaan, it is also understood as the renewal of God's creation:

> This is the word of the Lord to all Friends, and fellow-labourers in the truth, who are subduing the earth [Gen. 1:28], and its

earthly knowledge, and its carnal wisdom, and beating down
and threshing down that, in hope to get forth the wheat . . . .[26]

In answering that of God in every one, Friends are engaged in
nothing less than the eschatological work of God, reestablishing
and extending the garden of Eden amidst the briars and thorns
of a fallen world, and participating in God's harvest of the earth
(Rev. 14:14ff).

EARLY QUAKER PREACHING

A central issue in Fox's understanding of apostolic preaching is
that the true apostle of Christ is *sent* by the Lord. "So all that
succeed the apostles, they must be sent of Christ in the same
power and spirit" (see Rom. 10:15) . . . ."[27] Christ's call is pre-
requisite not only for one's original leading into ministry in the
first place, but for *every instance* of preaching. Those who
preach without this immediate sense of leading are false
prophets; those who are led yet do not speak "despise the
prophecy" (1 Thess. 5:20).

This is a sense of preaching that defies the established role of
preaching in Christian worships. Fox advises his fellow Quaker
ministers:

> . . . always be ready to preach the word, and be instant in
> season and out of season [2 Tim. 4:2]. He that observes the
> wind or storms, will not sow the seed; and he that regards the
> clouds will not reap [Eccles. 11:4].[28]

Fox views preaching as a divine event which does not follow the
times appointed by human schedules — the month, day or hour
— but the time revealed by Christ's light; it is not this Sunday's
sermon but the day of the Lord revealed:

> For it is a weighty thing to be in the work of the ministry of the
> Lord God, and to go forth in that. It is not as a customary preach-
> ing, but it is to bring people to the end of all outward preaching.[29]

This understanding places great responsibility upon the preacher
to be sensitive and obedient to Christ's leadings. Fox counsels
his fellow-laborers to "speak the word of the Lord faithfully,
neither add to it with your reason, nor diminish from it with a

disobedient mind . . . ."[30] He points to Philip in Acts 8 as an explicit example of apostolic preaching by immediate guidance:

> Philip was sent to a place, and then it was told him what to say, when he came to it . . . . And they that speak as the spirit gives them utterance, and moves them, take no thought but it is given to them in the same hour [Matt. 10:19; Luke 12:11f] . . . .[31]

This preaching places radical trust in the risen Christ to send the right person to the right place at the right time.

Preaching Christ, then, cannot be reconciled with the regular expounding of scriptural texts, which may be planned out for every Sunday and holy day of the calendar, according to a lectionary. One must preach him who gave forth the scriptures. Doing this, the scriptures are brought into the use of the preacher to confirm the witness to Christ. In a style basically like his writings, Fox's sermons[32] are packed with phrases derived from throughout the Bible. His approach is much like the use of scripture in the Gospel of John. The Fourth Gospel does not so much *cite* scripture as *breathe* it, showing Jesus to *embody* the Word of God. Jesus does not defend himself with scripture so much as show how it testifies of him. Likewise, Fox allows Christ risen up in him to speak through him. The words are pulled from throughout the Bible, like amino acids being appropriated by DNA to form new life, as the Word is made flesh through the obedient speaking of his human instrument in outward words. Fox's organic use of scripture and his apocalyptic viewpoint often lead him to give his hearers the entire panorama of history, from Eden in Genesis to the New Jerusalem in Revelation. Again, this approach is in line with Fox's belief that the work of the light recapitulates and resonates with the history described in scripture.

LANGUAGE AND RHETORIC

Fox's preaching often went on for hours. This is not surprising, given the scope of his message and his commitment to improvisation in the Spirit. Michael Graves[33] has written a very helpful study of the extant sermons of Fox and other early Friends. He agrees with Jackson Cope's analysis[34] of the early Quaker linguistic style. Cope calls this style "the epistemology of verbal incantation."[35] Words drawn from scripture are repeated and recombined in an improvisational manner which becomes not so much ungrammatical as agrammatical[36] (a manner which the reader may well have noticed in the quotations from Fox in this study).

Graves compares this style with what Ian Ramsey[37] has noted about the early sermons of Peter, as recorded in Acts 2 and 3. Ramsey describes Peter's message as a "riotous mixture of phrases," derived from a wide range of sources, mainly from the Old Testament. "This riotous mixing is in effect a rough and ready attempt to secure that special logical impropriety needed to express the Christian message."[38] The effect of this use of language, Ramsey states, is "to evoke the distinctively Christian situation," one of "challenge and response."[39] It is Graves' judgment that early Quaker preaching combines elements of this pure proclamational style with more explanatory language, which is also to be found in the New Testament, in the form of gospel preaching such as Paul's letters.[40]

This comparison to the early apostolic preaching in Acts is revealing. The distinctively Christian "situation" which is present in both early Christian and early Quaker preaching is, more specifically, the day of the Lord, the apocalyptic situation in which God's judgment and salvation are revealed. Preaching *from* the light *to* the light in others, the Quaker preacher's "incantation" is the attempt to "reach" beyond the outward, rational processes of the human mind, to the witness of God within.

Graves also examines Quaker preaching in comparison to Puritan preaching in terms of rhetorical approaches. During the rise of Puritanism in the early seventeenth century, English preaching shifted from the high, Renaissance style of ingratiation (techniques of flattery and supplication, which reflected the stratification of society) to a "plain style" in which classical values of persuasion, based upon logic, proofs, and reasons, were restored, favoring simplicity of speech (and perhaps reflecting the rise of a more broad middle class). Universities trained ministers in these techniques. But the untrained "mechanic preachers" of the Baptists represent probably the furthest progression of this trend toward plainness and simplicity.

Quaker preaching shares with the Baptists a strong tendency toward plainness and disregard for training in rhetorical techniques of argumentation. Yet, in breaking with the Protestant concept of preaching as the exposition of scripture, Fox and the

148

early Friends adopted a style which leaves all the disciplines of argumentation behind. The only guide to follow in this style is the shape of history as recorded in the whole Bible and as incarnated in the life, death, and resurrection of Jesus Christ, which they were confident would resonate with the shape of Christ's working in men and women. This resonance is the "situation" of faith.

THE ITINERANT ASPECT

Given that Quaker preaching was to be led by the light's commands and that its goal was to bring people to their inward teacher and leave them there, it is logical that the preaching of early Friends was strongly itinerant. A broad segment of the early Quaker movement took some part in this testimony to the world, whether interrupting established Church services, speaking in market places, going naked for a sign (see Isa. 20:3; 30:1), or addressing assembled groups in open fields. This broad participation is indicative of the very central role of preaching in the life of early Friends.

No one was barred from participation in the witness to the world; yet the need to exercise restraint was crucial. Friends sometimes ran into excesses in public ministry. It was the responsibility of the local meeting to be a check against false leadings. Fox counsels Friends to be careful to see that their calling to speak is from the Lord. Friends travelling in the ministry should not proceed aimlessly or beyond their call; when the work commanded is finished, they should go back home. Meetings are warned to be watchful for Friends unclear in their travelling ministry and to urge them homeward. Travelling ministers are advised to carry a letter of recommendation from their home meetings. Thus, while early Quakers were firm in their commitment to Christ's spiritual leadership in ministry, they recognized that the guidance of Christ in the wider Christian body must counter the misled motions of individual members. Beginning in 1654, travelling ministry was given overall coordination from Swarthmoor Hall.

Friends steadfastly resisted professionalizing their ministry. Most early travelling Friends travelled at their own expense, though some were supported by their home meetings or by a special fund first collected at Swarthmoor Hall. But again, the travel of these Friends, self-supported or not, was to continue only as long as the call was distinctly and specifically felt. A professional, regularized ministry thus stands diametrically opposite to the concept of a ministry led by Christ's Spirit. Preaching for a living will conflict with one's sense of this Spirit. Fox writes that the free ministry is concomitant with the free grace of God: Jesus sent his own disciples into the world to preach without any dependable income (Luke 10:4; 22:35), yet they lacked nothing. "Here you may see that Christ's disciples wanted nothing, who freely had received, and freely did give" (Matt. 10:8).[41] Those who follow the apostles' life and Spirit must trust in the Lord and in the people.

Not surprisingly, this stubbornly non-professional approach to ministry also disregarded the standards of the time for training ministers. Like the Baptists, Quakers were adamant that Christ, not schools, equips ministers. This did not prevent some theologically trained converts to Quakerism, like Samuel Fisher and Robert Barclay, from taking part in the ministry as well. Yet some of early Quakerism's most inspired and brilliant preachers, like James Nayler, came from the humblest backgrounds, without any formal training.

WOMEN IN THE MINISTRY

These criteria for ministry, while also held up by some radical Puritan contemporaries, were taken to revolutionary conclusions by the early Quaker movement, particularly in the role of women as ministers. The pioneering attitude of Quakerism toward women began with their participation in preaching from the very beginning. Elizabeth Hooten, a former Baptist, is the first person Fox names as convinced by his preaching and was an important early Quaker preacher. Margaret Fell was a preacher and key coordinator of the movement long before she married Fox.

Puritan critics rebuked Quakers on this issue, citing Paul's admonition for women to keep silence (1 Cor. 14:34f; also see 1 Tim. 2:11f). For Friends, the admonition to keep silent from one's own words applies to both men and women; "but Christ in the male as in the female . . . may speak, Christ in the male and female who are in the spirit of God . . . ."[42] Fox's main defense of women's ministry is found in a tract with the rather unpromising title, "The Woman Learning in Silence."[43] Here he marshals a broad array of biblical support for the ministry of women and

150

gives inspired interpretations to both the 1 Corinthians 14:34f and 1 Timothy 2:11f texts as well. After a brilliantly developed set of arguments, Fox concludes with a searing counter-rebuke to his Puritan opponents:

> Who is it that dare limit the Holy One of Israel? . . . you are against the scripture, and will not have [Christ] to reign over you; for that male in whom Christ doth reign, rule, and speak [2 Cor. 13:3], he will own Christ in the female, there to rule, to reign, and speak . . . . Christ is come to reign . . . in the male and in the female . . . .[44]

The apocalyptic perspective puts all things in a new light, judging the world's judgments. This is by no means a humanistic liberation; the Quaker witness was less against the limiting of human freedom than for the freedom of the Spirit, with human freedom as a corollary. Both women and men must live in subjection to Christ's authority. Yet those who are obedient to their Lord are given a power and authority to speak a mighty Word to the world.[45]

PROPHETIC MINISTRY TO THE WORLD

In the final analysis the prophetic character of early Quaker ministry lies not in features such as its anticipation of an accepted ministry of women long before it would become stylish among other churches. This feature is only a secondary ramification of a more fundamental orientation. That orientation is the acceptance of the prophet's mantle as the unglorious vestment of a servant. Modern New Testament interpreter Paul Minear[46] has shown that Jesus and the apostolic Church that succeeded him revived the prophetic ministry as servants to the inhabitants of the earth, humbling themselves below the basest condition, willing to suffer the reproach and rejection of the world. In sharp counterpoint to the scriptural authority and power of the Scribes, Jesus and the apostles exercised no personal power or prestige, but simply practiced a radical dependence upon the Father for their words and deeds.

Fox calls Friends to a new apostolate with exhortations such as this:

> Stand up ye prophets of the Lord, for the truth upon the earth; quench not your prophecy, neither heed them that despise it;

but in that stand which brings you through to the end. Heed not the eyes of the world, ye prophets of the Lord, but answer that in them all, which they have closed their eye to, that ye may tell them of things to come, answering that of God in them that shall remain.[47]

This singular vision created a singular ministry, not only during the heady days of the 1650s, but also during the grimly repressive times of the Restoration. While other nonconforming groups went underground, the Quakers maintained a stubbornly public ministry despite the sufferings that it brought. Fox describes one such meeting in London, 1670: as soon as one Friend was arrested and taken away for preaching, another would rise and begin. "And many Baptists and other sectaries forsook their meetings and came to see how the Quakers would stand both in city and country."[48] Scenes like these evoke the words of the prophet Amos, who declares, "the lion hath roared, who will not fear? The Lord God hath spoken, who can but prophesy?" (Amos 3:8).

The message of early Quaker preaching likewise echoes the prophetic call to the people for a direct knowledge of God's will. It pronounces God's indictment against those who have not taken the counsel of the Lord. They are clothed, like Adam and Eve, in their own works, not in God's Spirit; this is why they "add sin to sin" (Isa. 30:1). Nowhere is the primacy upon hearing God more forcefully stated than by the prophet Jeremiah. Here Israel's sin is summarized not only as a disobedience to the commandments of the law, but also that "ye have not obeyed my voice, saith the Lord" (e.g., Jer. 3:13). Early Friends believed that the way the prophets and apostles preached was not incidental to the message itself; in the particular circumstances of their day, they arrived at a fresh realization of that same stature of ministry.

Ye turned to God from idols to serve the living and true God; and to wait for his Son from heaven, whom he raised from the dead, even Jesus, which delivered us from the wrath to come [1 Thess. 1:9f].

9.   THE MEANING OF QUAKER WORSHIP

The ultimate goal of Quaker preaching is to "Bring all into the worship of God."[1] When Fox uses the phrase "the worship of God," the preposition is intended both as objective and as subjective genitive; not only is God the object of this worship, but this is the worship of God's choosing. It is Fox's claim that Quaker worship is unique in both cases.

Of course, Quakers were not the first to raise the question of what kind of worship pleases God, and seventeenth century England was the scene of unprecedented experimentation in Christian worship. From the beginning, a primary focus of Puritan reform was the effort to break from the strong formalism of the Anglican prayerbook. Early Puritan emphasis centered upon the role of pastoral preaching, according to the Calvinist tradition. But, as we have seen in our historical chapters, by the mid-seventeenth century, when Puritans finally gained freedom in worship, there was a growing trend among the more radical groupings in the Puritan spectrum toward less formalism in all aspects of worship. Separatists such as the Baptists insisted that not only preaching but praying and singing as well must be left to the spontaneous leadership of the Holy Spirit.

This trend reached its most radical Puritan expression with the Seekers, who questioned all practices of worship, no matter how spontaneously arranged. Some came to meet often in silence, with individuals occasionally offering a prayer. Hugh Barbour[2] points out that the Seekers were not a distinct sect, but a growing aggregation of spiritual pilgrims weary of their wandering through successive enthusiastic but short-lived gatherings. Their meeting in silence was less an outright commitment to an innovation in worship than a worshipful expression of the "holding pattern" in which they found themselves. Seekerism was characterized partly by despair, but also in part by an expectation that God would give a new revelation of his will for Christian worship and order.

George Fox does not claim silent worship as his innovation, nor does he describe how early Friends came to worship in silence. It appears that Quaker worship probably did originate from the practice of the Seekers. But it would be wrong to assume, as the Protestant interpretation of Quakerism seems to do, that Fox simply galvanized the Seekers and other radical Puritans into a new burst of radical Protestantism, based upon Spirit-led worship.

The meeting of Fox and the Seekers represents a significantly providential encounter. Unlike most of the encounters between Fox and existing Christian gatherings, his confrontation with the Seekers was one characterized by mutual respect and fellowship, as evidenced by the Sedbergh and Firbank Fell gatherings. This harmony arose from what both parties recognized in the other. In the Seekers, Fox recognized a group that had come to the end of the Reformation experience. They had rejected both liturgical formalism and the spiritual enthusiasm which often amounted merely to an impromptu reshuffling of the same activities every time the group gathered to worship. It was not enough to believe that the Spirit would guide the people as to which hymn to sing next. The Spirit must guide a person in what words to speak, *if one was to speak at all.* So the Seekers had assumed a radical dependence upon the Holy Spirit, in which the Spirit no longer served to inform and supplement the conventional building blocks of Christian worship, but the entire service was abolished in order to give full reign to the Spirit's leading. This surely represents the "Land's End" of the broad and varied continent of Protestant worship.

In Fox, the Seekers recognized an apostle whose message confirmed and focused the direction of their worship, while at the same time placing it upon different assumptions which utterly transformed its meaning. When Fox proclaimed to them that "Christ is come to teach his people himself," the implications for worship in this statement were tremendous. It meant that the Spirit which they sought to lead their worship is not simply an animating presence for the Church in the interim between Christ's resurrection and his return. This Spirit is the presence of *Christ himself* come to gather and minister to his Church.

Christ the Word of God thus having returned by his Spirit, the Word and the Spirit are witnessed to be one "on earth as it is in heaven." Similarly, worship and ethics are fused, as worship comes to serve the paramount purpose of Christian existence — the hearing and obeying of God's Word — "thy kingdom come, thy will be done." No longer does scripture, seen as the Word, serve as the code of Christian ethics, which believers are given courage to follow by the inspiration of Spirit-led worship. The living Word, who gave forth the scriptures, is present in worship to *command* his followers and give them the *power* to obey in unity.

Hence, the Seekers' willingness to let formal Christian worship grind to a halt in expectation of something truly new was fulfilled in the revelation of Fox's preaching. As with all apocalyptic fulfillment, the thing fulfilled (in this case, radical Puritanism) is fundamentally transformed into a new being by the power of God (the Word Fox preached). The gathering of the Westmorland Seekers into the Quaker movement transformed a loose collection of weary pilgrims into a dynamic, gathered community of faith that gave the Quaker movement a center and momentum that up to that time Fox's scattered and limited successes in preaching had not yet achieved. The Seeker community provided Fox's gospel with a peculiar worship that it perhaps had not yet found. The message and the worship together produced a mutually-informing unity that marks the full blossoming of the Quaker movement.

The encounter of the Seekers with Fox contains overtones suggestive of the linkage between John the Baptist and Jesus. John's ministry appears to have represented a rebellion from the established religious and political leadership of Judaism — from Sadducees and Pharisees alike (Matt. 3:7f). An ascetic living in the desert (Matt. 3:4), John preached repentance to Israel, a turning not simply from personal sins but, in fact, from the whole nation's sense of identity and purpose (Matt. 3:9f). John's effort was to baptize the entire people (Matt. 3:5f) into repentance, an utter negation of its religious and socio-economic life (Luke 3:10-14), leaving the people with nothing but an intense expectation of "he that cometh after me" (Matt. 3:11).

In Jesus, John saw his mission fulfilled and ended, as he encountered the one for whom his work had prepared a way. In John, Jesus affirmed a way that was essential and requisite to his own message of salvation. Therefore, upon John's imprisonment Jesus began to preach: "The time is fulfilled, and the kingdom of God is at hand: repent ye, and believe the gospel" (Mark 1:15).

With critique as sweeping as that of John and Jesus, Fox finds apostasy in all the existing worships of the Church. Their order is not God's order, because they are based upon a gospel that is not of God. The true gospel will bring not peace but division, as Jesus said (Luke 12:51):

> . . . and so the peace of all religions must be broken, before they come to the true religion from above; and the peace of all worships must be broken, before they come to the worship in spirit and truth the devil is out of; and the peace of all ways must be broken, the men and people are in, before they come into the way of Christ Jesus . . . .[3]

So the gospel (or true religion from above) leads to the worship, which in turn leads to the way of life that is God's. Fox and early Quaker preachers repeatedly broke the peace of existing worships throughout England to proclaim this gospel and gather people into the worship in Spirit and truth.

Fox sees that there are many nations and many worships (see Mic. 4:5), like those of the Jews at Jerusalem and the Samaritans at Mount Gerizim. These are *particular* worships; and like all the children of Adam and their nations (or cultures, as we might say today), they vie one against the other. But Christ is come to end these worships and to set up his own worship in spirit and truth (John 4:19-24). Fox calls this the true *public* worship, because it

> hits all men and women; they must come to the spirit in themselves, and the truth in their inward parts . . . . And this worship

156

is over the worship that was at Jerusalem, and over the worship
that was at the mountain; so by this must every man, every son
of Adam, and daughter, come to the spirit in their own particulars; and the truth in themselves . . . .[4]

This worship is universal because it seeks the truth revealed in
every individual who will come to the Spirit within. Those who
come not to this Spirit will worship in "blind zeal." Fleeing
from the inward revelation, "they have worshiped images, they
have worshiped the works of their hands; they have worshiped
the dragon; they have worshiped the beast; they have worshiped
creatures . . . ."[5] Whether with stone idols or with incessantly
devised liturgies, they have worshiped *their own wills.*

> Now will-worship is among them that have the scriptures given
> forth by the spirit of God in their own wills . . . and can sing,
> pray, preach, and read in their own will, and are out of the
> spirit that gave [scripture] forth . . . . And such are opposite to
> the scriptures, that are fighting about words, falling into sects
> and heaps about the words.[6]

The hearers of these words would be painfully aware not only of
the religious wars fought over worships, like the Thirty Years
War, but also Puritanism's own quest for worship "according to
the Word of God," which led to endless splintering. Like the
ancient Jews and Samaritans, the Puritans worshiped in enmity
with one another.

All outward places of worship are incidental to the pure
worship of God, thereby obviating the socio-economic weight of
the established churches: "the public and universal worship . . .
brings all to know their bodies to be temples of the holy spirit [1
Cor. 3:16; 6:19; 2 Cor. 6:16] in which they worship, as the Jew
outwardly worshiped in his outward temple."[7] So we find this
tension in the universal worship of God — it is public, yet inward;
it is universal in its radical particularity:

> The worship in the truth never changeth . . . and this is the per-
> fect standing worship, which will stand when all worships in
> the fall are gone, devil, dragon, beast, and will-worship; for
> truth was before they all were . . . .[8]

Here, then, is a worship for all seasons, and for all men and
women, whatever their condition, to hear their heavenly

prophet who will tell them all things.

> So this is a true, certain, standing, infallible, and perfect wor-
> ship; for the truth and spirit of God are certain, infallible, and
> perfect . . . .[9]

The infallibility of this worship is limited only by the worshipers'
obedient willingness to come under its discipline.

The meaning of this worship and its unique discipline are laid
out most extensively in an early tract by Fox entitled, "To All
People on the Earth."[10] Addressing the Christian worships of the
world, Fox invokes Jeremiah's condemnation of the false
prophets: "ye are such as . . . say the Lord saith, when the Lord
never spake to you" . . . (Jer. 23). They have not known the
Word of the Lord because they have not known the time to keep
silence before the time to speak (Eccles. 3:7). They have not
cared, or dared, to stand in the counsel of the Lord in order that
they might *hear* his Word (Jer. 23:18,22). Contrary to the
apostle's advice, they are quick to speak and slow to hear (James
1:19).

Fox goes on to build his case, starting with the proclamation of
Zechariah 2:13 — "Be silent, O all flesh, before the Lord." "Now
here is a birth born of the flesh, and this birth born of the flesh,
will persecute that born of the spirit; now come all to know the
birth silent which is born of the flesh . . . ."[11] The men and
women of the Old and New Testaments display the knowledge
of this second birth of the Spirit and witness to the silence,
waiting and watching that bring it forth. After the resurrection of
Jesus, the apostles waited in Jerusalem for the promise of the
Father (Acts 2:17). This promise was fulfilled in the pouring out
of Christ's Spirit upon them, according to Joel 2:28 (Acts 2:17).

Fox also cites some of the many references in the Psalms (Pss.
25, 27, 37) to waiting upon the Lord and the strength and
salvation which are witnessed and promised there. Lamentations
3:25ff similarly testifies that

> The Lord is good unto them that wait for him, to the soul that
> seeketh him. It is good that a man should both hope and quietly
> wait for the salvation of the Lord . . . . He sitteth alone and
> keepeth silence . . . .

Fox combines this witness with that of Paul: "For the earnest
expectation of the creature waiteth for the manifestation of the

Son of God, who groan within themselves for the adoption, to wit, the redemption of the body" . . . (Rom. 8:19, 23).[12] Here we see clearly how Fox takes a passage with a clear salvation-historical horizon and finds in it a grounding and present realization in the worship experience.

Fox draws attention to the many admonitions of the apostles to watchful waiting (e.g., Matt. 25:13; James 5:8; 1 Pet. 4:7). He summarizes this posture of wakefulness thus:

> Now mind where the watching is, and the praying is, they are in the light, in that which silences all flesh . . . . Therefore come to know that watch set before every one of your mouths, so to keep that silenced which must be stopped; so what Christ saith to one, he saith unto all, watch.[13]

As the first function of the light is to judge, it brings the thoughts and words of the flesh under silent scrutiny. Those who wait in this light will receive Christ's Spirit, as the disciples did at Pentecost:

> . . . for they spoke as they were moved by the Holy Ghost, and as the spirit gave them utterance [Acts 2:4]; and they prayed in the spirit, and it helped them in their infirmities, for they could not tell what to pray for as they ought; but he that searcheth the heart, knoweth the mind of the spirit that teacheth to pray [Rom. 8:26f]. And here comes to be known the birth born of the spirit, which God the Father of spirits hears, which is not of that birth born after the flesh, but is with that persecuted.[14]

The new birth, born by the will of God to know the will of God, comes to be known in the Spirit. In silence,

> the birth is brought forth, and the light springs, and that is known and seen, that must speak, and that is known that must keep silence. Praises arise to the Lord God for ever, who is exalting the birth born of the spirit, which is feeding upon the bread of life [John 6:51], which is nourished with the life in the bosom of the Lord God of life, and the elder is become servant of the younger.[15]

In the apocalyptic modality by which the separation of the ages is seen, the pure worship of God lets one see two separate births. As with the ages, one is passing away as the other is emerging.

Yet the Christian life is lived between the two, with the first birth subjected to the second.

As always, this discernment is the result of Christ's return which reveals the end of the world:

> . . . for God is coming to take his people off from the teachings of men, and to teach his people himself, and the Lord's children shall be taught by him; and they shall cease from man, whose breath is in his nostrils [Gen. 7:22], and come to know their strength renewed [Isa. 40:31], and come to know the prophet's life . . . .[16]

Here is teaching that truly nourishes those who "in one half hour have more peace and satisfaction, than they have had from all other teachers of the world in all their life time . . . ."[17] In God's immediate teaching, "every particular comes to a particular satisfaction."[18]

Yet the religions of the world resist this teaching; people will not stop themselves in order to wait upon the Lord:

> . . . all the world's teachers, people, and professors, you are far from silence, and the silent meeting together, and waiting upon the Lord in silence, you have too much flesh in you, which speaks, and so are too full of words . . . .[19]

In their refusal to silence the words of the flesh in favor of the incorruptible seed born of the Word (1 Pet. 1:23), they continue in the first birth, which Fox finds typified by Cain, Esau, and Ishmael, the elder brothers in Genesis.

> Cain was the first birth . . . now tell Cain the envious murderer of a silent meeting or waiting upon God, when he is a vagabond from that of God in him, and so from God [and] would slay and murder them that are [like Abel] in the life; it he will slay and yet sacrifice, to which sacrifice God hath no respect [Gen. 4:1-16].[20]

Fleeing from the presence of God within, the offspring of Cain devise their own sacrifices and worships, which will not please God (also see Amos 5:21-24). "And likewise wild Ishmael the mocker [Gen. 21:9]; tell these of silent meeting and waiting upon God; nay [these] will boast and mock and scoff at that which brings to wait upon God in silence . . . ." The same holds for Esau: "now tell Esau of silence; a silent meeting is wonder to

Esau, that despiseth his birthright [the light that is given to all], and would sway the sword, and slay his brother Jacob, the second birth."[21] So the world's responses to Quaker worship find their antitypes in the three elder brothers of Genesis, who rebelled from God and did not partake of the promise.

To come to the second birth is to mortify the first birth, the earthly and natural knowledge:

> And tell you that are in your own wisdom, and in your own reason, tell you of a silent waiting upon God, that is a famine to you; it is a strange life to you to come to be silent, you must come into a new world. Now thou must die in the silence, to the fleshly wisdom, knowledge, reason, and understanding . . . . Keep to that of God in you, which will lead you up to God, when you are still from your own thoughts, and imaginations and desires and counsels of your own hearts, and motions, and will; when you stand single from all these, waiting upon the Lord, your strength is renewed; he that waits upon the Lord, feels his shepherd, and he shall not want [Ps. 23:1]; and that which is of God within every one, is that which brings them together to wait upon God, which brings them into unity, which joins their hearts together up to God.[22]

Here the apocalyptic horizon of this worship comes fully into view. A separation is seen between two differing times, worlds, and births. To come into the new world, one must die in silence and be born anew of the Word. Fox understands that the Christian sense of anthropology (that is, of human being and experience) is, as Ernst Käsemann has called it, "crystallized cosmology."[23] The insistent New Testament emphasis, that one must die to the self and be born anew to God, is made within this cosmic horizon; the individual participates in the cosmic transformation that God has promised — a new heaven and a new earth. Stated in another way, the apocalypse which shall redeem the entire creation centers on and must begin with the *apokalupsis*, the revelation, of God's righteousness in Jesus Christ to those who believe, who come to his light. Hence, the revolution which turns the world upside down (Acts 17:6) is a revelation that begins from the inside out. This explosive force shatters the self as one has formerly known it; and as one is obedient to the new knowledge given by the light, one shatters the structures of the old world.

This apocalyptic power has been definitively revealed in the cross of Christ, the wisdom of God which makes foolishness of the world's wisdom (1 Cor. 1f). Fox states mordantly the relationship between the self, the cross, and the world:

> The cross is to the carnal part, which is the ground of images, the ground of seducers, and the ground of the false prophet and antichrist; the cross is to that ground, to the root and life of it. This being minded, which is pure and eternal, it makes a separation from all other lovers, and brings to God, and the ground of evil thoughts come to be opened, and the cross is to that ground; which cross overturns the world in the heart. Which cross must be taken up by all, who follow Jesus Christ out of the world which hath an end, into the world which is without end; and all the evil things of the world must be denied. For "who loves the world, the love of the Father is not in him;" [1 John 2:15] . . . where the world is standing, the cross is not lived in. But dwelling in the cross to the world, here the love of God is shed abroad in the heart, and the way is opened . . . .[24]

Waiting upon the Lord, stopping one's self, is the taking up of the cross in worship. The power of the cross breaks the shackles of the world's sense of time, which captivates the mind,[26] and brings one to the beginning — the hearing and obeying relationship with God known in Eden. Bereft of their own words, casting off outward knowledge, all are "to stand naked and bare and uncovered before the living God. For woe is to every one, that is covered, but not with the spirit of the Lord . . . [they] will not stand in his counsel."[26] Adam and Eve covered themselves only when they had departed from his counsel (Gen. 3:7); and when God approached them, they hid from his presence.

In silence, waiting, and watching, the new time comes to be known — God's time for speaking and acting, revealed by the light. The old birth is thus laid down and a new birth raised up: "for feeling God's word in the heart to obey it, you come to know that which the prophets and apostles witnessed, the word of life which became flesh, which is Christ in us; [therefore] know him in you all upon the earth . . . ."[27] Could this experience be what the second century Christian, Ignatius of Antioch, calls "the incarnation wrought in silence" (Ephesians 19:1)?

George Fox claims that this is the worship set up by Christ sixteen hundred years before, that it was practiced by the apostles, but that it was lost by the end of the first century.[28] Could such a claim be justifiable? We have no clear record of the style of Christian worship in the first century, either from the New Testament or any other source. Nor does the Old Testament give us many clues about the worship of ancient Israel.

Biblical scholars have sometimes presented their own impressions of what the worships of Israel and the early Church were like. These models have tended to be strongly liturgical in flavor, finding blocks of biblical materials to be the hymns and litanies of early worship. The high-church backgrounds of many of these scholars may well be inducing some fanciful reconstructions. But given the paucity of information that we have, the "argument from silence" is no stronger for a thesis of early silent worship than it is for a liturgical one.

Yet could it be that, whatever the historical details of early Christian worship, Fox and the early Friends captured the essential *spirituality* of the worship and life of the apostolic generation? Fox's numerous references to the apostolic emphasis on waiting and watching remind us that the first Christian generations were saturated with expectation. There is wide agreement in New Testament scholarship that the first century lived in fervent anticipation of Christ's return to bring the entire world to an end, setting up his everlasting kingdom. This hope of the Church is most frequently ascribed to Paul, the earliest of the New Testament writers. Yet even with Paul, we find ample testimony to Christ's presence with his believers already; sometimes the language is incarnational ("Christ in me" — e.g., Rom. 8:10; 2 Cor. 13:3, 5), sometimes it is participational ("in Christ" — e.g., Rom 8:1; 2 Cor. 5:17). This language cannot be discounted as vague metaphor. Whatever and whenever Christ's final, culminating work in history might be, Paul finds Christ now present and transforming the lives of his faithful, and that corporately, these faithful incarnate Christ's presence and power in the social order. The posture of hopeful expectancy is also clear in the later writings of the New Testament, though in some, like the Gospel of John, the emphasis upon Christ's present transforming power is further amplified.

It therefore seems altogether plausible, if not necessary, to conclude that the early Church's general attitude of expectancy did inform and infuse its worship in some manner, that their watchful waiting included some conscious and disciplined intentionality of waiting upon Christ's presence to quicken and rule over worship and daily actions. Returning to Schweitzer's concept of the consistent apocalyptic viewpoint of early Christianity, surely the posture of early Christian worship was in some way informed by this end-time consciousness. Again, while we have no satisfactory description of Christian worship in the New Testament, there are some pregnant allusions made, particularly by Paul. He connects waiting for Jesus with turning from idols to serve the living God and deliverance from the wrath to come, suggesting waiting as an agenda for worship (1 Thess. 1:9f). The most descriptive references to worship are found in 1 Corinthians 14, where silence is suggested by Paul at least three times (vss 28, 30, 34). We will touch upon this passage again in our next chapter.

But let us pursue this question further back in the history of the Bible. Fox claims that this was the worship known and practiced by the prophets as well. What, then, of the worship of Israel? It does seem likely that the temple cult at Jerusalem was dominated by liturgical formulas accompanying its ritual sacrifices, anointings, etc. But what of the repeated references to waiting upon the Lord in the Psalms and the prophets? What of those few enigmatic injunctions to silence before the presence of the Lord, like the one already cited in Zechariah 2:13, or Habakkuk 2:20, or in Zephaniah 1:7 — "Keep silence at the presence of the Lord God; for the day of the Lord is at hand"? Gerhard von Rad suspects that this silence may have constituted the highest moment of the temple worship.[29]

Yet the point of silent worship, hearing and obeying, is most definitively the concern of the prophets of Israel. Jeremiah's emphasis upon standing in the counsel of God (Jer. 23:18, 22) and hearing the voice of God (Jer. 3:13, 25) may well suggest some self-censoring discipline in the prophetic vocation. Then, of course, there is the great story of Elijah's reception of new instruction in the *qol demamah*, the "voice of silence" (1 Kings 19:12). It seems altogether likely that the prophets received not only their intense moral clarity, but also their future vision, from some practice of waiting for the Word, whatever relation this practice may or may not have had with the public worship at Jerusalem. Like the New Testament Church, the prophets appear to testify to some worshipful attitude of waiting, an attitude which T. Canby Jones has called "holy expectancy."[30]

Ultimately, the dynamic of hearing God in silence surely goes back to the very bedrock of Israel's experience, to the lives of the wandering nomadic patriarchs of the desert. The great historical work of God with his people begins with Abraham, who heard God's promises and guidance as he wandered through the deserts of the ancient Near East. Anyone who has been to the desert knows the vast silence of it — almost completely devoid of even natural sounds like the rushing of streams or the rustling of leaves. This is where God first made himself known to his people. Until the conquest of the Promised Land, the Hebrew people were wandering, shepherding people, far from the uproar of the city.

The prophetic tradition in Israel maintained this desert nomadic faith of hearing God and following his leadings, even as the rest of the nation moved into more established traditions of temple cult and monarchy — practices borrowed from Canaanite neighbors. When the nation went astray, it was the prophets who stood firm and pronounced God's Word of judgment upon Israel. The prophetic faith, extending back through Moses to Abraham, is the tap root of Israel's experience of God. Israel's creation stories extend this hearing and obeying relationship back to Eden and the beginning of all things, as God's intent in creating humanity.

Before going on, let us consider one more aspect of the meaning of Quaker worship in relation to the life of Israel and the Church. We turn now to the Incarnation, the decisive revelation of God's Word in Jesus Christ. The last centuries before this event were characterized by a silence, the lack of any recognized prophetic voice in Israel. A late Psalm laments that "there is no longer any prophet" (Ps. 74:9). The same theme is found in the intertestamental literature. 1 Maccabees records decisions made by religious leaders in the absence of a prophet to give more definitive guidance (1 Macc. 4:46; 14:41). The Dead Sea Scrolls testify of the Essenes' expectation of a coming Prophet-like-Moses. Late pre-Christian Judaism thus languished without prophetic leadership up to the time of John the Baptist and Jesus. In Jesus the prophetic tradition is fulfilled and ended, in that the Word that the prophets spoke is now known in the person of Jesus Christ, who is proclaimed anew by the apostles. So the revelation of Jesus Christ marks the reappearance, death, and new birth of the prophetic faith in Judaism after a long, silent period of waiting.[31]

Unfortunately, the religious leadership of Judaism by this time had abandoned the prophetic hope, moving into a more exclusive concern with the temple cult and the legal rulings of the Scribes. Others had been seduced by the political aspirations of the Zealots. Thus we find the very limited response to the new call to prophetic faith which the gospel proclaimed to Israel and the tragic split of the early Church from its great parent. This tragedy, however, was soon compounded by the Church's own apostasy from the prophetic faith as it developed its own cultic ritual, legalism, and hierarchy in the second century.

If we accept Fox's preaching that salvation history is recapitulated in individual spiritual experience, we may see that the silence and waiting which preceded the Incarnation is answered by a silent waiting which allows the light to reveal Christ incarnated and raised up within. This revelation ends all forms of outward religion, whether Hebrew worship in the first covenant or the outward conventions adopted by the Church.

In this chapter we have examined the historical roots of Quaker worship, Fox's theological understanding of it, and his claims to biblical precedents for this worship. Finally, in pondering the relation of silent worship to the Incarnation in history, we have seen that "waiting upon the Lord" fits with Fox's teaching that the Christian experience relives the history of salvation recorded in scripture. This makes expectation — and its fulfillment — a matter of present knowledge, rather than speculation. In our next chapter we can now examine further the way in which this theological framework is put into practice in the early Quaker approach to worship and ministry.

And in his name keep your men's and women's, and all your other meetings, that you may feel him in the midst of you, exercising his offices; as he is a prophet, which God has raised up to open to you, and as he is a shepherd, who has laid down his life for you, to feed you, so hear his voice [John 10:1-18]; and as he is a counsellor and commander, follow him and his counsel; and as he is a bishop to oversee you, with his heavenly power and spirit; and as he is a priest, who offered up himself for you, who is made higher than the heavens [Heb. 7:26] . . . so, I say, know him in all his offices, exercising them amongst you, and in you. [1]

---

10. WORSHIP AND MINISTRY
IN THE COMMUNION OF CHRIST

As John's ministry of repentance prepared a way for Jesus' preaching of the Kingdom, so the Quaker practice of waiting upon the Lord clears a space within and among men and women for Christ's risen ministry to reach its full stature. When Fox writes of "meeting in the name of Jesus," he has specifically in mind this spiritual discipline by which the full *power* of Jesus' ministry may be experienced. It is his claim that only by this resolute repentance of human activity and human mediation can Christ be known in the totality of his offices, as summarized in the quotation above. This understanding of worship has revolutionary implications for the use of sacraments.

THE SACRAMENTS

Friends today sometimes interpret Quaker worship in terms of its attitude toward the sacraments, as if this were the key difference between Friends and other Christian worships. But Fox's writings do not devote much attention to the sacramental question at all. This may be partly due to the already reduced emphasis laid on sacraments in the Puritan world of Fox's day. But more to the point, if we look at the overall prophetic framework of Fox's thought, we see that sacramentalism simply becomes moot: Christ's inward presence constitutes a radical sense of communion and baptism, quickly moving the believer on to the more pressing questions of hearing and obeying.

Early Friends rejected water baptism as an outward ritual that detracts attention from Christ's true baptism by his Spirit. Fox points out that this outward-mindedness has led the Church into an apostasy of many religions with many baptisms. But "there is one faith which Christ Jesus is the author and finisher of; and there is one baptism, and by one spirit we are all baptized into one body (1 Cor. 12:13) . . . ."[2] He finds the problem of water baptism portrayed in the New Testament itself. Admitting that certainly water baptism was practiced in the early Church, Fox nevertheless points out that it became the occasion for a sectarian spirit at Corinth, leading Paul to thank God he baptized only a few, and that he was sent to preach the gospel (1 Cor. 1).

Friends were determined not to follow in what Paul evidently saw as a problematic practice, but to emphasize with him the ministry of the Word. This brings people to the true baptism of Christ, the experience of Christian worship, the death of the first birth and the raising up of the second. Christ's baptism is not a celebrative day of ritual performance, but the awful day of the Lord: "And Christ did baptize them with the Holy Ghost and with fire, and burn up their chaff with unquenchable fire" (Matt. 3:11f) . . . .[3]

Fox's views of the eucharist, or communion with bread and wine, follow the same lines. He allows that Jesus told his disciples that when they took bread and wine, to do it in remembrance of him (Luke 22:19), and that Paul repeats this command (1 Cor. 11:24f). At the same time, he points out that this practice, like water baptism, was already established in the Judaism of Jesus' time; thereby nothing really separates this act from regular Jewish feasting. So Fox does not deny feasting as a Christian fellowship; "but," he suddenly challenges his opponents:

> will you come no nearer to Christ's death than to take bread and wine in remembrance of his death? For after you have eaten in remembrance of his death, then you must come into his death and die with him if you will live with him as the apostles did . . . .[4]

Allowing a Lord's Supper of remembrance, Fox questions, however, the need of bread and wine "to show forth Christ's death till he come" (1 Cor. 11:26); for "if he be witnessed within, and known within, then he is come, then what need you have bread and wine to put you in remembrance of him?"[5] Outward rites are superfluous at best when Christ has come. More seriously, outward rites, like the outward rites of Moses, may be used by men and women to devise a righteous status of their own and not God's; a scrupulous devotion to the eucharist may blind one to the inward imperatives of Christ's own teaching.

Fox points to another supper witnessed in the New Testament, one revealed by Christ to John, in order to bring the Church off the "many outward things":

> Behold I stand at the door and knock: if any man will hear my voice, and open the door, I will come in to him, and sup with him, and he with me; he that hath an ear to hear, let him hear what the spirit saith to the churches [Rev. 3:20, 22].

This "inward and heavenly supper" can be entered only by faith. It is therefore a "higher supper" than the outward Last Supper, which was and still may be entered by betrayers and denyers of Christ. The true communion with Christ is found as one enters into a hearing and obeying relationship with him. This understanding reaches to the real significance of Jesus' last meal with his disciples; it was not the institution of a ritual observance, but the last in a long series of table fellowships in which Jesus taught his friends.[6] The fellowship with the risen Lord is a communion in which his teaching continues with those who will hear him and open the door.

But the communion of Christ is not limited to his speaking to men and women individually in their silent waiting. Christ also speaks *through* men and women as he anoints them to speak his Word in the meeting for worship.

VOCAL MINISTRY IN THE MEETING

The function of vocal ministry within the Quaker meeting for worship is to *gather* the worshiping fellowship into a common understanding of the gospel and of Christ's will for that group. Thus, Quaker ministry serves twin purposes of teaching and exhortation. Early Friends believed that since the light of Christ enlightens all, then all who have come to that light share in Christ's work of edifying his body (see 1 Cor. 14). Fox quotes 1 Peter 4:10f in this regard:

> "As every man hath received the gift, even so minister the same to another, as good stewards of the manifold graces of God; if any man speak, let him speak as the oracles of God; if any man minister, let him do it as of the ability which God giveth, that God in all things may be glorified through Jesus Christ." So here you may see the ministry is not limited to one sort of people or tribe . . . . And the apostle saith, "God hath dealt to every man a measure of faith: and he that ministered, was to wait upon his ministry; and he that exhorteth, on his exhortation; and he that teacheth, on teaching; and he that giveth, he must do it with simplicity" [Rom. 12:3-8] . . . .[7]

Quaker ministry is shaped by a radical dependence upon Christ's own ministry carried out through human instrumentality. Ministry is not a human office, but an *event* of God's grace working through his chosen vessels. All are to wait upon him in readiness for service. Hence, as we have noted earlier, the goal of Quaker worship is that Christ should be the only one to speak in the Church.

Another New Testament precedent for Quaker ministry is found in 1 Corinthians 14:29-31, Paul's advice on edifying worship:

> Let the prophets speak two or three, and let the others judge. If any thing be revealed to another that sitteth by, let the first hold his peace. For ye may prophesy one by one, that all may learn, and all may be comforted.

The powerful effect of this free ministry is also described by Paul (vss 24f):

> . . . if all prophesy, and there come in one that believeth not, or one unlearned, he is convinced of all, he is judged of all; and thus are the secrets of his heart made manifest; and so falling down on his face, he will worship God, and report that God is in you of a truth.

We see how carefully Fox and early Friends absorbed Paul's thought. New Testament interpreter Clarence Tucker Craig has commented that Quaker worship resembles Paul's description in

1 Corinthians 14 more closely than does any other modern form of Christian worship.[8] The silent restraint of prophetic worship serves two purposes: the speaker is given time to consider the validity of his or her leading before daring to speak it; and the hearer is given the time for the message to reach to the witness within and edify. Many of the unconvinced and those newly drawn to Quakerism visited the silent meetings of the early Friends and had just the kind of experience described above by Paul.[9]

While vocal ministry serves to gather the local meeting in its faith and practice, it also must gather the entire Church into the same unity. This goal was achieved in part by the wider gatherings of Friends into monthly, quarterly, and yearly meetings, where both Christ's teaching and his reign were carried out in the ministry and eldership of Friends. But these occasional gatherings were not sufficient to knit the Society together into a single body. Friends whose gifts in ministry were proven to be helpful were often sent by their local meetings on travels in the ministry, visiting other meetings, as well as witnessing the gospel to the world. Thus, Lucia Beamish[10] suggests, ministry in the meeting and ministry to the world formed a unity among early Friends, evangelism being the work of gathering men and women into meetings, and meeting ministry being the equipping of some eventually to take their message back into the world.

All this being said, and its great worth and gospel validity recognized, it is also obvious that this concept of ministry runs enormous risks. A non-professional, untrained ministry, shared by all, might easily become a "free-for-all." Indeed, in the heady days of Quakerism's first growth, particularly as many former Ranters joined the ranks, meetings were troubled by chaotic messages from minds not yet established upon the foundation of Christ's teaching. For this reason, many of Fox's epistles to Friends include large buckets of cold water for fevered brows. Nevertheless, his commitment to the free ministry is unwavering. In 1656, Fox wrote a general epistle to Friends advising meetings on how to handle unhelpful ministry. His counsel is to avoid judging any openly during the meeting, unless they be "openly profane, rebellious":

> But such as are tender, if they should be moved to bubble forth
> a few words . . . suffer and bear that, that is, the tender. And if
> they should go beyond their measure, bear it in the meeting for

peace sake, and order, and that the spirits of the world be not
moved against you. But when the meeting is done, then if any-
thing should be moved of anyone to speak to them between
yourselves or one or two of you that feel it in the life, do it in
love and wisdom that is pure and gentle from above. For love is
that which edifies . . . .[11]

One could hardly ask for a more kind and compassionate
approach to what must have been at times an exasperating
problem. Yet there is a firmness, not an indulgence, in this love.

The attitude of ministry in the meeting is one of *servanthood*
to the Word, not the mastery of one's own words:

In all openings and speakings let not the man be lifted up, for
that will not be the servant, but the master; which is to be
thrown down with that from whence the openings come. Therefore keep down that which would be lifted up in the sight of
the world; but that being lifted up which answereth that of God
in every man, this is the Son of God . . . .[12]

The declaration of the Word is not an occasion for self-glorifica-
tion; it may in fact be a matter of self-denigration in the sight of
the world. The gospel is the Word of the cross (1 Cor. 1:18), and
this Word *is* a cross to deliver: "To speak of truth, when ye are
moved, it is a cross to the will; if ye live in the truth which ye
speak, ye live in the cross to your own wills."[13] So the cross that
is first taken up in the silent waiting upon the Lord is carried
forward in vocal ministry as the meeting follows Christ out of the
present world order and into the new. The motion of the Spirit
to minister, then, is not a license but a command which must not
be refused, as long as it is clearly felt.[14]

Fox repeatedly warns against "running out ahead of the
guide," enthusiasm leading into "high words." Spirit-led
ministry lightens hearers' burdens, bringing them to Christ's
yoke, which is easy. The kingdom stands in power, not in words
(1 Cor. 4:20). The gospel preaches liberty to the captives when it
is communicated in simplicity and without pretense; impressive
intellect and eloquent words may titillate the mind, but they do
not reach to the witness of God.

Speaking the Word of the Lord therefore is a matter for
considerable circumspection. Yet when it comes, it must not be
saved for another time:

> If any have been moved to speak and have quenched that which moved them, let them not go forth afterward into words until they feel the power arise and move them thereto again. For the other part gets up, and if any go forth in that, he goeth forth in his own, and the betrayer will come in.[15]

It is the apocalyptic character of the Word's revelation that it reveals not only the Lord's *message* but also the Lord's *time* in which to declare it.

Early Quaker ministry carried a strongly prophetic consciousness, one in which those who minister bear a great responsibility for faithfulness to their revelation. In a worship that is understood to be the experience of one world passing away as a new world begins, vocal ministry can either thrust the Church forward into the Heavenly Jerusalem or send it reeling backwards to Babylon. It is not strange, therefore, that early Friends trembled frequently at the Word of the Lord (Isa. 66:2) in worship. Indeed, Paul also bids Christians to "work out your salvation in fear and trembling" (Phil. 2:12).

REJOICING IN QUAKER WORSHIP

In our examination of early Quaker worship and ministry, it would be a great mistake to give the impression that this worship was an utterly dour experience. While early Friends certainly understood it as a matter of life and death, it was also an occasion for great joy. When entire meetings would "melt into tears," it was more often than not at the experience of Christ's overwhelming love and overcoming power in their midst. Time and again in his *Journal*, Fox describes worship experiences with Friends as "brave," "glorious," and "precious" meetings.

It was not unusual for early Friends to break out in songs of praise while worshiping. But even singing was to be done in a peculiar way. It was to be a singing in the Spirit, with understanding (1 Cor. 14:15). Just as Friends rejected formulated creeds which could be mouthed as a "profession without possession," they also refrained from traditional Psalm and hymn singing for the same reasons. They instead chose to sing praises aloud spontaneously, "making melody in their hearts" (Eph. 5:19).[16] We have little idea what this early Quaker singing was like but we gain the strong impression that it did not aspire to artistry.

While Fox seems to be oblivious to the Hebrew poetic and musical conventions that underlie the Psalms and does not show any interest in what role they have played in the temple worship at Jerusalem, which certainly included singing, musical instruments, and dance, his critique of aesthetics in worship is squarely in the prophetic tradition, as succinctly stated by Amos: "Take thou away from me the noise of thy songs; for I will not hear the melody of thy viols. But let judgment run down as waters, and righteousness as a mighty stream" (Amos 5:23f). Artistic inspiration must not be equated with the Spirit of Christ. To sing in the Spirit may not sound graceful to the world's ears, but if one does not sing "with the grace that comes from Jesus,"[17] then one will eventually be found honoring God with the lips while the heart is far off (Isa. 29:13). Beautiful choirs and magnificent pipe organs, like sounding brass and tinkling cymbal in another era, may seductively displace the crucial experience of God's world-transforming love (see 1 Cor. 13).

The early Quaker understanding of a true, universal worship is thus unsparing of all forms and conventions in worship. All must be sacrificed, regardless of their particular merits, because conventions with their particular merits will appeal to peculiar tastes, and with peculiar preferences come styles, sects, and divisions. The power of the gospel is not tied to styles or cultural preferences; it is the righteousness of God revealed to men and women to receive and perform.

There is a popular notion, even among some Friends, that the Quaker "brand" of worship is not for everyone; that it requires a cool, detached, middle- to upper-class Anglo-American temperament. Not only is this notion implicitly classist and racist, it constitutes a terrible misunderstanding of what Quaker worship means. What makes this worship difficult for people of all races and temperaments to accept is the way it brings the experience of the cross into worship itself. No one takes up this cross easily. Yet it is in this quiet, sometimes desperate, prayerful attitude that one may give up one's self to God and say, "nevertheless, not my will, but thine, be done" (Luke 22:44). Here the cross is taken up and carried into the world.

Early Friends were led to make a desert of Christian worship. In so doing, they returned to the desert faith in which this strange, different God first came to be known. The desert is a harsh, unyielding place, yet its pleasures are out of this world. In the stern early Quaker denunciation of all outwardly-oriented

Christian worships, outrageous though it sounds, can we not hear the echo of the prophet Samuel, as he questioned the worship of his own day?

> Hath the Lord as great delight in burnt offerings and sacrifices as in obeying the voice of the Lord? Behold, to obey is better than to sacrifice, and to hearken than the fat of rams [1 Sam. 15:22].

THE PURITAN-QUAKER DEBATE ON THE MINISTRY

It now remains for us to examine briefly the debate which took place between Fox and his Puritan contemporaries regarding the ministry of the gospel. Among the leading Puritan figures whose criticism of Quakers we have reviewed, none makes any direct comment on Quaker worship itself, except for John Owen, who briefly allows that silent meetings might have some edification.[18]

The most extensive and substantial attacks come from Richard Baxter, who seems to have been deeply scandalized by the Quaker criticism of the established professional ministry. He responded to this criticism in four different anti-Quaker tracts.[19] Due either to seventeenth-century polemical style or to the possibility that he simply did not encounter any adequate interpretation of Quakerism, Baxter does not display an incisive understanding of Quaker ministry or its critique of Reformed ministry.

It is Baxter's apparent impression that while the Quakers revile the Church and ministers of Christ, they offer no alternative. The Quakers' "prating against God's servants" is much worse than that of any other group; this cannot be the language of the Spirit of Christ. Baxter connects the Quaker attack upon the clergy with their refusal to give honor (hat honor and titles) to civil authorities; in dishonoring both magistrates and ministers, they were said to be breaking the fifth commandment (honor thy father and mother), suggesting that they may be enemies of the Commonwealth.[20] He remarks with incredulity that he has been called a devil and a dog by Quakers because he is called "Master" and stands above the people, preaching by the hour glass and by doctrine: "Doth the Christian Religion consist in such ridiculous accusations as these?"[21] Thus, respected ministers are damned by "a boy or a wench that's but a Quaker, as confidently as if God had bid them to speak it."[22]

More than once, Baxter defends scripture as the Word (together with the preaching of the Word) against Quaker accusations. Along with the Puritan doctrine of an extraordinary bestowal of the Spirit in New Testament times, Baxter affirms that the apostles had an extraordinary ministry. Since that generation, only an ordinary gift of the Spirit is known, and an ordinary ministry is provided until Christ comes. God calls these ordinary ministers himself, commanding that they be ordained according to qualifications. The Church cannot subsist without these officers; the people are "bound to know, honor, and obey them in the Lord."[23]

Though he can call ministers "the humble, holy servants of God," Baxter clearly views the clergy as socially, intellectually, and spiritually exalted above their congregations. This is apparent, for example, when Baxter states that his reason for writing against such a ridiculous people as the Quaker is that "they are attracting the gullible in droves,"[24] and that they take advantage of the ignorance and ungodliness of the common people.[25] He bids faithful Christians to hold to the Word of God (scripture, of course) and listen to their ministers and their doctrines.[26]

Richard Baxter was one of the great pastors of the Puritan watershed, and his many other writings contain a wealth of passages far better than the ones found in these controversial tracts. Yet even with Baxter we find this theme of clerical elitism which was not uncommon in Puritanism. This elitism became a central focus of the Quaker protest against the clergy. The light of Christ had revealed to Friends the way in which the rule of ministers mocked the lordship of Christ.

> In the eternal light . . . we see the priests bear rule by their means [Jer. 5:31] now, and seek gain from their quarters [Isa. 56:11] now, and are greedy dumb dogs [Isa. 56:10f] now . . . we see teachers who profess they are sent of Christ, to be in the seat of the Scribes and Pharisees, and are called masters, and have the chief places, going in their long robes, love salutations in the markets, have the uppermost seats at feasts, and under pretence making long prayers, devouring widows' houses, which Christ cried against [Mark 12:38-40; Matt. 23:2-8; Luke 20:41f].[27]

We see early Friends shared with Jesus himself "such ridiculous accusations as these.'' Like Jesus, Fox proclaims woe and a day of reckoning to those who covet the world's glory.

As always, Fox connects the leadership of the established Church with that of the Scribes and Pharisees in New Testament times. In both cases, their rule is too often by virtue of their *command* of the letter of scripture, rather than through *obedience* to the Spirit that gave forth scripture.

> So they that had the letter knew not the word, and they that have the letter know not the voice now, nor the word, but fly to the priest's lips and synagogues, and temple, and there the priest's lips that takes the tithes must preserve their knowledge, and so will not hear the word Christ, nor the voice, but imprison and persecute them that come to tell them of this word . . . .[28]

Though Fox's most severe attacks focus on the tithe system supporting the state church, he is generally critical of the social and economic franchise that the established ministry, whether state supported or not, has made of its teaching of the scriptures. Fox records his revulsion at the ''making a merchandise of the scriptures'':

> . . . and when I heard the bell toll to call the people together to the steeplehouse, it struck at my life, for it was just a market-bell to gather people together that the priest might set forth his ware to sale. Oh, the vast sums of money that are gotten by the trade they make of selling the scriptures, and by their preaching, from the highest bishop to the lowest priest! What trade else in the world is comparable to it, notwithstanding the scripturtes were given forth freely, and Christ commanded his ministers to preach freely, and the prophets and apostles announced judgment against all covetous hirelings and diviners for money.[29]

Baxter was right in his observation that the Quakers made the greatest protest against the established ministry of that day. They did so because they questioned not only the increasingly maligned tithe system but even the very idea of a professional guild of ministers, standing more above the people than under the Lord.

The term ''hireling'' became the favorite Quaker appelative for the clergy. The term is, of course, derived from John 10:12f, in which the hireling shepherd is the one who will not guard the flock against the wolves. He will not lay down his life, as Christ the true shepherd does, but flees. Friends saw the truth of this teaching in their own time when the Restoration outlawed not only Quaker gatherings but many Puritan fellowships, as well. Their leaders either returned to the state Church or carried on their ministry secretly. Quaker ministers of Christ, however, continued their ministry in the open, preaching publicly. For this witness they suffered imprisonments and even death.

In professionalizing the ministry, Quakers asserted that the Church had created a guild, operating within a framework of its own traditions. Professional preaching could so easily become preaching *for* a commission, rather than *by* a spiritual commission, like Isaiah had (Isa. 61:1f). The hour glass became the perfect symbol to Friends of a ministry that subsists too much by the world's reckoning. Anxious about the world's time, anxious for the world's sense of security, rather than first seeking the kingdom of God and his righteousness (Matt. 6:31-33), the professional ministry will find itself concerned with its own perpetuation instead of laboring in service to the Lord. It is important to remember that Fox's critique of the established ministry, like the established Church, is not a condemnation of all *individuals* therein; he encountered many "tender" Puritans, some of them ministers. His critique is of the *institutions* of the Church and ministry, the powers and principalities which mock the power of the gospel and restrain people (ministers included) from it.

Nevertheless, Fox did encounter many clergymen who were very jealous of their power and prestige. Setting up the outward letter in place of the true Word revealed within, these ministers were in fact engaged in the trade of idolatry, the worship of the creature in place of the Creator (Rom. 1:25):

> . . . now the doctors and teachers of the world, who be in the nature of the Jews, have given the writings the name of Christ, whose name is "The Word of God" [Rev. 19:13], and persecute them that do not bow to their image.[30]

Here Fox's critique of the Church and its investment in the Bible as the Word comes into its sharpest focus. The charge of idolatry is more radical than even Paul's charges against his legalistic opponents. Yet Fox is simply applying Paul's own insights on the inwardness of the Spirit *versus* the outwardness of the letter and fleshly reckoning in Romans 2:29.

In 1655, Fox and a companion rode into Cambridge, where they were physically attacked in the streets by the seminarians,

> for they knew I was so against their trade, which they were there as apprentices to learn, the trade of preaching, that they raged as bad as ever Diana's craftsmen did against Paul [Acts 19].[31]

Fox understands the hostility of the clergy to the Quaker message and ministry as arising from the same spiritual condition as those idol-makers of Ephesus were in, as they saw their position endangered by the gospel.

Fox and the early Friends preached this gospel, not in order to set up their own tradition and teaching establishment, but in order that men and women might also receive this same gospel by the same revelation of Jesus Christ. Their task, therefore, was to lead people to Christ's direct and free teaching within them. That "Christ is come to teach his people himself" represents the most radically disenfranchising power that has ever confronted the social and economic structures of the Church.

Pastors like Richard Baxter simply could not believe that Christ's teaching could so transform the "gullible," "ignorant," "ungodly," "common people" — especially a mere "boy" or "wench." Early Friends knew otherwise, but not because of some proto-liberal view of a great inherent worth and dignity of each person; quite the opposite — all are ungodly, spiritually ignorant, and gullible without Christ's light, regardless of their education or social background. If God is no respecter of persons (Acts 10:34), then Friends felt bound not to be either. Their attack upon the clergy, therefore, had to be sharp and relentless or this point never could have been made adequately. The day of trial which Quaker preaching revealed must indict especially those who have been most honored in the world's eyes. This indictment went far beyond social and religious protest. It constituted revolutionary spiritual warfare. Friends understood their witness as part of a conflict that would determine the course of the Church, the people of God.

For I was made to open the state of the Church in the primitive times and the state of the Church in the wilderness, and the state of the false Church that was got up since; and that now the everlasting Gospel was preached again over the head of the beast, whore, and false prophets, and antichrist, which had got up since the apostles' days.[1]

11. THE LAMB'S WAR
AND THE CONSUMMATION OF HISTORY

George Fox's message offered an understanding of Christ's work that stands distinctly apart from those of Catholicism and Protestantism. The key to this difference is the way Fox places the Christian experience in a thoroughly apocalyptic framework that, while witnessed and interpreted by scripture, is decisively independent of scripture or the tradition of the Church.

The unique message Fox preached contained strong implications for the relationship of the Quaker movement to the Catholic and Protestant churches. It could not simply be a *renewal* movement within established Church structures, something like the function of the Protestant and Catholic charismatic movements of today. Neither could it see itself as a further refinement of the *reform* motives of the Protestant watershed. Instead, Fox and the early Friends saw their message and mission in the most radical terms. It was their calling to raze the structures of the churches to their foundations and to *restore* men and women upon the foundation of Christ's direct teaching, for which there can be no substitute (see 1 Cor. 3:10f). This calling demanded nothing less than *revolution*[2] among the churches in all their social, economic and political aspects.

Early Friends were not satisfied simply to break from the existing churches and go their own way, following the sectarian trend of mid seventeenth-century England. Nor did they entertain dreams of attaining state power with which to enforce their vision upon the nation. Unwilling to accept either denominational relativism or state church absolutism, they advanced upon the world trusting solely in one power, the power of the gospel. This gospel they knew to be a revelation which had overthrown them in their own personal lives, bringing them into subjection to Christ. It had brought them to a new order of Church government radically at the disposal of Christ's leadership. Now they were confident that this power should overthrow the established church structures which stood in opposition to Christ's immediate reign.

Fox claims this revolutionary vision to come from Christ's inward teaching, especially as it opened to him that most exotic book of the Bible, the Book of Revelation. This book has always posed the greatest challenges for interpretation, probably accounting in part for the hesitance with which it was accepted into the New Testament canon. It constitutes a highly developed example of apocalyptic literature, which flourished in Jewish and Christian circles approximately from 200 B.C. to 200 C.E. Over the centuries, it has received a diversity of interpretations rivalled by no other book of the Bible. Today it remains a closed and forbidding text to many. For these reasons, it is important that we give an overview of Revelation, the Apocalypse of John, before moving on to Fox's interpretation of it. In this overview we are informed most by the work of Elisabeth Schüssler-Fiorenza,[3] a leading modern interpreter of the Book of Revelation.

THE BOOK OF REVELATION

Revelation is a text heavily laden with symbolism; it draws upon images and mythological traditions from many sources — Old Testament, Jewish, pagan. While these appear to pour forth in a wild, incoherent stream, they are in fact highly structured to give the book a singular and compelling message to Christians living in a time of growing persecution, probably in the last decade of the first century. The book's overall structure is commonly seen as dividing into seven parts. Indeed, the number seven, symbol of totality and completion in Jewish tradition, is a key theme in Revelation; sequences of seven seals, seven trumpets, and seven bowls, as well as figures with seven eyes or seven heads, communicate to the Christian community that forces of absolute good and absolute evil are coming into a conflict that will consume the present world order and consummate world history. Therefore, Revelation is a prophetic interpretation of the Christian community's present situation in terms of God's ultimate future.

This book must be interpreted as a whole, unified statement; its rich symbolism can inspire all kinds of interpretations if any part is taken out of the context of the whole. At the same time, the progression of visions in Revelation does not describe a linear sequence of future historical events. The visions instead portray in tableaux the dynamic of struggle between the forces of Christ and those of Satan, with the earthly actors in this struggle as the Christian community and the Roman Empire.

The apocalyptic question — who is lord of the universe? — was painfully pressed upon the Church in Asia Minor as Rome, under the Flavian emperors, demanded that all its subjects participate in the imperial cult, the offering of divine honors to Caesar as lord and ruler. While this rite was put in religious dress, it clearly amounted to little more than a political "pledge of allegiance." Evidently, some Christians were willing to make this compromise, feeling that it did not seriously contradict Christ's power and kingdom among them. Moreover, those who would not comply apparently suffered Rome's economic and social sanctions against them (13:5). Some faced imprisonment or even death (13:10).

Against this accommodating trend in the Church, John presents his visions as a stern warning and exhortation to radical witness to Christ's lordship. John himself has suffered exile to the island of Patmos "for the word of God, and for the testimony of Jesus" (1:9). The Church as a body must witness the kingdom of the risen Christ now or be excluded from his reign when it covers the earth in the future. Christ is coming to reign with justice; he will judge Rome for its blasphemies and for its oppression of the nations. Churches which cooperate with Rome shall be judged with Rome. Schüssler-Fiorenza points out that it is the centrality of this question of lordship that makes the *throne* the central symbol of Revelation.

Scholars vary in the way they divide up Revelation's seven

sections. We will follow Schussler-Fiorenza's concentric scheme of sections, which she outlines as A B C D C' B' A'. Section A (1:1-8) sets forth the book as both an apocalyptic vision and as a general epistle to the churches of Asia Minor. Verses 7f set the book's sights upon the key reference point, Christ's return in glory to reign on earth. Everything that follows about the present situation has been laid out from that perspective.

Section B (1:9-3:22) addresses the present crisis. John has been banished to Patmos for his witness (1:9f). He has a vision of the risen Christ, who tells him to write down what he sees and to send it to the seven churches of Asia Minor (1:11). That Christ is present with these churches is symbolized by his walking among seven candlesticks (1:13, 20). He dictates to John a short epistle to each of the seven churches (2:1-3:22). These contain a mixture of condemnations and promises. The seventh letter, to the Church at Laodicea, contains the most severe condemnation — for their wealth and ease as other Christians suffer (perhaps they have most accommodated the imperial cult?). Yet this letter also contains Christ's most sublime promise: if they will open the door to him, he will sup in intimate communion with them; persevering in the faith, they will ultimately share his throne with him (3:20-22).

Section C (4:1-9:21; 11:14-19) takes John up to heaven to view the divine court of God and Christ. In the right hand of God is a book which no human can open. But the Lamb, a figure with seven horns and seven eyes, signifying Christ in his omnipotence and omniscience, comes forward to receive and open the book. The Lamb receives cosmic authority as he receives the book and breaks its seven seals in order to open it. This opening reveals the conflict that will decide the world's outcome. Since much of what follows is described in imagery drawing from the Old Testament, the book may also be seen as the scriptures themselves. The Lamb thus takes power over history in this act. The breaking of the first six seals unleashes a series of catastrophes upon the earth. The seventh seal, the breaking of which opens the book, is followed by half an hour's silence in heaven.

With the opening of the scroll, seven angels blow seven trumpets, unleashing more cataclysms upon the earth and its inhabitants. The effect of each of these trumpets is to reverse the order of God's creation in Genesis 1, until with the fifth trumpet the bottomless pit is opened and chaos overcomes the earth again. These trumpet visions echo the plagues upon Egypt in

Exodus; they are not to be taken as literal predictions, but instead thematize the demand for repentance (see 9:20f). All those who repent and turn to God will be received (11:18).

Section D (10:1-11:13; 12:1-15:14) forms the center and pivot point of Revelation. It focuses attention upon the earthly conflict between the Church and the satanic power of Rome. These crucial visions begin with a second commissioning of John to prophesy (10:1-11:13), in which he is given a scroll to eat. It is sweet in his mouth, as God's Word of salvation to proclaim; but in his stomach it is sour, suggesting the persecution which the Word can bring (cf. Ezek. 3:1-4). The power and the suffering of the Christian prophet are dramatized in the succeeding vision of the two witnesses.

Next comes a vision in heaven of a conflict between a woman and a dragon. The woman, symbolizing the faithful Israel, gives birth to a child, to be understood as the Messiah. The dragon, identified as "that old serpent" (see Gen. 3) and Satan, deceiver of the world, attacks the woman and attempts to devour the child. The child is caught up to the throne of God, symbolizing Christ's resurrection. The woman flees to the wilderness, where she is protected and nurtured by God for a prescribed period of time. The dragon is cast down to earth, where he makes war upon God's faithful.

The nature of this war is amplified as John sees two beasts raised up by the dragon to persecute the remnant of the woman's seed (13:1-18). The first beast represents the oppressive political power of Rome. The beast and the dragon form a demonic counterpart to the divine power and relationship of Christ and God. The beast has power over the nations and people, who worship him. The beast *parodies* Christ with its powers, which are oppressive rather than liberating, claiming names that are a blasphemy against God. The second beast extends and enforces the parody of Christ. He appears like the Lamb, but speaks like the dragon (13:11), and in later references is called the false prophet (16:13; 19:20; 20:10). Representing the imperial cult, this beast forces all to worship the imperial power of the first beast, persecuting and even murdering those who refuse.

Over against this terrible power, John's next vision portrays the Christian community of faith (14:1-5) as one hundred and forty-four thousand standing on Mount Zion with the Lamb. They sing to the Lord a new song, being freed of sin, following the Lamb wherever he goes (14:4). Though this Zion is in the middle of the beast's dominion, these faithful have resisted the beast, its deception, and its worship. Immediately after the revelation of this opposition community, John sees an angel with an everlasting gospel to proclaim to every nation, kindred, tongue, and people (14:6). The content of this proclamation is this: "Fear God, and give glory to him; for the hour of his judgment is come" (14:7) . . . . Thus, with the revelation of the two powers in conflict, the decisive hour of judgment is proclaimed.

First announced is the judgment upon Babylon (14:8-13). Babylon is a new figure, that of a prostitute, which also represents Rome. She is the demonic counterpart of the woman seen in Chapter 12. Whereas the beasts represent Rome's brute force of repression, Babylon portrays Rome's seductive power. She has offered her cup of wine to all the world, to seduce the nations into worshiping the beast. All those, including Christians, who accept this cup will be judged with Babylon.

Section C' (15:5-18:24) initiates the resolution of Revelation with the judgment and execution of Babylon. This begins with the emptying of seven bowls, or vials, of God's wrath upon the earth (15:5-16:21). Again, themes from the Exodus plagues are recalled, and the emphasis is upon the refusal of the beast's worshipers to repent; in the end, they only curse God (16:21). Now follows the destruction of Babylon (17:1-18:24). First, the tremendous wealth and magnificence of Rome are portrayed, with "the great whore" riding upon the beast, dressed gloriously, holding her wine cup. She is drunk with the blood of the prophets, saints, and inhabitants of the earth (17:6; 18:24). She sits upon many waters, representing the peoples, nations, and languages of the earth. As her destruction is described, the prophetic warning goes out to all who cooperate with the Roman Empire: "Come out of her, my people, that ye be not partakers of her sins, and that ye receive not of her plagues" (18:4). Like the call to Israel to come out of Egypt, this cry declares not only the oppressor's judgment but the liberation of God's people as well.

This liberation is envisioned in Section B' (19:1-22:9), beginning with the announcement of God's reign on earth and the invitation to the wedding feast of the Lamb (19:1-10). This reign is consolidated in a great battle (19:11-21). In this vision, heaven opens to reveal Christ as a horseman whose name is the Word of God. Out of his mouth comes a sharp sword. Christ and his army battle with the forces of the beast and false prophet. These two figures are captured and thrown into a lake of fire. After this, the Abyss below the earth is opened and the dragon is thrown into it. After a thousand years, Satan is loosed upon the earth once more for a final battle, in which he is thrown into the lake of fire (20:1-11).

With evil finally and utterly defeated, the heavens and earth pass away and the final resurrection of the dead takes place, in which all — Christians and others — are judged according to their deeds (20:11-15). Even Hades and death itself are now cast into the lake of fire. This makes possible the appearance of a new heaven and a new earth, along with the establishment of the glorious city of God (21:1-22:5). The New Jerusalem comes down from heaven as a bride prepared for her wedding. This feminine figure, though not explicitly linked with the woman in Chapter 12, is logically to be identified with her as the true Israel/Church, whose undying love for Christ, the Word and Lamb, is now consummated. This heavenly city is described in terms which express the immediate presence of God and Christ with the faithful; its center is the throne of God. The return to Eden is suggested by the presence of the tree of life, available to all. There is no temple; the presence of the Lord is throughout the city, giving continuous light.

The angel who has shown John the glory of this great city now speaks to John, and we are suddenly reminded that this is a message to the churches in a present time of temptation and suffering. Section A' (22:6-21) brings us "back to earth," making this sublime vision an urgent exhortation to hold fast to the faith. Christ comes soon to fulfill all these visions; the Spirit, the bride, and the faithful all say "Come!" (22:17).

FOX'S INTERPRETATION OF REVELATION

George Fox writes that in 1647, at the age of twenty-three,

> I had great openings concerning the things written in the Revelations; and when I spoke of them, the priests and professors would say that was a sealed-up book, and would have kept me out of it, but I told them Christ could open the seals, and that they were the nearest things to us, for the Epistles were written to the saints that lived in former ages, but the Revelations were written of things to come.[4]

186

Though Fox clearly has a singular grasp of scripture as a whole, Revelation is the only text for which he particularly notes a breakthrough in interpretation. It is also the only book of the Bible to receive an extended, point-by-point interpretation in his writings.[5] But its significance to him is best revealed by the way its language infuses and informs page after page, volume after volume of his works.

As we examine Fox's use of Revelation, we shall again see that he finds the inward experience of Christ informing his understanding of God's ultimate future, even as God's ultimate future, as seen by John, informs his inward experience, interpreting it and leading it into religious and political action in history. This is the same apocalyptic resonance we have described in a number of ways already, suggesting that the Christian experience participates not only in the past history of God's acts as recorded in scripture, but in the future, final acts promised there as well. When Fox declares "now the ages are come"[6] (see 1 Cor. 10:11; Eph. 2:7), he witnesses to an experience that has taken him to the end of the world, where he may *see* not only God's acts up to the end of the apostolic generation, but also the apocalyptic struggle described by John in Revelation. Therefore, John's assertion that he is *in* the kingdom of Jesus Christ (1:9) comes as no surprise to Fox. If John were not standing at this eschatological vantage point, he could never have had the revelations that follow. John "is not only an heir to the kingdom, but in it. And this many witness, that are witnesses to Jesus Christ . . . ."[7]

The Lamb's Power. Fox finds the opening of scripture and the future of the world witnessed in John's vision of the Lamb breaking the seven seals on the book in Revelation 6:1-8:1. "And it is he that opens to his people now the book of the law and prophets, and the gospel and revelation, and the book of life, which we witness."[8] This revelation is to be sought in the discipline of Quaker worship, a practice which affords men and women a companionship with John in both the kingdom and the tribulation (1:9). The judgments upon the earth that are described by John with the breaking of the seven seals are known in the practice of waiting upon the Lord. Here the birth according to the flesh is silenced and judged, so that the birth according to the Spirit may be raised up. Fox describes this event in a 1648 vision:

I saw there was a great crack throughout the earth, and a great smoke to go as the crack went; and that after the crack there should be a great shaking. This was the earth in people's hearts, which was to be shaken before the Seed of God was raised up out of the earth. And it was so; for the Lord's power began to shake them, and great meetings we began to have . . . .[9]

This shaking fulfills the breaking of the sixth seal, the penultimate of the series; John sees a great earthquake which displaces and darkens the natural order (6:12-14). Fox and the early Friends understood their frequent experiences of quaking in worship as this earthquake, in which the seed begins to break free of the earthly, fleshly birth.

Fox stresses that this experience is not new with the Quakers; quoting from scripture, he notes that Moses, David, Job, Jeremiah, Isaiah, Habakkuk, Joel, Daniel, and Paul were all quakers,[10] trembling at the same power of Christ.

. . . and the trumpet is blown in Zion, and the alarm is sounded in his holy mountain, which makes the earth to tremble [Joel 2:2, 10], and it doth tremble at the word of the Lord [Isa. 66:2] . . . at whose voice Moses exceedingly did quake [Heb. 12:21], which power and voice now is known among us, which doth not only shake the earth but the heavens [Heb. 12:26], which power removes that which may be shaken, that that which cannot be shaken may remain and appear [Heb. 12:27].[11]

Again, Friends testified to a Spirit and power that had been known by the apostles *and* the prophets; they shared the same inward revelation of God's Word.

Quakers were scorned by Puritans as enthusiasts for this testimony of their bodies. Fox answers with a stern warning during the height of Quaker persecutions in the 1670s:

. . . the wrath of the Lamb shall find you out [Rev. 6:16]. When the sun is turned black as sackcloth of hair, and ye shall know the great earthquake [Rev. 6:12], then ye will not scoff at, nor persecute the people of God, in scorn called Quakers.[12]

To deride those whose very bodies witness the terrifying power of the Lamb is to reveal that one simply does not know the Lamb.

The earthquake, however, is not the revelation of Christ himself, but only the judgment that is the prelude to the seventh seal, which opens the book. Like the experience of Elijah at

Mount Horeb (1 Kings 19), where cataclysms of earthquake, wind, and fire precede the true revelation of God in silence, so the breaking of the seventh seal by the Lamb is followed by half an hour of silence in heaven (8:1). This is the breakthrough of Quaker worship: "He that hath an ear to hear, let him hear: such as know the seven seals, shall know the silence in heaven."[13] In this silence, the scriptures are at last opened to spiritual understanding, and the ages are seen and comprehended.

As the seed is raised up, the believer is "redeemed from the earth" (14:3), to see the old world passing away and a new creation beginning. Dwelling in the power of Christ, one dwells in the end of all things: "They that live in it may take a prospect of these wonderful things and workings of the Lord God and his power in this age."[14] So the kingdom and fulfillment in Christ are known now. But this sublime experience does not remain a private domain; as in what follows in the Book of Revelation, a vast world-historical panorama of apocalyptic conflict unfolds in this "prospect," one in which Christ's followers are called to participate.

> And all you that have received the power of Christ in your hearts, have you not seen what wars, and what rumours, and nation against nation [Matt. 24:6f; Mark 13:7f], as it was in the two births in the womb, that came forth . . . and so here he being received, here is people against people, and nation against nation, and earthquakes, and shakings within and without. They that receive the Lord's power must feel this, and know this, and see the fulfilling of it, and not look out, for his kingdom without, like a company of Pharisees, lo here, lo there [Luke 17:20f], but as Christ, the power of God, is known within . . . and as they come to feel it there, they shall know the shakings and earthquakes . . . and that part that pertains to nations, that must be shaken [cf. Hag. 2:7] before they come to be of the holy nation, which is against the other; and this is to be known, and seen, and felt, and fulfilled with the power of Christ Jesus, and by his spirit . . . .[15]

> Therefore, as I said, keep in Christ's power, in which the kingdom stands, and not in words, that you may see the fulfilling of the scripture . . . .[16]

The inward experience of the war between the fleshly birth and the spiritual birth, which Fox describes in the discipline of Quaker worship, brings one to see his or her part in a wider cosmic conflict. The reception of Christ's power and authority forms a holy nation, the Church, which finds itself in opposition to outward kingdoms and authorities of the world as they stand against Christ's kingdom. The power of Christ, in which the Church stands, is an unshakeable force which shakes the outward powers until they shall become of Christ's holy nation. This view of the apocalyptic struggle brings us now to Fox's interpretation of the pivotal section of Revelation, the vision of two authorities.

The Beast and False Prophet. As we have seen throughout this study, Fox maintains a relentlessly critical view of the established churches of his day, both Catholic and Protestant. His opposition arises from his view of the primary source of authority in the Church. It is neither the hierarchy of the Roman Church, established upon the concept of apostolic succession; nor is it scripture, taken by Protestantism to be the Word of God, rule for all matters of doctrine and practice. Looking at these positions historically, we can see that they were derived from a shift in the Church's devotion — from the authority of *revelation* by which the apostles had formulated their teaching, to the authority of *tradition* and *succession* of that teaching and authority. The tradition and authority of the apostles became a commodity that could be possessed by "successors" without the revelation — even in *alienation* from that revelation — of the living Christ. In Fox's view, the authority of the Church must be the *living* authority of Christ's living Word to his people, to be heard "in all things." In his declaration that "Christ is come to teach his people himself," Fox sets all matters of faith and practice in a consistently apocalyptic framework. Just as the symbol of the throne is central to Revelation, challenging Christians to witness the heavenly authority of Christ above the earthly authority of Caesar, so Fox challenges the churches in their choice of the earthly authority of scripture and Church tradition over the divine authority of Christ's own teaching.

In one of his more "ecumenical" moments, Fox can allow of Luther and Calvin that "something was stirring in them. Luther was true in his place, but it was but a little . . . ."[17] He asserts that the Quakers have made a more thorough job of Protestantism in that they "protest against all that which the apostatized spirit hath set up, which is erred from that power and spirit the apostles were in."[18] Ultimately, however, the Quakers in their sense of revelation cannot be fundamentally linked with Catholicism or Protestantism, "but they are of the apostles' stock, and of Abraham, and of Christ . . . ."[19] Fox particularly attacks Protestantism's failure to abolish the professional clergy, the tithe system, and the national church.

George Fox sees the beginnings of a great apostasy in the Church witnessed in Revelation's portrayal of Christians who have compromised Christ's lordship. This was the beginning of the false Church and "the false prophets, which Christ said should come [Matt. 7:15; 24:11, 24], and John saw were come, and how all the world wondered after them [Rev. 13:3]; how they filled the world with false doctrines, ways, worships, and religions . . . ."[20] Just as some Christians in John's time were coerced and seduced into worshiping a vain idol representing a human ruler, Fox describes the false Church that followed them thus: "the eyes of the people have been after men, and not after the Lord."[21]

This turning away occurred when the Church began to value the apostles' words, or writings, more than the Spirit that the apostles were in. The Church set up human rulers as successors to these apostles who themselves had never exercised such authority. With many human rulers, the Church became like the beast, having many heads, rather than the one head, Jesus Christ. These heads became authoritative interpreters of the apostles' writings, much as the Scribes had exercised power in their expertise in the laws of Moses. And where apostolic tradition was insufficient or unspecific, pagan inventions were sometimes adopted in worship and Church government. Thus, "the apostate Christians have sat since the apostles' days, in their rudiments, inventions, handiworks, and traditions, and cannot sit long in them, therefore turn one against the other."[22] With many heads, many bodies soon follow in the false Church.

The leaders of the false Church are, like the second beast in Revelation 13, justly named "false prophets" because they profess to succeed and follow the apostles, yet they do not know, and may even "quench," the prophetic Spirit of the apostles. The false Church, seen as the beast, or antichrist, and its leaders, the false prophets, therefore *parody* the true Church and true prophets. The false prophet looks like the Lamb but speaks like the dragon (13:11), deceiving the Church, turning it from

Christ's direct rule in order to follow, at best, a human rule.

The beast utters blasphemies against God (13:3). Fox finds this blasphemy most succinctly in the Church's denial of a present power of God to overcome sin.

> Now since the apostles and martyrs were killed, and true ministry, and the church fled into the wilderness, do not you and your false church say, that people must sin while they be on the earth, and so preach up sin? . . . and what good doth your preaching do, if they must have sin while they are upon the earth?[23]

This denial of a perfecting faith in the power of the gospel succeeds the Roman Empire's blasphemy against God, denying God's power and kingdom on earth, causing men and women to submit in their hopelessness to the authority of men. Fox invokes Jesus' own invectives against the earthly religious rulers of his day:

> Woe unto you, scribes and Pharisees, hypocrites! for ye shut up the kingdom of heaven against men: for ye neither go in yourselves, neither suffer ye them that are entering to go in [Matt. 23:13] . . . Woe unto you, lawyers! for ye have taken away the key of knowledge; ye entered not in yourselves, and them that were entering in ye hindered [Luke 11:52].[24]

The priesthood of the false Church is therefore the same as the priesthood of the first covenant, which made nothing perfect (Heb. 7:19). Ironically, Friends themselves were accused of blasphemy for preaching perfection. Fox counters, "Doth not Christ say, 'Be ye perfect as your heavenly Father is perfect' [Matt. 5:48]? Is that blasphemy? . . . Whose ministers are you?"[25] Again, we see Fox adapt the accusations of his opponents to show that *they* are ignorant of, and in opposition to, Christ's power.

With the rise of the false Church and the deceiving ministry of the false prophets, the dragon has driven the woman, the true Church and true ministry into the wilderness (12:6). The people who know and do God's will, "Christ in the flesh, the true church fled into the wilderness."[26] This is the remnant of true Christian faith, weltering in a wilderness as it is scattered, repressed, and persecuted by the earthly powers of the false Church. Though Fox in general consigns sixteen centuries of Church history to this long, dark night of apostasy, it is not without its faithful individuals and even some glimmerings of the true Church gathered. While Fox makes no effort to compile a listing of these, he regards the persecuted gatherings of the Waldensians and Lollards as evidence that "God left not himself without witness" (Acts 14:17).

Babylon. When the issue of religious persecution arises in Fox's writings, it is often described in connection with the figure of Babylon, portrayed in Revelation as drunk with the blood of the saints, martyrs, and prophets (17:6; 18:24). Symbolizing Rome's tremendous social, economic, and political power, Babylon is seen in Revelation riding upon the beast (17:3). To Fox this union represents the demonic marriage of the Church and the state. In this union the Church not only keeps people from the power of the apostolic faith, but it also subjugates them into its false gospel and false order. Babylon's earthly power and glory are so great that even John marvels and wonders "with great admiration" (17:6) upon seeing her, as one might admire a great cathedral. She has used her splendor to make the kings and inhabitants of the earth "drunk with the wine of her fornication" (17:2). Like John, Fox uses the term "fornication" to speak of the apostasy from the Spirit of Christ. "This woman, the false church . . . is whored from the spirit of God . . . ."[27]

Having forsaken the prophetic order of the apostles, the Church was bound eventually to turn to state authority to settle its differences and fight its battles:

> And they confess, they have not the same power and spirit of the apostles; so then it is true for them to say, we are not spiritual men, we have not spiritual weapons to fight withal; if ye do not help us, higher powers, we fall. For we hold our traditions by the earthly powers . . . and to them we go with our packet of letters, as Saul did; for we are not spiritually weaponed men as Paul was.[28]

The Babylonian splendor of the state churches is a triumph gained by the help of earthly powers, but the true Church must triumph by the power of God alone.

Babylon's Constantinian juggernaut is spread over many nations, peoples, and tongues (17:1,15), and though she has been shaken and broken into separate parts (16:19) by schisms and reformations, her power and persecutions persist, even under as tolerant a regime as Cromwell's. Thus, even English Separatism was not fully free of Babylon's thrall. Francis Howgill, a former Seeker who became a leading figure in the early Quaker preaching movement, wrote that the Separatists had not yet come to deny the *ground* of apostasy, only some of its *practices;* even the best of them had not escaped Babylon, but were "yet in the suburbs thereof."[29]

The True Church, Lamb's War, and Harvest. The Quaker experience of Christ's teaching and the preaching of this experience as Christ's return formed a community which believed itself fully free of Babylon's empire. This community believed itself to stand in the power of Christ's kingdom, gathered around their king on Mount Zion. Fox understands this gathering in terms of John's vision in Revelation 14:15. This is a Church no longer condemned to sin in captivity to the beast and Babylon; it is without fault or guile before the throne of God (14:5) insofar as they "follow the Lamb withersoever he goeth" (14:4).

This community represents a *revolution*, overturning the world, the leadership, and the practices of the established churches: "the Quakers have revolted from you apostates . . . as the converted Jews did that were turned to Christ . . . ."[30] It has been *restored* to the hearing and obeying relationship to God, which reveals other fellowships for what they are:

> . . . and the Quakers are risen up in the night of apostasy, and discover you all what you are in, and what you went from, and what hath been lost since the days of the apostles. And an earth-quake is coming upon you that hath not been since the foundation of the world [16:18], out of which earthquake we are come into that which cannot be shaken.[31]

Dean Friday[32] has helpfully shown that the early Quaker use of the term "true Church" had the biblical meaning of "truth" in mind. It is not a matter of right doctrines or methods. As the Hebrew word for "truth" is the same as for "faithfulness" *('amun)*, so the true Church is the gathering that subsists in the unsublimated reality of its relationship with Christ. And as the most literal meaning of *'amun* is "solidity," the faithful, responsive relationship with God is more solid than any rock or foundation on earth; it cannot be shaken. With this discovery of true and false, the lines of conflict are drawn:

194

> ... and now the gospel of God is known, the power of God, and now is the mystery of the fellowship [Eph. 3:9] known, by which shall all the mysteries and fellowships upon the earth be broken, which are not in the power of God: and now vials [15:1-16:21], plagues, and thunders, and woes is coming upon the world, and the smoke of the bottomless pit hath ascended [9:2] ... on this the Lamb's day, whose sceptre of righteousness has gone forth, who will rule the nations with a rod of iron [12:5; 19:15], and make war in righteousness [19:11]. There is a people come forth of the north [i.e., the North of England] that shall spoil Babylon.[33]

As we noted earlier, the revelation of the Lamb's community is immediately followed by John's vision of the angel with an ever-lasting gospel to proclaim, then by the announcement of judgment upon Babylon (14:6-8). Fox understands this juxtaposition to indicate the kind of conflict which must take place between the community of the Lamb and that of the dragon. The apocalyptic battle that will decide the lordship of the universe is to be waged through the revelation of the gospel. This preaching offensive is what Fox means when he speaks of "The Great Mystery of the Great Whore of Babylon *Unfolded;* and Antichrist's Kingdom *Revealed* unto Destruction." This preaching is understood as a battle of liberation, to free the inhabitants of the earth from the repressive doctrines of the false prophets, the ruling clergy, the merchants of the apostles' words who have kept people in Babylon's captivity. This liberation looks forward to the day of total victory when "the merchants of the earth shall weep and mourn for her, for no man buyeth their merchandise any more" (18:11).[34]

This struggle, known among early Friends as the *Lamb's War*, attempts to "confound deceit" perpetuated by the false Church's leadership, through preaching and debating; it also gives the call of Exodus to people captive under that leadership: "Come out of her, my people, that ye be not partakers of her sins, and that ye receive not of her plagues" (18:4). The approach of early Quaker preaching in the steeplehouses was aimed to call people "to come out of all national corrupt ways, religions, churches, worships, fellowships, and teachers."[35] Therefore, in the Quaker movement Fox sees a major event in history taking place:

> ... the everlasting gospel, which was preached in the apostles' days, and to Abraham ... was sent from heaven by the Holy

Ghost in the apostles' days, and is so now; and was not of man neither by man; but by the revelation of the Holy Ghost [Gal. 1:1, 11f]. And now this gospel is preached again (as John saw, and said it should be) to all nations, tongues, and people; and all people are now to hear Christ the prophet in this his gospel of the new covenant.[36]

In this statement, we again find Fox's insistence, following Paul, that the true gospel cannot be received by human traditions and authority but only God's direct revelation.

The terms Fox uses to describe the Quaker preaching of the gospel are sometimes strikingly martial in flavor. This sensibility is founded primarily in his understanding of Chapter 19, the decisive battle of Revelation. Here the figure of Christ, named "The Word of God" (19:13), descends from heaven to lead his armies in defeating the beast, false prophets, and those who support them. The white garments of his armies identify them as the community of faith (10:8, 14). They follow the Lamb as he makes war in righteousness, using the sword which comes forth from his mouth (19:15).

When Fox proclaims that "Christ is come to teach his people himself," he is announcing that John's vision of the great battle is now being waged. In our examination of Quaker preaching, we saw that it was carried out in such a way that it was understood to be Christ's own preaching through obedient instrumentality. Thus, the armies of Christ wage their campaign by the sword that comes from *his* mouth, and under his commands. This scene inspires some of Fox's most vivid imagery.

And God is coming to judge that great whore, all manner of opinions, and all manner of sects and fellowships (as you call them) all manner of her forms, as every one that lives in God is coming to overturn and overthrow, for [your fellowships] all lodge in her: all the foundation of them is in the earth, and earthly wisdom . . . he will overturn them, that he may establish his own truth, his own truth in righteousness, his own kingdom . . . great earthquakes shall be, the terrible day of the Lord draws near, the beast shall be taken, and the false prophet, into the fire they must go . . . . Now shall Zion arise and thresh to beat the hills, and thresh the mountains [Isa. 41:15], now is the sword drawn . . . for Christ is risen, the true light shines, the glory of the Lord appears, and you are discovered to him . . . .[37]

Fox sees revelation as creating revolution, an overturning in the Church as the Word of God has come to overthrow human ecclesiastical authority and wisdom in order to establish God's own truth, God's own kingdom. Threshing is one of the terms used by early Friends to describe their preaching to the world. Its imagery draws in part upon the announcement of the great harvest in Revelation 14:14-20, another vision of Christ's return. In 1647, Fox had envisioned the seed of God lying thick upon the ground, ready for harvest, but with no one to gather it; "and for this I mourned with tears."[38] But with the rise of the Quaker movement, many had been brought together for this task. Now Fox urges them on in this great work of the Lord:

> . . . the prophet is arisen and arising, and the everlasting gospel shall be, and is preached again . . . and the reapers are going forth to reap people down, and so up to God, and to bring them into his barn, and to gather the wheat into the garner. And people shall come to worship God . . . the beast's worship, and the dragon's worship, and the great whore's church is falling . . . .
> Reap out, reap out, reap out, I say (with the power of God) ye reapers unto the Lord, for here is the day of harvest; for as the other falls, the day of harvest is known, a day of gathering . . . .[39]

With breathless, triple imperatives such as these, Fox makes clear the timeliness of this moment in history.

Fox's epistles are often full of exhortations to faith and courage in the forces of Christ, as the sword of God's Word goes forth to cut down the inventions and worships of the false Church.

> Arm yourselves, like men of war, that ye may know what to stand against. Spare not, pity not that which is for the sword (of the spirit) plague, famine, and set up truth, and confound deceit which stains the earth and cumbers the ground [Luke 13:7]. The dead stinks upon the earth, and with it the earth is stained, therefore, bury it.[40]

Here, drawing upon Jesus' parable of the unfruitful fig tree, Fox combines horticultural and martial imageries.

As martial as this imagery is, early Friends were very clear that theirs was a spiritual warfare. Just as they knew Christ's return to be inward and spiritual, they carried out this warfare with spiritual weapons, not outward force. Fox repeatedly quotes 2 Corinthians 10:3f and Ephesians 6:10-17 as the apostolic precedent for this spiritual weaponry, contrasting it to the imprisonments and physical abuses inflicted by the opponents of

Quakerism. He warns Friends never to rely upon their own strength, either physical or intellectual, in this spiritual battle; it is by God's power and the Lamb's authority that victory over the world is obtained. He exhorts them on, despite the earthly cost of this discipleship:

> And so be of good faith and valiant for the truth; for the truth can live in the jails. And fear not the loss of the fleece [i.e., the confiscation of your possessions], for it will grow again; and follow the lamb [14:4], if it be under the beast's horns, or under the beast's heels; for the lamb shall have the victory over them all.[41]

It is Fox's firm conviction that "as the gospel, the power of God is preached and received, Babylon falls."[42] And he places most of his emphasis on the Lamb's War with the preaching campaign of Friends. But he also sees God working out his judgments upon Babylon in other ways, with or without human agency. In this area, he echoes Revelation's theme of plagues and woes, brought upon the earth to inspire repentance. He often views the political upheavals of his day as such judgments; Christ will summon all forces to "shake the foundation of all false religions, ways, worships, churches, and teachers, and will make the pillars of them to totter, and they must be at their wit's end, before they see another foundation."[43] For example, Fox in 1660 could view the Restoration of monarchy as the "day of the Lord," even though it meant trouble for Friends, because he saw in it God's judgment upon the political and religious bankruptcy of the Puritans. Like the Pharoah in ancient Egypt, these "powers had hardened themselves" against the witness of God within themselves, as well as the public witness of Friends. In these actions the Commonwealth had failed to become a nation unto the Lord. At the same time, Fox's view of God's judgments is usually positive, rather than punitive. He urges Friends to "delight in judgment, which leads to the door of mercy."[44]

The New Jerusalem. The new gathering of the Church grows and is settled under the ministry of Christ as the false Church's teachings, worships, and government are "revealed unto destruction." And "from amongst them will God fetch his royal seed with his own hand, and with his might power will he fetch it."[45] In this gathering, the true Church is "come and coming out of the wilderness, which is the bride, the wife of Christ the Lamb. And so Christ is the speaker again unto his church, and who should speak unto his wife, his church, but himself?''[46]

This gathering under Christ's teaching represents the reconciliation of men and women through Christ to their heavenly Father, with whom they are to live in obedience. At the same time, the body of the Church represents their heavenly and ultimate Mother.[47] In the prophetic Church, which relies utterly upon the felt leadings of the light, that latter *corporate* authority stands equal to the *inwardly* received authority of Christ, so that the leadings of one individual may be checked with the leadings of the whole body (in Quaker terminology, the "sense of the meeting"). Thus, while Fox is a radical exponent of the authority of personal experience, at the same time he knows that it is the corporate unity of the Church that makes that experience a powerful force in the world. Therefore, he counsels Friends, "all children of New and Heavenly Jerusalem, that is from above, and is free, with all her holy spiritual children [see Gal. 4:26], to her keep your eyes."[48] The Church which finds unity in its experience of Christ is "the pillar and ground of Truth" (1 Tim. 3:15), not a "mixed multitude" (Num. 11:4).[49] So the "children of the light" are to grow to spiritual maturity under the loving authority of both of these parents, the heavenly Father *and* the heavenly Mother.

Though Babylon is far from completely overthrown, the marriage supper of the Lamb (Rev. 21) is already celebrated wherever the true Church is gathered. Fox connects this gathering with the worship of God which allows him to minister directly:

> . . . and there is no true church but where Christ exerciseth his offices in and amongst them, and they are asking their husband at home [i.e., within themselves; note the interpretation here of Paul's admonition to women in 1 Cor. 14:35], and he is their head, and the true marriage to Christ the heavenly man is witnessed by such as are flesh of his flesh, and bone of his bone . . . .[50]

Fox testifies that this wedding feast is promised by Christ in Revelation 3:20 — "if any man will hear my voice, and open the door, I will come in to him, and will sup with him and he with me."[51]

Fox often criticizes the custom of calling earthly tabernacles the Church, insisting that the Church is God's *people*. Of course, this equation is by no means new with Quakerism. Nevertheless, it is taken to radical conclusions in Quakerism, where the lack of a professional clergy places the responsibility of ministry upon all members of the body. Though the gifts of the Spirit may be revealed more strongly in some, "the least member in the church hath an office, and is serviceable; and every member hath need one of another."[52] This Church in its totality "is called a royal priesthood, offering up spiritual sacrifices [1 Pet. 2:5]; and his church are his believers in the light. And so in the light every one should have something to offer . . . ."[53]

So radical is this trust in the light to lead God's people, that the business meetings of the Church are in fact times of worship, in which the believers gather to wait upon the Lord for him to guide their actions. This is to be the practice not only of the monthly meeting but the wider geographic gatherings of the quarterly meetings and yearly meetings as well, so that the Church is gathered in the light *in every case*, and the decision-making is left to the whole body as much as possible. Fox understands this Church order to be the order which *embodies* the revelation and promises of the gospel. It is the gospel order of the Church gathered around the throne of God, as seen by John:

> . . . behold the tabernacle of God is with men, and he shall dwell with them, and they shall be his people, and God himself shall be their God with them [21:3]. And this we witness, blessed be the Lord forever, who dwelleth with his people.[54]

This reality is most beautifully described by Fox in a vision that he had during one of his grave illnesses (1671) from overwork and stress during the persecutions. This sublime vision bears quoting at length:

> And whilst I was in my travails and sufferings I saw the state of the city New Jerusalem, which comes out of heaven . . . which the professors had looked upon to be like an outward city or some town that had come out of the elements . . . . The spiritual reign of Christ Jesus in this great city . . . is within the light, the city of the living God . . . . So here is the city within the light [where] there is no place or language, but there his voice may be heard. The gate stands open night and day that all may come in here . . . . Without the city are dogs [22:15] . . . within this city, here is light, here is life, here is the heavenly bread and

blood of the Lamb to eat and drink of . . . . I am just in the city. Oh the heavenly Jerusalem, the bride is come down, the marriage of the Lamb that must go over all the false cities that have gotten up since the apostles' days . . . . This true city is come down since the apostles' days and is coming down from God . . . . All that are within the light of Christ and his faith . . . and within the Spirit and the Holy Ghost that Christ and the prophets and apostles were in . . . all that come to this heavenly city, New Jerusalem, that is above the old [and] which is the mother of all true Christians . . . must come to the truth and light in their hearts . . . if they come to be members of this city . . . and so grafted into [Christ Jesus (see Rom. 11:17-24)] that they might bring forth heavenly fruit to the heavenly Father that has begotten them and drawn them unto Christ.[55]

As with John's visions, Fox's visions are revelations in spatial terms of the spiritual and moral dimensions of the gospel. Those who are in the light, "the life in the Word," are in this city; its entrance is open to all who will come to the truth and light in their hearts.

THE RESTORATION OF ALL THINGS

The life in the Word does not amount solely to the evangelical campaign we have discussed so far. Those in the city are engaged in the *restoration of all things* to God's order and kingdom. This means the restoration of God's justice and creative purpose in all aspects of life. All the work of restoration is grounded in the restoring of the hearing and obeying relationship man and woman had with God in Eden. One primary aspect of this restoration is the return of a mutually-informing relationship is to inform not only the marriage relationship but all aspects of Christian life. Men's and women's separate monthly meetings were established to fulfill this relationship on the corporate level, developing leadership among women.

The new ordering extends into social and economic relationships of various kinds. Attention is to be given to the needs of the poor, a task especially taken up by the early Quaker women's meetings. Relief work was concentrated within the early Friends' own ranks, particularly due to hardships under persecution; but it extended into the world as well. Children of poor Quakers were set up in trade apprenticeships, so that the root of poverty could be removed.

While Fox maintains a consistent witness both to Friends and to the government for the needs of the poor and oppressed, it must be said that his vision at times falls short of total fulfillment. He advises Quaker plantation owners in Barbados to free their slaves and give them money to begin independent life — but after thirty years of service. Fortunately, there was more light on this issue coming from other quarters among Friends; there were some Quaker leaders, such as William Edmondson, condemning all slavery in the seventeenth century.

In all their efforts at social and economic re-ordering, Fox exhorts Friends as "heirs of the power of God to take their possession of the Gospel . . . ."[56] This *taking possession* is the conquest of God's kingdom upon the earth. Without taking possession, the gospel amounts only to words without power.

Since Christ the Word is the creator of the universe (John 1:3), his reordering in his kingdom by his light constitutes a new creation. Fox often speaks of the Christian stewardship of the creatures in terms of the *wisdom* of God that is revealed in Christ. When Fox speaks of the creatures, he has in mind not only plants, animals, and other material things, but also human beings in their material needs.

> This is the counsel of the Lord to you all, who are brought into the eternal truth of God, whose minds are guided out of all the earth up to God, and have received their wisdom from God; which wisdom orders all the creatures; that with it you may come to know how to order in the creation, with the wisdom by which all was made. This I charge you, and warn you all, in the presence of the living God, that you suffer no creature to perish for want of the creatures [i.e., sustenance], and that none be lost through slothfulness, laziness, and filthiness . . . .[57]

The beginnings of a Christian environmental ethic may be seen, for example, in Fox's warning to those who do not live simply:

> . . . are not these the spoilers of the creation, and have the fat and best of it, and waste and destroy it? Do not these cumber God's earth [Luke 13:7]? Let that of God in all consciences answer, and who are in the wisdom, judge.[58]

Since the actions and lives of Friends are to be a witness of the gospel to the world, these matters of restoration cannot be truly separated from the preaching campaign of the Lamb's War. The

Lamb has come to make war in righteousness (19:11); this means that he is bringing people to God's justice — in relationships between men and women, in economic matters, and in all dealings with the creatures. As the Lamb claims new territory upon the earth, his new creation unfolds, and every aspect of the heavenly city makes it a "light unto the world" (Matt. 5:14), reaching to the witness of God in all.

THE CHURCH AND THE STATE

The restoration of God's reign on earth is in process in the midst of a world torn by strife and injustice. Setting the restoration in this wider social and political context raises another important question: what is the relationship of the Church, in its attempt to establish God's order, to the state, in its attempt to maintain its own sense of order? As we saw in the historical chapters of our study, Fox did not share the Puritan hope of England becoming the kingdom of Christ through the leadership of a Parliament of "saints." He could not see the kingdom of Christ arising through a coalition of political forces, even if they did consider themselves Christian. All his apocalyptic hopes were placed upon a Church gathered into the authority of Christ's light. He parted ways with both Oliver Cromwell and Henry Vane, political leaders with sympathies toward Quakerism over the very issue of Christ's light.

Fox delivers a promise and a warning from God to all religious and political powers: "I will exalt my kingdom and set it upon the highest throne, to tread dominions and principalities under my feet, who put down the authority . . . ."[59] No political "deals" or armed insurrections can achieve God's kingdom. Fox warns Friends, "Ye must do nothing for the Lord by earthly policy, nor trust to that; but wait in the power of the Lord God, and be ordered by that to his glory. Ye will never be right, till then . . . ."[60]

Due to this understanding of God's power and kingdom, Fox's interpretation does not focus on the geo-political speculation so popular among the Puritans, but places sole emphasis upon the Church and its apocalyptic conflict. *All true hope rests with the future of the Church, which must be neither aided nor compromised by the support of earthly power.* Partly because of this conviction, early Friends, more than any other religious movement, were decisive in sundering the Church-state alliance in England.

Moreover, through Penn's experiment, Friends played a major role in establishing the posture of the Church in America.

T. Canby Jones sums up Fox's understanding thus: Christ "begins his rule in the hearts of his saints and through them he will reign over all the world."[61] But this does not mean that early Friends saw no relationship between the kingdom of God and the kingdoms of this world; if Christ's kingdom is not of this world (John 18:36), it certainly must be *in* this world, if it is more than an interior kingdom of private experience. Fox and early Friends made a vigorous prophetic witness to the civil powers of their day, demanding social, economic, and political reforms. In the 1680s, they focused their efforts upon lobbying in Parliament for toleration. Friends clearly hoped for the fulfillment of the words of Revelation, that "the kingdoms of this world are become the kingdoms of our Lord and of his Christ; and he shall reign forever and ever" (11:15). This hope can never be fulfilled by governmental decree or by *coup d'etat*. It is best articulated by the Declaration of 1660, of which Fox was a co-author, to King Charles II:

> As for the kingdoms of this world, we cannot covet them, much less can we fight for them, but we do earnestly desire and wait, that by the Word of God's power and its effectual operation in the hearts of men, the kingdoms of this world may become the kingdoms of the Lord, and of his Christ, that he may rule and reign in men by his spirit and truth, that thereby all people, out of all different judgments and professions may be brought into love and unity with God and with one another . . . .[62]

This statement emphasizes the transformation of societies by the inward work of God's Word and the leadership of the Church, a spiritual renewal which organically brings communities and nations to achieve God's justice and to do his will.

The political power of the Church lies less in an engagement with the political process than in its power to shift the social context of that process, thereby destabilizing sinful policies. For example, the early Quaker non-cooperation with tithes and restored national worship created a disruption in the English judicial system and jarred the nation's sense of an orderly Restoration. The graphic *social fact* of the government's intolerance of Quakers and Baptists was more decisive in bringing Toleration than political lobbying efforts, though these latter played an important role.

Friends were often faced with leadings of Christ's light which countermanded the laws of the state. In these cases of conflict, the kingdom of God must be exalted above earthly rule:

> and to every ordinance of man we are subject, for the Lord's sake; but should we bow to the spirit of pride we should betray the Lord and give his honour to another . . . so what we see for the Lord and of him in every ordinance of man, we subject to for the Lord's sake; and what is against him, for his sake we deny, and with him suffer under it, as witnesses for him against it.[63]

Thus, part of the Lamb's War is to witness for Christ against unjust laws of the state. Thousands of Friends took up their share in Christ's cross as they refused to comply with laws requiring military service, giving of oaths, and the paying of tithes — witnessing Christ's ultimate lordship over their lives. While the prisons of England sometimes overflowed with Friends, Fox insists that Quakers are not against the laws of the land. Their witness to the Spirit of God in people is a service to the state:

> . . . this brings them into the well-doing which eases the magistrates who are for the punishment of evil-doers. And so people being turned to the Spirit of God which brings them to mortify deeds of the flesh, this brings them from under the occasion of the magistrate's sword . . . . So we establish the law and are an ease to the magistrates, and are not against it, but stand for all good government.[64]

We can see that Fox affirms both the fierce opposition to state oppression found in Revelation and the exhortation of Paul to be subject to the earthly powers (Rom. 13).[65]

Given this stance, early Friends sought to close the gap between the two kingdoms in two ways. First, they sought to bring men and women to the Spirit of God within themselves, which would bring them "from under the occasion" of any punishment by "good government." At the same time, they witnessed to the government to make its laws good and just for all, thereby taking away the occasion not only for the lawlessness of the oppressed, but also of the civil disobedience of Christians. Fox exhorts Cromwell and Charles II alike to wait in the fear of the Lord and order the creatures according to his wisdom. He warns a persecuting judge to "take heed what thou doest, for in the light of the Lord God thou are seen, lest the hand of the Lord be turned against thee."[66] Friends are to live peaceably under every government. But where the state's actions are against God's justice, the Church is joined in an apocalyptic conflict with the state, waged by the sword which comes from the mouth of Christ.

THE FINAL FULFILLMENT

The hope that the world's kingdoms might ultimately become the kingdoms of the Lord raises the question of the final consummation of history in Fox's thought. Throughout this study, we have seen Fox's great emphasis upon God's promises fulfilled in present Christian experience and incarnated in the Church, all the way to the New Jerusalem in Revelation 21. If men and women come to the same Spirit and power that John was in, it will take them to this city just as it took him (21:10). And the intensity with which Fox and early Friends pursued the Lamb's War, against powers of both Church and state, and the extent to which they were willing to suffer and die in this struggle suggest that they were not satisfied to let this experience remain a private possession.

Early Friends looked forward to a day when God would indeed restore *all* things, according to the preaching of Peter (Acts 3:21). Fox testifies that Christ is

> risen, is ascended far above all principalities, powers, thrones, and dominions, and is set down at the right hand of God, and remaineth in the heavens till all things be restored [see Eph. 4:10]. And he is restoring with his light, grace, truth, power, spirit, faith, gospel, and word of life; so that you read of some that came to sit together in heavenly places in Christ Jesus [Eph. 2:6].[67]

According to Fox's understanding of Revelation, relationship with the risen Christ draws men and women out of the earth (14:3) and into heavenly fellowship with him (i.e., into a new order and quality of life). In this heavenly fellowship, they are engaged at the same time in an earthward restoration of all things to his dominion through preaching and re-ordering his creation. So the Church incarnates Christ's restoring work, which looks forward to a final perfection of all things. Christ is

restoring all things into their place, as they were in the beginning,
and reconciling in one, by his power, things in heaven and
things in earth, destroying that which made the separation, and
broke the unity, which is the enmity in people's minds, which
the light which doth enlighten every one that cometh into the
world destroys . . . . So spread the truth abroad, and be valiant
for it upon the earth . . . .[68]

The final victory over evil is assured in Christ's resurrection; yet
there is no speculation in Fox's writings about when this might
be, or exactly how it shall happen. The Christian is to be content
with his or her part in the restoration as Christ commands it *now*.
The vital and triumphant message of Quakerism is that *the
work has already begun*. Fox expresses this repeatedly in his
proclamations that Christ "is come and coming to reign,"[69] "the
church in her glory and beauty is appeared and appearing," [70]
"the mighty day of the Lord is come, and coming to all the
world, and his salvation shall be known to all the ends of the
earth,"[71] "now is Babylon confounded and confounding."[72]
With this figure of speech, he grounds ultimate future in an
unfolding present. He appears to have derived his usage here
from John 4:23 and 5:25 — "the hour cometh, and now is."

Thus we see that just as Fox's concern with the past acts of
God in history is defined by what may be known "experimental-
ly" of them now, his concern for the future is likewise defined
by what can be known and fulfilled of it now. "As "faith is the
substance of things hoped for, the evidence of things not seen"
(Heb. 11:1), Fox exhorts Friends to dwell in Christ the substance
of the scriptures *and* of the new world. His emphasis upon this
palpable substance is so great that he gives almost no attention to
the resurrection of the dead. However, he does affirm this
promise and even had a vision of his dead parents with himself
in the resurrection.[73]

Elisabeth Schüssler-Fiorenza notes that Revelation proclaims
Christ's victory in three stages. The first stage is in heaven, as the
Lamb receives cosmic power with the seven-sealed book in
Chapter 5, and as the child is caught up to Gods' throne, with
Satan cast down to the earth in Chapter 12; these visions
represent Christ's decisive victory over Satan in his crucifixion
and resurrection. The second stage is upon the earth, with the
return of Christ in Chapter 19 to make war upon the beasts and
Satan; this represents the victory of Christ with his saints. The

final stage is Christ's victory over the underworld, as Satan, death, and Hades are forever destroyed in Chapter 20, making possible the new heavens and the new earth seen in Chapter 21.

It is clear that in terms of this scheme, Fox's main concern is with the second stage of Christ's victory, the movement of his reign from heaven to earth. "Christ is come to teach his people himself;" however long this conquest may take, Fox is confident of the outcome:

> And the Lamb shall have the victory; and this we believe, let the beast and whore make ever so much war against him and us, I say, the Lamb shall have the victory . . . . Christ is a-top of the head of them all, for he was before they were, and will be when they are gone, glory to God forever. Come, therefore, let us sing the song of Moses, and of the Lamb [Rev. 14:3; 15:3] . . . .[74]

CONCLUSION

It remains now to summarize the key features of the life and message of George Fox and to offer some conclusions about the significance of Fox and early Quakerism in the history of the Church. George Fox grew up the son of exemplary Puritan parents. Even so, he was uncommonly grave and scrupulous as a child. His description of himself as a young man resembles in some ways Paul's own self-portrayal before his conversion, so that we might typify the young Fox as "a Puritan of the Puritans;" regarding the teachings of Puritanism he was "blameless" (cf. Phil. 3:5f).

Yet, beginning in his nineteenth year, Fox was overcome by a chronic "temptation to despair." This malaise appears to have arisen from a sense of hollowness in the Church's teaching of Christ's victory. It seemed to him a salvation *in* sin rather than *from* sin; Fox felt that forgiveness for sin still left him miserable in a sinful *condition*. He was desperate to overcome this condition; but his Puritan mentors taught that it is impossible to do so in this life. Thus, he found those around him comfortably resigned to a condition he could not accept.

Fox continued in this desperation until he finally gave up on *all* forms of Puritan teaching, both conservative and radical. It was at this point that he heard a voice that said, "There is one, even Christ Jesus, that can speak to thy condition."[1] this experience initiated a process by which "the Father of life drew me to his Son by his spirit."[2] It gave him a sense of Christ's presence and love far beyond what his Bible reading and the hearing of "outward teachers" had been able to offer; it led him to conclude that only this totally "inward," or immediate experience can truly save men and women.

The revelation of Christ's light over succeeding months led Fox through a series of spiritual states which he felt inwardly recapitulated the outward history of God's dealings as recorded in scripture. He was thus drawn out of Adam's alienation from God, through the experience of Moses and the prophets, through John's baptism of repentance, to the new life and will of Christ risen up within himself, and finally into the intimate unity with God in paradise.

Fox realized that this new creation of Christ within must be the Christian's ultimate authority, the true Word who interprets the scriptures and gives an understanding of their meaning through an experience of the history they record. At the same time, the scriptures, as that record, also help give an understanding of the experience of the Word within. In giving this understanding of experience, the scriptures name the God of this experience and gather a community of shared understanding which will fulfill God's stated purposes in history.

The experience of Christ, therefore, is the revelation of history — not only the history *recorded* by scripture, but also the end of history *foretold* by scripture. Christ first reveals one's alienation from God, giving an understanding of Adam's Fall in Genesis. If one remains in the light of this revelation, Christ will empower one to enter the city of New Jerusalem, as envisioned by John at the end of Revelation. Thus, men and women are brought to the end of history by the revelation of Christ. This relationship between experience, scripture, and history led Fox to understand Christ's revelation as an *apocalyptic* event. And while the revelation of the end may remain in the personal realm, the thrust of Fox's work was to gather a new community through the public preaching of the apocalyptic gospel. This Church would take Christ's revelation into social and historical realms by establishing Christ's rule, the kingdom of God, on earth.

To state this important point in another way, just as Christ is incarnated within the individual in the raising of the seed (the new will in that person) the gospel gathers individuals into a unity of common experience, understanding, and obedience which corporately incarnates Christ. The Church as the body of Christ that does the will of its head creates social, economic, and political transformations that change the course of history according to Christ's commands. History, as the vast realm of human activity carried out by men and women in alienation from God and from one another, is *ended* as they hear and obey the voice of Christ, who reconciles them to God and to one another.

Therefore, it is a strongly apocalyptic perspective that lies behind Fox's famous declaration that "Christ is come to teach his people himself." In that single statement, Fox binds into a dynamic unity the intimacy of personal experience with the broadest world-historical expectations of the Church. Fox's message began to gather a powerfully prophetic Church in the Quaker movment of the 1650s. The implications for preaching, worship, and Church order that Fox and other early Quaker leaders found in this message are no less revolutionary than the message itself.

In terms of preaching, Fox saw that Christ's coming to teach his people meant an end to biblical preaching as such; the Quaker preacher must preach from the Word's voice within. Christ himself must preach through human instrumentality, bringing the scriptures to bear as he will, in an organic, rather than exegetical, fashion. The preaching of the gospel constitutes an outward witness in words which will answer the witness in all people; that is, it will answer their inward experience of the Christ who can speak directly to their own condition. The function of prophetic preaching therefore is to call forth this revelation into the consciousness of individuals so that they may begin the same process of spiritual transformation that Fox and the other early Friends had known.

This preaching, then, cannot be a "customary preaching," regularized in weekly installments and arranged by a calendrical series of Christian festivals and holy days. The Word of the Lord proclaims the day of the Lord, an end to the world's sense of worship. Hence, this preaching does not seek to establish or regularize itself, but must be carried out whenever, wherever, and to whomever Christ leads the prophetic preacher. Its paramount aim is to settle men and women under their teacher, Jesus Christ, and to leave them to him.

The goal of early Quaker preaching clearly suggests great implications for Christian worship. If Christ is come to teach his people himself, then the most important task is to allow him the *opportunity* to be heard. This meant to Fox that the sacraments, liturgy, formal hymn-singing, preaching, and prayers stand in interference to the unmediated hearing of Christ's own voice. They must be abolished, or else defined as something other than the worship of God. Fox defined the true, catholic worship of God as *waiting upon the Lord*. He understood this approach in apocalyptic terms as the silencing of the first birth according to the flesh so that the second birth according to the Spirit may be heard. As the fleshly birth dies in silence, so the old world begins to pass away; as the spiritual birth is raised up, a new world comes into view. In other words, the new creation begins with the raising up of the new creature.

Friends insisted that this experience is the spiritual baptism that Christ bestows upon those who will wait upon him; water baptism becomes superfluous and can only diminish one's attention to the spiritual. Further, there is no need to remember Christ's death with bread and wine until he comes; *he has returned* to teach his people himself, nurturing by the intimate communion of his inward presence. "Behold, I stand at the door and knock; if any man *hear my voice,* and open the door, I will come in to him, and will sup with him, and he with me" (Rev. 3:20).

Christ alone may speak in this inward worship. But while this worship is inward, it does not remain private. In the context of the silence, Christ may move any man or woman to speak his message aloud to the gathered meeting. This vocal ministry in worship must be carried out with considerable gravity: to speak when not led or to speak beyond one's leading is to exalt one's self and not Christ; not to speak when one is led to speak is to "quench the spirit" and "despise the prophecy" (1 Thess. 5:19f).

Just as the act of vocal ministry in worship is guided by the knowledge that Christ is come to teach his people himself, so all actions of the Church are to be governed directly by Christ's present authority. The meeting for business, like the meeting for worship, is carried out in the same context of silent waiting upon the Lord, seeking his will in all things. Decision-making is entrusted to the local meeting as a whole, in the effort to gain as much light (i.e., revelation) as possible on matters of concern. Decisions are reached not by majority vote but by "the sense of the meeting;" there must be unity behind the actions taken in the name of Jesus, since in the one seed there may be only one will.

The wider business of the Church is to be carried out through the broadening geographical authorities of the monthly, quarterly, and yearly meetings. Local meetings send representatives to participate in the same business process as used on the local level. Thus, the Church gathers anew under its head at every level. The authority is Christ's own present guidance. All forms of clerical and hierarchical status are rejected as impediments to the Lord's own ministry and government.

From the individual's first experience of the light as a revealer of sin to the broadest range of the Church's witness and actions in society, the work of Christ is to reveal the righteousness of God (Rom. 1:17), to teach his people his ways (Mic. 4:2), to establish on earth his everlasting kingdom of peace and justice. These qualities must characterize not only the actions of members toward one another within the body of Christ, but also their actions in relationship to the world. Members are to be a leavening agent for peace and justice in society, while maintaining a prophetic witness to the state to govern mercifully and justly. This witness in both actions and words is as much evangelical as it is political, since the Church looks forward ultimately to a day when the kingdoms of this world become the kingdoms of the Lord (Rev. 11:15).

In the meantime, however, any practices of the Church which impede the Lord's immediate work among his people constitute an obstruction of his justice, a quenching of his Spirit, and a thwarting of his divine will for all the world. Fox and the early Friends, therefore, could not maintain a neutral stance toward practices of the Protestant and Catholic churches which they saw as standing against Christ's direct rule. They charged that these churches continued and expanded upon practices which had begun shortly after the apostolic era and that these practices were in apostasy from the direct ministry and rule of Christ to which the apostles witnessed. These inventions included not only coercive state religion, but also the very institutions of clergy and Church hierarchy. Such institutions had arisen when the Church began to venerate the *words* of the prophets and apostles (i.e., the scriptures), instead of seeking the *experience* of Christ that lay behind those words. Early Friends understood themselves as nothing less than restorers of the apostolic life, message, and Church order.

Fox understood the problem of the Church in terms of the Book of Revelation and its portrayal of a demonic religious and political force in conflict with the rule of Christ. This power is seen to be at war with the true Church, attempting to break the obedience of the faithful through coercion and seduction. Early Friends believed that, as the prophetic and apostolic Church restored, they incarnated Christ's life-and-death battle against Satan as envisioned in Revelation. Christ had come to teach his people himself, fulfilling the vision of Revelation 19 of the divine warrior come down from heaven to war against the false religion. This cosmic conflict, which Friends called "the Lamb's War," was not a battle waged with carnal weapons, but a spiritual warfare carried forth in the preaching and adamant nonconformity of Friends under first Puritan and then Anglican persecutions. Fox made no bold predictions about the time or manner of the final outcome, but it was his repeated assertion that "the Lamb shall have the victory."

The Church that was gathered around the preaching of early Friends must be termed a *prophetic* Church. It is a Church gathered by a direct revelation of God's Word, unmediated by either scripture or the tradition of Church teaching. This experience recalls the testimony of the Old Testament prophets, fusing the Word with the Spirit (e.g., Isa. 59:21; 61:1; Ezek. 3:1-14), as well as the experience of the apostles at Pentecost (Acts 2:1-4) and the nature of the authority which Paul claims (Gal. 1:1, 11f). This fusion of Word and breath is the hearing of God's *voice*.

Moreover, in the revelation of God's voice, this Church is gathered for the purpose of declaring and incarnating God's ultimate purpose in history. That purpose is characterized by his justice, and all aspects of the life of his Church are given over to the embodying of this justice. Its preaching brings men and women to the judgment bar of God. Its worship seeks a sense not only of God's presence, but especially his *will* in all things. In this concern, the Church echoes the Old Testament prophets' distrust of cultic ceremony (1 Sam. 15:22; Amos 5:21-24) and Paul's insistence upon worship that builds up the Church (1 Cor. 14:12). Further, the Church's government seeks the unmediated rule of Christ through an openness to his revelation through all its members, following Moses' openness to the leadership of *all* who prophesy (Num. 11:29).

Finally, the prophetic Church as the cutting edge of God's new order in the midst of the old can be expected to generate conflict. In this role, it follows the example of the prophets' suffering. But pre-eminently, it bears the cross of Christ, accepting the world's scorn and abuse. By so absorbing the destructive force of the world, it incarnates the hope of Christ's resurrection, that death may be swallowed up in victory (1 Cor. 15:54).

The prophetic Church is therefore gathered and defined by the *apocalypse* of the Word of God — an immediate revelation whose content is the end of the world. Our entire exploration has amply shown that Fox's message unfolds most fully and meaningfully within this apocalyptic horizon. Other interpretations of Fox and early Quakerism have successfully highlighted certain aspects while failing to do justice to the whole. The two major interpretations that have dominated twentieth century Quaker thought have manifested this problem. (The *mystical* interpretation, advanced by Rufus M. Jones, and the *Protestant* interpretation, best articulated by Geoffrey

Nuttall and Hugh Barbour, were summarized and appraised in my Introduction.)

But there is more at stake in the study of Fox and early Friends than simply an adequate historical and theological assessment. Both of the interpretations just mentioned have had considerable effect upon the modern Society of Friends. Together with cultural trends, these interpretations have helped foster distorted views of Quakerism both within and without the Society of Friends.

MYSTICAL AND PROTESTANT QUAKERISMS

Rufus M. Jones' mystical interpretation attempted to unite Quakerism with the best of world religions by placing them all on a common metaphysical grounding, "life itself at the highest inward unity and its most consummate attainment of Reality."[3] Jones' attitude toward the early Quaker use of biblical language was essentially that of liberal theology's attitude toward biblical language itself — a secondary husk circumstantially attached to some core of universal meaning unrelated to history. The conclusion follows that Jesus spoke as a Jew only because of his culture, and early Friends spoke as Christians only because of their culture.

This loss of prophetic/apocalyptic perspective in liberal Christianity has contributed greatly to the individualistic relativism that has sapped the Church's strength so much in this century. This lack of prophetic power is seen acutely in the modern Society of Friends. The legacy of Jones' mystical interpretation has dominated major portions of Quakerism in this century, particularly the unprogrammed (silent) Friends meetings in the United States. While Jones remained steadfastly Christian in his own viewpoint, his interpretation of Quakerism has led the way for many modern Friends to conclude that there is no essential identity between the person of Jesus and the experience of the light within. Furthermore, Jones' rationalistic explanation of "that of God in every one" has led Quakers of succeeding generations to conclude that the light need not be understood in theistic terms at all. Without the language of the gospel, meetings are not gathered into a community of shared understanding of the light or obedience to it. Consequently, the transforming social power of Quakerism in history has been greatly diminished in Friends meetings, despite growing political activism in the secular sphere among many Friends. Worship too rarely becomes a "gathered" experience; it is more often simply a "forum" for the sharing of different religious, philosophical, and political perspectives. An early Friend visiting such a meeting today might well feel something like Paul at the Areopagus of Athens (Acts 17). And *he* didn't stay there long.

It would be unfair to ascribe to Rufus Jones all the excesses of his followers or to ignore his many important contributions, such as his helping to found the American Friends Service Committee. But his interpretation of Fox and early Quakerism not only missed the early Quaker vision, it imposed upon Quakerism a liberal philosophical agenda, carrying Quakers along with a cultural tide that has proven ultimately unfruitful. Liberal Quakerism partakes of an early twentieth-century optimistic humanism that seems woefully inadequate to the problems of this nuclear age.

The Protestant interpretation of Quakerism has not so much helped create a new mutation among modern Friends as given sanction to existing mutations. Nineteenth-century Protestant revivals and awakenings on the American frontier created a cultural dynamism that moved many local Friends meetings to more Wesleyan conceptions of faith, worship, and ministry. These continue to predominate in major sectors of the modern Society of Friends. Consequently, scripture as primary authority developed concomitantly with a return to professionalism in ministry. A programmed "service" of worship thereby replaces the apocalyptic event of waiting upon the Lord.

Protestant Quakerism pictures the early Quaker Lamb's War as a form of revival and so imposes the individualistic piety of Protestant revivalism upon the more corporate vision of early Friends. Moreover, the influence of Christian ecumenism has made the Protestant reading of Quakerism all the more palatable among Friends concerned for an inter-denominational dialogue.[4] But if one assumes a *denominational* definition of Quakerism, one has already greatly revised the early Quaker self-understanding.

Protestant Quakerism has produced a message and worship intelligible to the Protestant culture of America, bringing more new converts to Quakerism than any other approach since the seventeenth century. It has also produced greater dialogue between Friends and Protestants than at any time since those days. But while membership rolls have swelled, the witness to the world has weakened. Apart from their disuse of ritual sacraments, there is little that these Friends can recognize in their faith as unique. The world-transforming fervor of early Quakerism is today a foreign language to a people transformed by cultural religious norms.

THE CURRENT SITUATION

As the cultural tides of liberalism and Protestantism have receded since the middle of this century, the fortunes of the liberal and Protestant Quakerisms have similarly ebbed. Yet during this same period, a third major interpretation of Fox and early Quakerism has arisen with increasing influence. Its leading figure, Lewis Benson, has made several key insights into early Quakerism. His interpretation has informed the approach and conclusions of this study at many points. Benson terms his interpretation of early Quakerism *prophetic*, citing particularly Fox's prophetic Christology. He has provided several key critiques of the mystical and Protestant interpretations of Quakerism.

Benson's painstaking work of reading and correlating Fox's unsystematic writings, together with his keen theological insights, have given his prophetic interpretation strongly convincing weight for an increasing number of Friends today. Over the past decade, this groundswell has created a renewal movement among Friends, known as the New Foundation Fellowship, a network of speakers and writers who are reacquainting modern Friends with the early Quaker vision and reviving the travelling ministry among Friends.

Thus far, this movement has remained largely within Quaker circles, not yet sure how to present its witness to a wider society. The fuller fruition of this movement remains to be seen. Its message may be able to converge with the findings of wider Christian scholarship on the New Testament, or with other Christian movements, to find a wider audience. Or, it may become overwhelmed by the weight of its historical reference and prove to be simply an antiquarian interest group, harkening back to a Quaker Golden Age.

George Fox provided a radical, coherent answer to the burning questions of his time and place. Assuming that the theological framework of that answer is valid today, the burning questions are nevertheless different. Empty forms, repressive doctrines, and authoritarian leadership may still be problems in some cases today, but they do not represent the most pressing dilemmas. The issues of Church *versus* state, servanthood *versus* power, and revelation *versus* tradition remain crucial. Yet they arise in a different historical context. For example, the state's guarantee of relgious freedom has come along with a circumscribed role for the churches in society. Denominational pluralism has made Church traditions and the expertise of clergy more a matter of comparative shopping for the religious consumer than a matter of authority. How does Fox's message move men and women beyond a view of religious experience as personal preference and private consumption? Denominational Christianity represents Babylon's most clever maneuver; the inversion of Church-state relationship is but a new permutation of the Constantinian settlement. How does Fox's message speak to this dilemma? Such questions must be addressed if the full power of prophetic faith is to be regained.[5]

The basic orientation of Fox's vision is too important to be ignored by anyone who understands the New Testament message. It is helpful to recall the thought of Albert Schweitzer, whose research identified the pervasively eschatological character of New Testament proclamation. Schweitzer analyzes Paul's "mysticism" (a catch-word in the early decades of this century, similar to "spirituality" today) as eschatological in character, differentiating it from the mysticism of other religious traditions. While other approaches seek union with mythic beginnings or metaphysical groundings in God, "Pauline mysticism is concerned with the passing away and restoration of the world, and the fate of the Elect amid these events."[6]

This eschatological quality makes Paul's emphasis world-historical rather than metaphysical, corporate rather than individualistic, features that have been lost in subsequent ages of Christian thought.

> The great weakness of all doctrines of redemption since the Primitive Christian is that they represent a man as wholly concerned with his own individual redemption, and not equally with the coming of the Kingdom of God. The one thing needful is that we should work for the establishment of a Christianity, which does not permit those who allow their lives to be determined by Christ to be "of little faith" in regard to the future of the world . . . to be a Christian means to be possessed and dominated by a hope of the Kingdom of God, and a will to

work for it, which bids defiance to external reality. Until this comes about Christianity will stand before the world like a wood in the barrenness of winter.[7]

Any attitude within the Church that argues for the essential harmony of all Christian approaches manifests not only this barrenness before the world, but a "separate peace" among the churches that turns its back upon the hope of the kingdom. It is a resignation to despair.

Referring not only to Paul's own battle with legalism but also to his influence upon the Reformers, Schweitzer concludes,

> Great has been the work as a reforming influence which Paul, by his doctrine of justification by faith alone, has accomplished in opposition to the spirit of work-righteousness in Christianity. Still greater will be the work which he will do when his mystical doctrine of being redeemed into the Kingdom of God, through union with Christ, begins to bring quietly to bear upon us the power which lies within it.[8]

This prescription for a renewed Christian hope finds a fleeting fulfillment in the writings of George Fox and the historic witness of the early Quaker movement. Their example, together with the New Testament proclamation itself, can provide two important historical reference points for all men and women in the Spirit of Christ who today seek first the kingdom of God.

Notes

NOTES TO INTRODUCTION

1. George M. Trevelyan, *History of England* (Garden City, New York: Longmans, Green and Co., 1965), Vol. II, p. 217.

2. Williston Walker, *The History of the Christian Church*, rev. ed. by Robert T. Handy (New York: Scribner, 1970), p. 420.

3. Rufus M. Jones, Introduction to *The Beginnings of Quakerism* by W.C. Braithwaite (New York: Macmillan, 1912), p. xxii.

4. *Ibid.*, p. xxxiv.

5. *Ibid.*, pp. xxxvii-xxxix.

6. *Ibid.*, p. xlii.

7. Rufus M. Jones, *Spiritual Reformers of the Sixteenth and Seventeenth Centuries* (London: Macmillan, 1919), p. xxx.

8. Rufus M. Jones, Introduction to *The Second Period of Quakerism* by William C. Braithwaite (London:Macmillan, 1919), p. xxx.

9. T. Canby Jones, "The Nature and Function of the Light in the Thought of George Fox," *Quaker Religious Thought*, Vol. XVI, Nos. 1 & 2 (Winter 1974-75): 53.

10. See Rudolf Bultmann, *Theology of the New Testament* (New York: Scribner, 1951), Vol. I, pp. 190-352.

11. J. Christiaan Beker, *Paul the Apostle: the Triumph of God in Life and Thought* (Philadelphia: Fortress, 1980), p. 154.

12. Geoffrey Nuttall, *The Holy Spirit in Puritan Faith and Experience* (Oxford: Blackwell, 1946), p. viii.

13. *Ibid.*, p. 13.

14. See the criticism of Lewis Benson, *Catholic Quakerism* (Philadelphia:Philadelphia Yearly Meeting, 1968), pp. 9f.

15. Hugh Barbour, *The Quakers in Puritan England* (New Haven: Yale University Press, 1964), p. 42.

16. Hugh Barbour, "Protestant Quakerism," *Quaker Religious Thought*, Vol. IX, No. 2 (Autumn 1969): 2.

17. *Ibid.*, p. 5.

18. Lewis Benson, "Response" to "Protestant Quakerism," p. 37.

19. Albert Schweitzer, *The Quest of the Historical Jesus* (New York: Macmillan, 1968), p. 360.

20. Lewis Benson, *What Did George Fox Teach about Christ?* (Gloucester: New Foundation, 1976), p. 3.

21. Ernst Käsemann, "Justification and Salvation History," *Perspectives on Paul* (Philadelphia: Fortress, 1971), p. 76.

22. See Oscar Culmann, *Christology of the New Testament* (Philadelphia:Westminster, 1959); Hans Joachim Schoeps, *Jewish Christianity* (Philadelphia:Fortress, 1969; Francis Glasson, *Moses in the Fourth Gospel* (London:SCM, 1963); Wayne Meeks, *The Prophet-King* (Leiden:Brill, 1967).

23. Paul Minear, *To Heal and to Reveal: The Prophetic Vocation according to Luke* (New York: Seabury, 1976).

24. See Culmann, *Christology*, p. 38; Minear, *Heal and Reveal*, pp. 49ff; and Schoeps, *Jewish Christianity*, p. 68.

25. Lewis Benson, "George Fox's Teaching about Christ," *Quaker Religious Thought*, Vol. XVI, Nos. 1 & 2 (Winter 1974-75): 34-37.

NÕTES TO CHAPTER 1

1. NJ:121.
2. Christopher Hill, *The World Turned Upside Down* (New York: Viking, 1972), p. 187.
3. Christopher Hill, *Puritanism and Revolution* (New York: Schocken, 1958), pp. 29, 31.
4. *Ibid.*, pp. 32-49.
5. Dean Freiday, *The Bible: Its Criticism, Interpretation and Use in 16th and 17th Century England* (Pittsburgh: Catholic and Quaker Studies, 1979), pp. iif.
6. Michael Watts, *The Dissenters* (Oxford: Clarendon, 1978), pp. 17f.
7. Hill, *Puritanism and Revolution*, p. 38.
8, John Punshon, *Portrait in Grey* (London: London Yearly Meeting, 1984), pp. 14-26 represent some original and very helpful work on this subject.
9. Christopher Hill, *Antichrist in Seventeenth Century England* (London: Oxford University Press, 1971), p. 13.
10. Peter Toon, *Puritans and Calvinism* (Swengel, Pennsylvania:Reiner, 1973), p. 13.
11. James I, quoted in Hill, *The Century of Revolution* (New York: Norton, 1961), p. 43.
12. *Ibid.*, p. 91.
13. Hill, *Puritanism and Revolution*, pp. 38f.
14. Hill, *The Century of Revolution*, p. 107.
15. See Hill, *Antichrist,* Chapter III.
16. See Geoffrey Nuttall, *The Holy Spirit in Puritan Faith and Experience* (Oxford: Blackwell, 1946), Chapter IV.
17. For an insightful and sympathetic treatment of Levellerism, see Hill, *The World Turned Upside Down*, Chapter VII.
18. Horton Davies, *Worship and Theology in England* (Princeton: University Press, 1975), Vol. II, p. 497.
19. Joseph Salmon, *Anti-Christ in Man* (1647).
20. Hill, *Antichrist*, pp. 171f.
21. Christopher Hill, *Puritanism and Revolution*, p. 51.
22. William Erbury, *The Testimony of William Erbury* (1658), pp. 263-265, 337f.
23. John Webster, *The Saint's Guide* (1654).
24. Joseph Salmon, *Heights in Depths and Depths in Heights* (1651), p. 28; quoted in Hill, *The World Turned Upside Down,* pp. 175f.
25. Hugh Barbour, *The Quakers in Puritan England* (New Haven: Yale University Press, 1964), pp. 30-32.
26. *Ibid.*, p. 31.

NOTES TO CHAPTER 2

1. VIII:61.
2. NJ:1f.
3. NJ:2.
4. NJ:11.

5. *Ibid.*
6. NJ:19.
7. NJ:27.
8. *Ibid.*
9. Rufus Jones, *Quakerism: A Spiritual Movement* (Philadelphia: Philadelphia Yearly Meeting, 1963), p. 120.
10. Hugh Barbour, *Quakers,* p. 28.
11. NJ:7.
12. This view is shared by W. C. Braithwaite, *The Beginnings of Quakerism* (London: Macmillan, 1912), p. 41.
13. NJ:33f.
14. Braithwaite, *Beginnings,* p. 47.
15. NJ:40.
16. NJ:52.
17. NJ:65.
18. Christopher Hill, *The World Turned Upside Down,* p. 189.
19. NJ:74.
20. NJ:83.
21. NJ:89.
22. NJ:109.
23. A few instances of this recurring formula are found in NJ:48, 74, 122, 190, 235-237.
24. Lewis Benson, *A Revolutionary Gospel,* (Philadelphia: The Tract Association of Friends, 1974), pp. 3-5.
25. NJ:158.
26. IV:28f.
27. George Fox, *To the Protector and Parliament of England* (1658), p. 12.
28. George Fox, *To the Parliament of England: Fifty-nine Particulars for the Regulating of Things* (1659).
29. Alan Cole, "The Social Origins of the Early Friends," *Journal of the Friends Historical Society* 48 (1957), pp. 99-118.
30. R. T. Vann, *The Social Development of English Quakerism* (Cambridge: Harvard University Press, 1969), pp. 47-87.
31. Barbour, *Quakers,* p. 164.
32. NJ:37.
33. Quoted in Hill, *The World Turned Upside Down,* pp. 198f.
34. Barbour, *Quakers,* p. 92.
35. John Bunyan, "A Vindication of Some Gospel Truths Opened . . . ." *Works* (London: Virtue and Yorston, 1859), Vol. I, p. 93.
36. NJ:79.
37. Barbour, *Quakers,* p. 160.
38. CJ I:24.
39. VII:70.
40. Barbour, *Quakers,* p. 65.
41. Our treatment of events of this year is greatly aided by James F. Maclear, "Quakerism and the End of the Interregnum: A Chapter in the Domestication of Radical Puritanism," *Church History* 19 (December 1950): pp. 240-270.
42. Frederick Tolles, *Quakers and the Atlantic Culture* (New York: Macmillan, 1960), p. 41.
43. Cited and described in part above.
44. NJ:353f.
45. VII:179.

222

46. NJ:334-336.
47. See particularly NJ:199f, 274f.
48. Braithwaite, *Beginnings*, p. 512.
49. W. C. Braithwaite, *The Second Period of Quakerism* (London: Macmillan, 1919), p. 115.
50. NJ:169f.
51. J. Louis Martyn, *The Gospel of John in Christian History* (New York: Paulist, 1978); *History and Theology of the Fourth Gospel* (Nashville: Abindgon, 1979).
52. NJ:317.
53. NJ:404.
54. There were, however, some gaps in the Quaker peace testimony during the 1650s, especially regarding the New Model Army. See Hill, *The World Turned Upside Down*, p. 194f; Barbour, *Quakers*, pp. 192, 196.
55. NJ:274f.
56. Braithwaite, *Second Period*, pp. 14f.
57. *Ibid.*, pp. 15f.
58. *Ibid.*, p. 114.
59. NJ:457-502.
60. R. T. Vann, *Social Development*, p. 94.
61. *Ibid.*, p. 78.
62. Quoted in Braithwaite, *Second Period*, p. 41.
63. NJ:517f.
64. NJ:511.
65. R. T. Vann, *Social Development*, p. 104.
66. NJ:667.
67. NJ:709.
68. Braithwaite, *Second Period*, p. 67.
69. NJ:643.
70. NJ:642.
71. Henry J. Cadbury, "George Fox's Later Years" (concluding essay in the Nickalls edition of the *Journal*, NJ:713-756), NJ:741.
72. Tolles, *Quakers*, p. 43.
73. *Ibid.*, p. 44.
74. Braithwaite, *Second Period*, p. 115.
75. NJ:752.
76. NJ:756.
77. NJ:48.

NOTES TO CHAPTER 3

1. NJ:312.
2. These views were preached by John Owen before Parliament in 1652. See Peter Toon, *Puritan Eschatology* (London: Clarke, 1970), p. 39.
3. IV:15.
4. See J. Louis Martyn, "Epistemology at the Turn of the Ages: II Cor 5:16, *Christian History and Interpretation: Studies Presented to John Knox,* Farmer, Moule, and Niebuhr, eds. (Cambridge: University Press, 1967), pp. 269-287.
5. NJ:9f.
6. NJ:6.
7. NJ:11.

8. *Ibid.*
9. NJ:11f.
10. *Ibid.*
11. NJ:13f.
12. NJ:14.
13. NJ:14f.
14. NJ:15f.
15. NJ:19.
16. NJ:21.
17. NJ:25.
18. NJ:27.
19. *Ibid.*
20. In developing this section, I found particularly helpful T. Canby Jones' article, "The Nature and Functions of the Light," *Quaker Religious Thought*, Vol. XVI, Nos. 1 & 2 (Winter 1974-75): 53-71.
21. NJ:34.
22. BJ I:274f.
23. IV:15f.
24. V:15f.
25. IV:17.
26. III:518f.
27. NJ:15f.
28. NJ:16.
29. See Jospeh Pickvance, "Convincement and Conviction," *New Foundation Papers*, No. 1 (July 1980): 8-10.
30. IV:21.
31. IV:303.
32. BJ I:67.
33. IV:17f; also see III:264.
34. VII:167.
35. VII:58.
36. IV:303f.
37. IV:18.
38. NJ:228.
39. VII:320.
40. IV:18.
41. NJ:17f.
42. VII:108f.
43. Barbour, *Quakers*, pp. 94-126.
44. III:487; also see III:463, 466.
45. NJ:34.
46. VII:296.
47. BJ II:272.
48. VI:388.
49. IV:148.
50. VII:300f.
51. VIII:59f, 175.
52. IV:18.
53. VIII:184.
54. Lewis Benson, "The People of God and Gospel Order," *The Church in Quaker Thought and Practice*, Charles Thomas, ed. (Philadelphia: Faith and Life Movement, 1979), p. 21.
55. CJ II:128.

56. BJ II:152.
57. VIII:62.
58. VII:328f.
59. VII:61.
60. VI:229.
61. VI:472; VII:259.
62. George Fox, "Wheeler Street Sermon," *Early Quaker Writings* (Grand Rapids: Eerdman's, 1973), p. 506.
63. BJ II:199-201.
64. VII:232.
65. VII:233.
66. III:198.
67. CJ I:69.
68. III:338.
69. III:148.
70. NJ:688.
71. John Owen, *Works,* William Goold, ed. (London: Johnstone & Hunter, 1853), Vol. III, p. 566.
72. Richard Baxter, *The Quakers' Catechism* (1655).
73. Richard Baxter, *One Sheet Against the Quakers* (1657), p. 8.
74. III:74, 79.
75. III:265.
76. VII:212.
77. IV:16f.
78. NJ:28.
79. IV:17.
80. BJ II:339.
81. VII:213.
82. VII:130.
83. VII:120.
84. VIII:26.
85. NJ:204.
86. III:508.

NOTES TO CHAPTER 4

1. VI:302.
2. This famous Quaker formulaton is quoted often among Friends today as "that of God in every *man*." T. Canby Jones, however, in an extensive study of Fox's epistles, finds "that of God in every *one*" to be Fox's most frequent usage, at least in those writings.
3. III:117.
4. III:117, 227; VIII:283.
5. NJ:11, 51, 699; VI:13.
6. VIII:16, 181.
7. III:100; VII:30.
8. BJ II:461.
9. VI:381.
10. NJ:8; IV:25; VI:56f, 247, 396f.
11. III:482; VII:225.
12. IV:62-64; VII:125.
13. BJ I:351; IV: 32-34.

14. VII:66f, 103.
15. VI:355f.
16. III:461.
17. NJ:33.
18. Richard Baxter, *The Quakers' Catechism*, pp. 8-11.
19. John Bunyan, "Some Gospel Truths Opened . . ." (1656). *Works*, Henry Stebbing, ed. (London: Virtue & Yorston, 1859), Vol. I, pp. 43ff.
20. John Owen, *Works*, Vol. XII, p. 12.
21. *Ibid.*, Vol. XVI, pp. 426-476.
22. See *Of the Divine Original, Authority, Self-Evidencing Light, and Power of the Scriptures* (1659), *Ibid.*, Vol. XVI, pp. 283-421.
23. I am greatly indebted to Philip Schwartz, teacher at the Upper School of the Friends Seminary in New York, for his very able translation of this material so that it could be reviewed for this study.
24. Geoffrey Nuttall devotes special attention to the universal light, seeing it as the truly "contradistinguishing character of Quakerism" (*The Holy Spirit*, p. 151) in relation to Puritanism. Like Baxter, Bunyan, and Owen, he sees this teaching as reducing the significance of Christ's incarnation; a "sense of a Christian watershed in history is lacking" (Ibid., p. 159). Following Baxter, Nuttall sees error in identifying the bestowal of the Spirit of the Creator with that of the Redeemer (Ibid., p. 174). Finally, Nuttall is concerned over a reduction of the difference between the creature and the new creation, leading to a neglect of repentance (Ibid., p. 175). Here he seems to miss Fox's overpowering emphasis on the judgment and mortification that precede true empowerment.
25. Owen was answered, however, by the Quaker Samuel Fisher in 1660, with a rather ponderous volume entitled *The Rustics to the Academics*. Fisher and other early Quaker contributors to the Quaker-Puritan debate are reviewed by Maurice Creasey, *Early Quaker Christology* (Pittsburgh: Catholic and Quaker Studies, 1956), pp. 143-192; also see Dean Freiday's helpful *The Bible*, pp. 69-103.
26. V:341-361.
27. IV:17.
28. NJ:316f.
29. NJ:103; BJ II:234.
30. V:199.
31. V:199; VI:391.
32. VI:390f.
33. BJ I:356.

NOTES TO CHAPTER 5

1. III:338f (answer to John Bunyan).
2. E.g., III:178, 246, 337, 342.
3. E.g., "A Visitation to the Jews" (IV:53-57); "A Looking Glass for the Jews" (V:61-84).
4. NJ:63; III:452f.
5. NJ:625f.
6. NJ:xxvii.
7. NJ:31f.
8. NJ:33.
9. See Ferdinand de Saussure, *Course in General Linguistics* (New York: McGraw-Hill, 1959); Roland Barthes, "Historical Discourse," in *Introduction to*

226

Structuralism, Michael Lane, ed. (New York: Basic Books, 1970), pp. 145-155.
   10. VII:263.
   11. III:403.
   12. III:409.
   13. III:353.
   14. George Fox, "Wheeler Street Sermon," Early Quaker Writings, p. 503.
   15. For Fox's treatments of the two covenants, see "The Second Covenant" (IV:144-159); "A Clear Distinction . . ." (VI:38-77); "Christ Jesus the Covenant of God" (IV:267-269).
   16. NJ:15.
   17. Ibid.
   18. I thank Joseph Pickvance of Birmingham, England, a long-time student of Fox's writings, for this helpful insight into Fox's hermeneutical language.
   19. IV:83.
   20. IV:82.
   21. IV:78.
   22. IV:86.
   23. BJ:364, 422, 458.
   24. IV:78.
   25. On the question of continuity and discontinuity I am helped by Graham Hughes, Hebrews and Hermeneutics (Cambridge: University Press, 1979), pp. 35-74.
   26. VII:234; also see III:33.
   27. VII:127.
   28. III:375f.
   29. IV:33.
   30. VII:122.
   31. NJ:699.
   32. NJ:109.
   33. BJ II:364, 422, 458; IV:53, 55, 64.
   34. BJ II:364.
   35. See NJ:23, 603.
   36. VIII:149.
   37. VII:206.
   38, NJ:617f.
   39. NJ:625.
   40. VI:48f.
   41. Ibid.
   42. NJ:109; VIII:250f.
   43. VII:202.
   44. VII:233f.
   45. VI:472.

NOTES TO CHAPTER 6

   1. "A Word from the Lord to All the World" (IV:32-39).
   2. IV:39.
   3. Gerhard von Rad, "Typological Interpretation of the Old Testament," in Old Testament Hermeneutics, Claus Westermann, ed. (Richmond: John Knox, 1963), p. 36.

4. IV:37.
5. IV:38.
6. VI:304.
7. IV:33.
8. IV:37.
9. NJ:33.
10. VII:263.
11. BJ II:418.
12. IV:18.
13. III:563.
14. IV:124.
15. VII:177.
16. VIII:51.
17. VII:240, 257, 258.
18. V:423.
19. NJ:55f.
20. NJ:159.
21. NJ:145f, 295f; III:467f, 507f.
22. Nuttall, *The Holy Spirit,* p. 31.
23. *Ibid.,* p. 29f.
24. Barbour, *Quakers,* p. 139.
25. *Ibid.*
26. *Ibid.,* p. 157.
27. Hughes, *Hebrews and Hermeneutics,* cited in the preceding chapter.
28. *Ibid.,* p. 90.
29. VI:56; VI:334f; VII: 124.
30. IV:267f.
31. IV:64.
32. III:314; For entire expositions with strongly parallel developments, see "A Visitation to the Jews" (IV:53-75), followed by "A Visitation to All You That Have Long Had the Scriptures" (IV:76-89).
33. For an excellent treatment of Fox's use of scripture, see T. Canby Jones, "George Fox's Teaching on Redemption and Salvation" (Ph.D. dissertation, Yale University, 1956), pp. 59-69.
34. NJ:34.
35. NJ:636.
36. NJ:134.
37. NJ:604.
38. III:462.
39. III:287, 322.
40. IV:34.
41. NJ:303, 471.
42. IV:127.
43. IV:18.
44. VII:17.
45. NJ:333.
46. George Fox, "Introduction," in *The Battle-Door* (1660).
47. VI:71-73.
48. NJ:30.

NOTES TO CHAPTER 7

1. NJ:123.

2. BJ II:271.
3. NJ:177.
4. III:127.
5. IV:178-193.

NOTES TO CHAPTER 8

1. NJ:103.
2. Benson, "That of God," pp. 14-17.
3. NJ:263.
4. BJ I:316.
5. BJ I:423.
6. III:240f; also see VII:186.
7. VIII:59.
8. VII:73.
9. III:144f.
10. VII:113.
11. VII:301.
12. *Ibid.*
13. NJ:36.
14. IV:46f.
15. VII:193.
16. VII:301.
17. NJ:263.
18. NJ:46.
19. John Calvin, *Institutes of the Christian Religion*, John T. McNeill, ed. (Philadelphia:Westminster, 1960), ¾ Vol. I, p. 501.
20. See NJ:11.
21. BJ II:386-389.
22. BJ II:502.
23. VIII:165.
24. VII:100.
25. NJ:263.
26. VII:78.
27. V:182.
28. VI:425.
29. BJ I:425.
30. VII:77.
31. III:495.
32. Fox, of course, did not write out his sermons. But a handful were recorded by hearers in shorthand. Eight of these are available to us in the Richardson MSS. These are to be found in the Quaker Collection of the Haverford College Library. The earliest of the sermons come from Fox's preaching to Friends in Barbados, 1671. The others are gathered from preaching in England. One of these latter, a sermon given at General Meeting in London, 1680, may also be found in print. See *Early Quaker Writings*, pp. 501-512.
33. Michael Graves, "The Rhetoric of the Inward Light: An Examination of Extant Sermons delivered by Early Quakers, 1671-1700" (Ph.D. dissertation, University of Southern California, 1972).
34. Jackson Cope, "Seventeenth-Century Quaker Style," *Proceedings of the Modern Language Association*, Vol. LXXI (September 1956): 725-54.

35. *Ibid.*, p. 736.
36. *Ibid.,* p. 735.
37. Ian Ramsey, *Religious Language: An Empirical Placing of Theological Phrases* (London: SCM, 1957).
38. *Ibid.*, p. 154.
39. *Ibid.*
40. Graves, "Rhetoric," p. 143.
41. VI:427.
42. III:453.
43. IV:104-110.
44. IV:109f.
45. For an excellent treatment of the early Quaker attitude toward ministry and the role of women, see Lisa B. Kuenning, "Christ's Wife: A Vision for All Women," *Quaker Religious Thought*, 48 (Summer 1979): 4-32.
46. Mark Minear, *To Heal and to Reveal: The Prophetic Vocation according to Luke* (New York:Seabury, 1976).
47. VII:43.
48. NJ:566.

NOTES TO CHAPTER 9

1. NJ:263.
2. Barbour, *Quakers*, pp. 31f; also see Watts, *Dissenters,* pp. 185f.
3. VIII:49f.
4. VII:229.
5. VII:323.
6. III:273.
7. VII:292.
8. VII:236.
9. VII:318.
10. IV:119-133.
11. *Ibid.*
12. IV:121.
13. IV:122.
14. IV:123.
15. *Ibid.*
16. IV:128.
17. IV:125.
18. *Ibid.*
19. IV:129.
20. IV:130.
21. *Ibid.*
22. IV:132.
23. Käsemann, *Perspectives,* p. 29.
24. VII:66f.
25. IV:124.
26. VII:35.
27. IV:127.
28. VII:323.
29. Gerhard von Rad, *Old Testament Theology* (New York: Harper and Row, 1962), Vol. I, p. 242.

30. T. Canby Jones, "Worship as Experienced," *Quaker Religious Thought*, vol. XV, no. 2 (Winter 1973-4):17-40.

31. See Brown, *The Gospel According to John*, Vol. I, p. 524; also Joachim Jeremias, *The Central Message of the New Testament* (London: SCM, 1965), pp. 71-90.

NOTES TO CHAPTER 10

1. VIII:54; also see VIII:70, 77f, 251.

2. VIII:277.

3. BJ II:390.

4. CJ I:253f.

5. IV:237.

6. See Norman Perrin, *Rediscovering the Teachings of Jesus* (New York: Harper and Row, 1976), pp. 102-105.

7. VI:425f.

8. See Craig's exegesis of 1 Corinthians 14 in *The Interpreter's Bible* (New York: Abingdon, 1953), Vol. X, p. 207.

9. See Robert Barclay's famous description of his early experiences among Friends in his *Apology for the True Christian Divinity*, Modern English Edition by Dean Freiday (Elberon, New Jersey: By the Author, 1967), p. 254.

10. Lucia Beamish, *Quaker Ministry: 1691-1834* (Gloucester, by the Author, 1967), p. 18.

11. NJ:282.

12. VII:144.

13. VII:38.

14. See Lewis Benson, "On Being Moved by the Spirit to Minister in Public Worship," *The Quaker Vision* (Gloucester: New Foundation, 1979), pp. 48-51.

15. NJ:341.

16. NJ:35, 541.

17. NJ:35; IV: 42.

18. Owen, *Works,* Vol. IV, p. 331.

19. "The Quakers' Catechism" (1655), "One Sheet Against the Quakers" (1657), "One Sheet for the Ministry against Malignants of All Sorts" (1657), and "A Second Sheet for the Ministry" (1657). The latter two are directed against both Seekers and Quakers principally.

20. "One Sheet for the Ministry," p. 5.

21. *Ibid.,* p. 6.

22. *Ibid.,* p. 7.

23. Baxter, "Second Sheet," p. 11.

24. Baxter, Preface to "Catechism."

25. Baxter, "Against the Quakers," p. 1.

26. *Ibid.,* p. 13.

27. IV:23f.

28. *Ibid.*

29. NJ:39.

30. IV:94.

31. NJ:219; also see NJ:291.

NOTES TO CHAPTER 11

1. NJ:444.

2. See Lewis Benson, *A Revolutionary Gospel.*
3. Elisabeth Schüssler-Fiorenza, "Revelation, Book of," in *The Interpreter's Dictionary of the Bible* (Nashville: Abingdon, 1976), supplementary volume, pp. 744-746; *Invitation to the Book of Revelation* (Garden City: Doubleday, 1981).
4. NJ:8.
5. V:127-141.
6. VII:233.
7. V:127f.
8. V:130.
9. NJ:22.
10. BJ I:238-243; IV:255-258.
11. IV:72.
12. V:130f.
13. IV:119.
14. VIII:50.
15. *Ibid.*
16. *Ibid.*
17. George Fox, *The Papists' Strength* (1658), p. 52.
18. VI:104.
19. III:191.
20. BJ I:420.
21. BJ II:270.
22. VII:234.
23. IV:188; also see V:132; VII:228.
24. BJ II:461.
25. III:375.
26. IV:187.
27. VI:158.
28. VII:163.
29. Francis Howgill, *Works* (1676), p. 210.
30. III:101f.
31. III:99.
32. Dean Freiday, *Nothing Without Christ* (Newberg, Ore: Barclay, 1984), pp. 11-16.
33. IV:229.
34. See title page of *Works,* Vol. III.
35. VII:278.
36. BJ II:364.
37. IV:18f.
38. NJ:21.
39. VII:262.
40. VII:70.
41. VII:241.
42. V:133.
43. VIII:129.
44. VII:115.
45. VII:262.
46. V:300.
47. CJ II:174; IV:364.
48. BJ II:528.
49. NJ:24.
50. VII:244.
51. VI:243.

52. VII:347.
53. VIII:19.
54. V:138.
55. CJ I:170-174.
56. NJ:517.
57. VIII:34.
58. NJ:206.
59. IV:102.
60. VII:85.
61. T. Canby Jones, *George Fox's Attitude Toward War* (Annapolis: Academic Fellowship, 1972), p. 87. Jones' study is an excellent resource on Fox's thought on war, Church-state relations and the Lamb's War.
62. NJ:400.
63. CJ I:131f.
64. NJ:460; see NJ:699.
65. For more of Fox's thought on this subject, see T. Canby Jones, *Fox's Attitude*, pp. 80-86.
66. NJ:470.
67. VIII:182.
68. VII:218.
69. III:251.
70. VII:157.
71. IV:242.
72. IV:241.
73. NJ:673.
74. V:151.

NOTES TO CONCLUSION

1. NJ:11.
2. *Ibid.*
3. Rufus M. Jones, Introduction to *The Beginnings of Quakerism* by W.C. Braithwaite (New York: Macmillan, 1912), p. xxii.
4. See the comments of Maurice Creasey in *Then and Now,* Anna Brinton, ed. (Freeport, New York: Books for Libraries Press, 1960), pp. 330-331.
5. My own recent article on the Church and the nuclear age is an attempt at this kind of translation. See "An Alternative Apocalypse: Gospel of Hope in an Age of Nuclear Despair," *Quaker Religious Thought*, no. 59 (Spring 1985): 3-19.
6. Albert Schweitzer, "Eschatological Mystic," in *The Writings of St. Paul*, Wayne A. Meeks, ed. (New York: Norton, 1972), p. 392.
7. *Ibid.*, p. 393.
8. *Ibid.*, p. 394.

SELECTED BIBLIOGRAPHY

BOOKS

Barbour, Hugh. *The Quakers in Puritan England*. New Haven: Yale University Press, 1964.

_____ and Arthur Roberts, editors. *Early Quaker Writings*. Grand Rapids: Eerdman's, 1973.

Beamish, Lucia. *Quaker Ministry: 1691-1834*. Gloucester: by the Author, 1967.

Benson, Lewis. *Catholic Quakerism*. Philadelphia: Philadelphia Yearly Meeting, 1968.

_____. *The Quaker Vision*. Gloucester: New Foundation, 1979.

_____. *The Truth Is Christ*. Gloucester: New Foundation, 1981.

_____. *What Did George Fox Teach About Christ?* Gloucester: New Foundation, 1976.

Braithwaite, William C. *The Beginnings of Quakerism*. London: Macmillan, 1912.

_____. *The Second Period of Quakerism*. London: Macmillan, 1919.

Creasey, Maurice. *Early Quaker Christology*. Pittsburgh: Catholic and Quaker Studies, 1956.

Doncaster, L. Hugh. *Quaker Organization and Business Meetings*. London: London Yearly Meeting, 1958.

Freiday, Dean. *The Bible: Its Criticism, Interpretation and Use in 16th and 17th Century England*. Pittsburgh: Catholic and Quaker Studies, 1979.

_____. *Nothing Without Christ: Some Current Problems in Religious Thought in the Light of Seventeenth Century Thought and Experience*. Newberg, Oregon: Barclay Press, 1984.

Jones, T. Canby. *George Fox's Attitude Toward War*. Annapolis: Academic Fellowship, 1972.

_____, editor. *Quaker Understanding of Christ and of Authority*. Philadelphia: Faith and Life Movement, n.d.

McCandless, John H. *The Quaker Understanding of Christ*. Philadelphia: Philadelphia Yearly Meeting, 1975.

Nuttall, Geoffrey. *The Holy Spirit in the Puritan Faith and Experience*. Oxford: Blackwell, 1946.

Pickvance, T. Joseph. *George Fox on the Light of Christ Within*. Gloucester: New Foundation, 1978.

_____. *George Fox and the Purefoys: A Study in the Puritan Background in Fenny Drayton in the 16th and 17th Centuries*. London: Friends Historical Society, 1970.

Punshon, John. *Portrait in Grey: A Short History of the Quakers.* London: London Yearly Meeting, 1984.

Tolles, Frederick. *Quakers and the Atlantic Culture.* New York: Macmillan, 1960.

Vann, R. T. *The Social Development of English Quakerism.* Cambridge: Harvard University Press, 1969.

DISSERTATIONS

Graves, Michael. "The Rhetoric of the Inward Light: An Examination of Extant Sermons Delivered by Early Quakers, 1671-1700." Ph.D. dissertation, University of Southern California, 1972.

Gwyn, Douglas. "The Apocalyptic Word of God." Ph.D. dissertation, Drew University, 1982.

Jones, T. Canby. "George Fox's Teaching on Redemption and Salvation." Ph.D. dissertation, Yale University, 1955.

ARTICLES AND TRACTS

Barbour, Hugh. "Protestant Quakerism." *Quaker Religious Thought* vol. XI, no. 2 (Autumn 1969): 2-23.

Benson, Lewis. "George Fox's Teaching about Christ." *Quaker Religious Thought* vol. XVI, nos. 1 &2 (Winter 1974-75): 20-42.

————. "The People of God and Gospel Order." In *The Church in Quaker Thought and Practice,* pp. 16-26. Edited by Charles Thomas. Philadelphia: Faith and Life Movement, 1979.

————. "The Relation of Quakerism to Its Own History." *Quaker Religious Thought* vol. III, no. 2 (Autumn 1961): 25-40.

————. " 'That of God in Every Man' — What Did George Fox Mean by It?" *Quaker Religious Thought* vol. XII, no. 2 (Spring 1970): 2-25.

Creasey, Maurice. " 'Inward' and 'Outward' — A Study in Early Quaker Language." *Journal of the Friends' Historical Society* supplement no. 30 (1962).

Freiday, Dean. "The Early Quakers and the Doctrine of Authority." *Quaker Religious Thought* vol. XV, no. 1 (Autumn 1973): 4-38.

Gwyn, Douglas. " 'Into That Which Cannot Be Shaken': The Apocalyptic Gospel Preached by George Fox." in *The Day of the Lord: Eschatology in Quaker Perspective,* pp. 61-96. Edited by Dean Freiday. Philadelphia: Faith and Life Movement, 1981.

Jones, T. Canby. "The Bible in George Fox and Contemporary Quakerism." *Quaker Religious Thought* vol. IV, no. 1 (Spring 1962): 18-36.

————. "The Nature and Functions of the Light in the Thought of George Fox." *Quaker Religious Thought* vol. XVI, nos. 1 & 2 (Winter 1974-75): 53-71.

Maclear, James F. "Quakerism at the End of the Interregnum: A Chapter in the Domestication of Radical Puritanism." *Church History* 19 (1950): 240-70.

SUBJECT INDEX

236

SCRIPTURE INDEX